Industrial Electronics

CET Exam
Study Guide

Industrial Electronics

CET Exam
Study Guide

Sam Wilson

TAB **TAB BOOKS**

Blue Ridge Summit, PA

FIRST EDITION
FIRST PRINTING

Copyright © 1990 by **TAB BOOKS**
Printed in the United States of America

Reproduction or publication of the content in any manner, without express permission
of the publisher, is prohibited. No liability is assumed with respect to
the use of the information herein.

Library of Congress Cataloging-in-Publication Data

Wilson, J. A. Sam.
Industrial electronics CET exam study guide / by Sam Wilson.
p.   cm.
ISBN 0-8306-9611-3   ISBN 0-8306-3311-1 (pbk.)
1. Industrial electronics—Examinations, questions, etc.
I. Title.
TK7881.W564 1990
621.381′076—dc20   89-29161
CIP

TAB BOOKS offers software for sale. For information and a catalog, please contact
TAB Software Department,
Blue Ridge Summit, PA 17294-0850.

Questions regarding the content of this book should be addressed to:

Reader Inquiry Branch
TAB BOOKS
Blue Ridge Summit, PA 17294-0214

Acquisitions Editor: Roland S. Phelps
Technical Editor: Laura J. Bader
Production: Katherine Brown

Contents

Acknowledgments

I WOULD LIKE to thank Joe Risse for his help in obtaining technical material for this book.

I would like to thank the following people at TAB for their help in getting this book published, and for waiting patiently through my months of illness for me to complete the manuscript:

Roland Phelps
Laura L. Crist
Laura J. Bader

Last, but certainly not least, thanks to my wife for typing the material. I am the president of my company, and she is everybody else.

Preface

IN ORDER TO become a Journeyman Certified Electronics Technician in any specialty, you must first pass an Associate-Level Test—a general test covering the broad subject of general electronics. Having passed that test, you are ready to take the Journeyman test. To do so, you must be able to show that you have four years of experience in your chosen field. A diploma from an electronics school or a degree usually counts as $1^1/_2$ years toward the 4 years of experience.

This book is a companion to *Industrial Electronics for Technicians (TAB No. 3321)*. It is written to help you review related subjects before you take the CET test.

My experience with study guides dictates that some instructions for the use of this book are necessary. You should not expect a study guide to be a textbook. It is called a *study guide* because it helps you to determine what subjects to review before taking a test.

If you miss a question in a study guide, make sure you understand why you missed it. You should also glance through the detractors and make sure you know what they mean. However, in a few cases, the detractors are nonsense words. In other words some terms have no physical meaning in industrial electronics.

Years ago I was lecturing to a group of ISCET technicians at a convention in North Carolina. During that lecture I told the following true story. I was working on a CET test. (At one time I wrote all of the tests.) I was nearly finished but I needed one more detractor; that is, an incorrect answer for a multiple-choice question. I came up with several ideas, but they were all too obvious. So, I gave *bead ledge* as one of the choices.

A bead ledge is actually a small ledge on a tire mold that is used for vulcanizing white sidewalls and other colored sidewalls to a tire. It has absolutely nothing to do with electronics, yet many technicians gave it as an answer. It was obviously a guess.

After I told this story, a technician in the audience spoke up and said that I was wrong. He claimed there really is such a thing as a bead ledge in electronics. I asked him what it was and how it worked, and he said he was not sure but he would write to me and let me know so that I could correct my lectures for the future.

That was nearly 20 years ago and I still haven't heard from him. I am beginning to think that I was right when I said there is no such thing as a bead ledge in electronics.

The reason I tell this story is that you may see a question that has a detractor which is meaningless in the field. Your experience should tell you that. If you have never heard of it before, it certainly isn't one of your choices for the answer.

When you miss a question and you are not sure why your answer is wrong, it is a good idea to go back to a textbook (like the companion book for this study guide or my book *Control Electronics with an Introduction to Robotics*). The fact that you missed the question is a good indication that some additional study would be of value.

One of the most common complaints of study guides goes something like this: "I read the study guide and answered all the questions, but I still saw questions in the CET test that I could not answer." Of course, that is very possible.

The CET tests are changed frequently. The questions given in this study guide are not the ones that you will see on the test. However, the range of subjects is usually the same, so, if you know the subject material and you review the questions that you are not sure about, you should be able to pass the CET test. Remember: your four years of experience is added background for taking the test!!

When you take the Journeyman Industrial Electronics CET test, you might encounter a range of subject headings, or the test you take might not be divided into subjects. The chapters in this study guide are equivalent to the subjects that were once used to divide the test. The same range of test subjects is still covered but they might not be titled in the test that you take.

You will note that there are two Programmed Reviews for each chapter. My suggestion is that you go through one of the Programmed Reviews immediately after you have read the chapter material—including the related material in *Industrial Electronics for Technicians*. Then, after you have reviewed all of the chapters in this book, go back and do all of the second Programmed Reviews at one sitting.

The reason for this is based on our experience with technicians who have not taken a long test during the interim between the Associate Level Test and the Journeyman Level Test. I know for a fact that fatigue sets in on long tests. Then, you will start answering questions too quickly in order to get finished. I know this from looking at many answer sheets and noting that more questions are missed on the last half of the test.

You might say that more questions are missed in the last half because the questions are more difficult. However, experienced technicians should find those questions easier than those in the first half. The first half of the test usually has material you have not looked at for a number of years.

Learn to pace yourself on a test. Do the second Programmed Reviews in this book at one sitting. Also, do the Practice Test in the back of the book at one sitting. It can result in a better grade!

Sam Wilson

1
Electric
Circuit Components

As with all fields of electronics, industrial electronics has its own *jargon* (technical terms that are not familiar to people who are not in the business). For that reason most of the chapters in this book start by defining some terms. Some of these terms are used in other fields such as physics, mathematics, and chemistry; however, most of the terms given here are directly related to industrial electronics.

TERMS

Transducers Transducers are very important to industrial electronics. You will also see them referred to as *sensors*. You can think of them as being the sense organs used for testing and measuring. Without them it is impossible to exert control over any kind of industrial electronic system.

For example, if you want to control the speed of a motor to a specific value of RPM, you must have some way of measuring that motor's speed. Otherwise you would not know if the motor is already going too fast or too slow, or if the speed is just right. You cannot exert speed control unless you know what has to be done to get the motor to the desired right speed.

Closed-loop Systems Transducers are often used in feedback control circuits. They are also known as *servo loops*, or *negative feedback loops*.

In a closed-loop system, the transducer signal is compared with a standard signal that is generated by a reference source. The two signals are compared, and the difference between them is a signal used to adjust the motor speed. The signal in the closed-loop system can be a dc voltage or an ac voltage or frequency.

Active and Passive Transducers   In addition to their use in closed-loop systems, transducers are used for making measurements. For example, if you want to measure temperature there are some obvious nonelectronic ways to do it. A thermometer is an example.

If you want to do it in such a way that you have a voltage that is directly related to the temperature, you will need an *active* transducer. A thermocouple can be used in that application.

Another way is to use a temperature-sensitive *passive* transducer. That way a circuit parameter—such as resistance—will be related to the temperature being measured. Passive transducers do not generate a voltage. *Thermistors* are passive transducers used for measuring or sensing temperature.

The thing being measured is called the *measurand*. So, in the example, the temperature is the measurand.

The word *active* applied to any device—not just transducers—means that a voltage is generated. It can be a dc voltage or an ac voltage, or it can refer to a signal frequency. Remember that *passive* means that the device changes a parameter such as resistance, capacitance, or inductance.

Open-loop Controls   Many open-loop control systems are used in industrial electronics. They are usually set manually. An example would be setting a motor's speed with a variable resistor. The motor may be operating in an application where speed is not crucial. So, an elaborate speed control system is not required.

Absolute Values   The term *absolute*—as in absolute pressure—refers to a value of pressure measured against, or relative to, some zero-pressure value. As an example, zero pressure may represent the pressure of the surrounding air. The surrounding air is referred to as the *ambient* air. If all other pressures are measured relative to that value, then the pressure of the surrounding air is the absolute value.

Another example is used for measuring temperature. The lowest possible temperature is $-473°$ Fahrenheit. This is called absolute zero. All temperatures on the Kelvin scale are measured with reference to absolute zero.

Parameters   A parameter is a value chosen in order to make something come out right. If you are asked to draw a circle that has an area of 10 square inches, the parameter you would choose would most likely be the radius, although you could also use the diameter. The parameter is chosen to get the right area, and this is true of parameters in electricity and electronics. For example, if you want a certain amount of current to flow, the parameters you choose will be the voltage and the resistance.

Motion   When you are talking about motion the parameters are *velocity* (the rate of change of distance) and *acceleration* (the rate of change of velocity).

If you are talking about rotary motion, then you are considering angular velocity and angular acceleration. The reason these terms are important is that there are some transducers designed to measure these quantities. For example, an accelerometer measures acceleration. A tachometer measures angular velocity. A speedometer measures linear speed.

Keep in mind the fact that velocity means a speed in some specified direction. However, speed is given without direction. You cannot say "my velocity was 30 miles per hour" because you are not specifying the direction. The correct terminology for velocity would be "my velocity was 30 miles per hour north."

The Bridge   Resistive transducers are usually placed in a bridge circuit which is sometimes referred to as a *Wheatstone Bridge*. Originally a Wheatstone Bridge was used for making accurate resistance measurements, but the term is now being used in industrial electronics for a measuring or sensing circuit.

The reason for connecting resistive transducers into a bridge circuit is that it cancels out the effects of changes in power supply voltage. Also, the effect of power supply current flowing through the transducer—and therefore, heating the transducer—can be eliminated by using a bridge connection.

A Wheatstone Bridge has an *active leg*. It is also called the *active arm*. That is the arm where the transducer being used for sensing or measuring is located.

Be sure you understand the uses of bridge circuits before you take the journeyman industrial electronics CET test!

Analog and Digital   The world of electronics is divided into two classifications: *analog* and *digital*. In an analog circuit, there is always an output change whenever there is an input change.

You can think of an analog display as being an analogy. The speedometer in a car, for example, may have a pointer that moves upscale in an amount that is related to the speed of the vehicle. A steady increase in speed will result in a steady increase in upscale movement. In order to make the measurement you must compare the position of the pointer by sighting the numbers behind the pointer.

In a digital display the output is a specific number. An example is the odometer that tells how many miles the car has traveled. The number of miles is displayed directly as digits.

Analog systems react to any small change. Most digital systems react only to two different inputs: 1 and 0. They do not respond to changes between those values.

The numbers 1 and 0 are *B*inary dig*ITS*—or, BITS. They often represent a full ON condition (1) and a full OFF condition (0).

Because of their higher efficiency, digital systems are favored in many industrial applications that once were accomplished with analog systems.

Telemetering A measurand may be sensed from a distant location. In that case the information is transmitted over a telephone line, or it is transmitted by radio waves. The technique is called *telemetering*.

Telemetering is necessary when the quantity being measured or sensed is in a dangerous location. Also, when the measurand is not accessible by a human, as in the case of the Mars landing, telemetering is necessary. Industrial electronics technicians must have an understanding of communications when working with telemetering equipment.

Transducer Compensation and Calibration When a transducer is *compensated* it means that some error or errors have been balanced out. A transducer is said to be *calibrated* when its output has been adjusted to be equal to a known standard.

When contracts are granted to companies it is sometimes a requirement that test equipment be periodically calibrated. Otherwise, a condition known as *creep* can occur. In other words, the equipment can drift off calibration over a period of time.

Damping Consider the case of a motor with closed-loop speed control. The motor starts to drift off the proper speed. The control circuitry reacts to correct the speed.

If the correction is too severe, the motor speed will go past the desired value. Correction is made again and the speed overshoots the mark. When this condition continues the system is said to be *hunting* or *oscillating*. It is avoided by properly damping the system to prevent the overshoot.

If the system reacts too slowly when a change is necessary, it is said to be *underdamped*. *Critical damping* occurs when the system reacts properly without overshooting or reacting too slowly. Normally, a closed-loop system is slightly underdamped.

Dynamic Whenever you see the word *dynamic* you should think about the word change. The word range also comes to mind. For example, the dynamic range in audio systems is the maximum change in volume that can occur from the weakest sound to the loudest sound.

Impedance In electrical systems, impedance is the combined resistance and reactance of the circuit.

In mechanical systems, impedance is the ratio of the applied force to the velocity when simple harmonic motion is under consideration. As an example, a loudspeaker offers impedance to the flow of signal current. It also has mechanical impedance in the motion of its cone when a pure sine wave is being reproduced.

Mechanical impedance can affect the electrical impedance of a system. It can also affect system damping.

Relative The word *relative* is sometimes used in regard to measurements. It means that the measurement is being compared with some standard value. An example is relative humidity which is a comparison between the amount of water vapor in the surrounding air divided by (or, referenced to) the amount of humidity required for air saturation at a given temperature. Relative humidity is usually expressed as a percent value.

In some applications, such as a clean room used for assembly, it is necessary to continually monitor and control the humidity. High humidity can be very detrimental to some types of operating systems. A system that is protected against the invasion of humidity is said to be hermetically sealed.

Differential When you see the term differential applied to an industrial electronic component you should think of the word difference. A differential transducer, for example, produces an output that is the difference between a fixed value and a variable value. A differential amplifier has an output that is the difference (or, related to the difference) between two inputs.

When a signal is applied to both inputs of a differential amplifier at the same time it is called a *common mode input*. That should produce a zero signal output. A measure of how well it accomplishes this is called the *common mode rejection*. Expressed as a number, it is the *common mode rejection ratio*.

Stress and Strain Do not use the terms stress and strain incorrectly. Strain is the amount of deformation of a body that is a result of a force called stress. A strain gauge measures the amount of twisting or bending of a body when a stress is applied.

Transient A transient voltage is a very short-duration rapid change in voltage level. It appears on an oscilloscope as a spike. It can also be a step voltage like the leading edge of a square wave.

Transient response is a measure of how well a system reacts to a transient condition. If you apply a step voltage to a regulated power supply it would be ideal if the supply could react immediately. However, in the real world it takes the power supply time to recover. The speed of recovery is called the *slewing rate*.

Slewing rate is also a term applied to operational amplifiers. It refers to the time it takes the output of the op amp to react to a step voltage at its input.

It is not intended that the terms listed here cover the complete gamut of terms in industrial electronics, especially as applied to electric and electronic components. However, this review should establish in your mind the range of subjects you should cover in these areas.

It is likely that you will be asked about mechanical devices even though you are taking an industrial electronics exam. Keep in mind the fact that an industrial electronics technician must be familiar with the environment of electronics. If you are working on a motor speed control, you should have an understanding of how the motor works, what controls its speed, and what its limitations are.

PROGRAMMED REVIEW NO. 1

Start with Block number 1. Pick the answer that you think is correct. If you select choice number 1, go to Block 13. If you select choice number 2, go to Block 15. Proceed as directed. There is only one correct answer for each question.

BLOCK 1

Sensors are also called:

(1) Feelers. Go to Block 13.
(2) Transducers. Go to Block 15.

BLOCK 2

The correct answer to the question in Block 7 is choice (3). You might run across this term on a test for industrial electronics because in other fields potentiometers are seldom used. So, it becomes part of industrial electronics jargon.

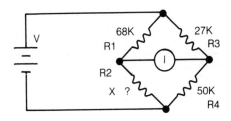

Here is your next question: *What value of resistance is needed in this bridge so that no current flows in the center leg?*

(1) About 126K. Go to Block 14.
(2) About 86K. Go to Block 22.

BLOCK 3

Your answer to the question in Block 18 is not correct. Go back and read the question again and select another answer.

BLOCK 4

Your answer to the question in Block 25 is not correct. Go back and read the question again and select another answer.

BLOCK 5

Your answer to the question in Block 6 is not correct. Go back and read the question again and select another answer.

BLOCK 6

The correct answer to the question in Block 28 is (2). Over long periods the time constant of the circuit becomes insignificant. However, for short periods of time the time constant becomes an essential part of the design.

If the time constant is too long, many changes will occur before the time cycle. If the time constant is too short, the circuit will not be able to reach its proper value of voltage. This is better understood from individual time constant circuits, but the case of the UJT is the one that can be easily understood. The frequency of the UJT is determined by the time constant as will be discussed in chapter 3. It can only be made correct if the time constant is the proper value.

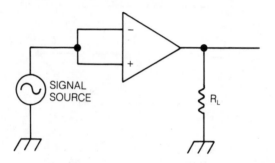

Here is your next question: *The operational amplifier in this block has a differential amplifier input. The connection shown is called a:*

(1) Difference input. Go to Block 5.
(2) Common mode input. Go to Block 18.

BLOCK 7

The correct answer to the question in Block 12 is (2). The voltage is being generated in accordance with Faraday's law which states that any time there is relative motion between a magnetic field and a conductor, a voltage is produced or generated. Lenz's law deals with the polarity of that voltage, not with the generation of the voltage.

Each time a magnet passes the coil, it induces a voltage pulse. Those voltage pulses are then used in a closed-loop circuit by comparing them with a fixed pulse frequency. If the pulses generated by the motor magnet are not equal to the fixed frequency, an adjustment will take place to correct the motor speed. Of course, the reason two magnets are used instead of one is to balance the rotating equipment.

Here is your next question: *The word potentiometer is used to mean a "variable resistor used to vary voltage."* Potentiometer *is a term also used for an instrument that measures:*

(1) Power. Go to Block 20.
(2) Resistance. Go to Block 24.
(3) Neither choice is correct. It is used to measure voltage. Go to Block 2.

BLOCK 8

Your answer to the question in Block 11 is not correct. Go back and read the question again and select another answer.

BLOCK 9

Your answer to the question in Block 10 is not correct. Go back and read the question again and select another answer.

BLOCK 10

The correct answer to the question in Block 15 is choice (2). Faying surfaces are shown in that block. They are very important in the electronics industry and also in many other industries.

When two metals are brought together this way they should be identical. Otherwise, the difference between the two metals can produce a galvanic action. Specifically, two different metals in an acid or alkali atmosphere become a battery. That battery produces a small circulating current that will eventually eat the metal away.

Faying surfaces that are bolted together are especially vulnerable to galvanic action. It is not necessary that the dissimilar metals be immersed in a solution, although, that is the way it is done to make a battery. Acids in the atmosphere (for example acid rain) can have a disastrous effect on faying surfaces because of the galvanic action.

As a technician you should be wary of bolting two surfaces together with a bolt made of a third kind of material. Some materials will react strongly with one or both of the metals and the galvanic action can weaken the bolt.

Here is your next question: *A servo control is also known as a:*

(1) Manual control. Go to Block 9.
(2) Closed-loop control. Go to Block 28.

BLOCK 11

The correct answer to the question in Block 17 is choice (1). The thermocouple produces a voltage when its junction of two metals is heated. The fact that it produces a voltage makes it an active transducer. The LDR, given as the second choice in the question in Block 17, stands for Light Dependent Resistor. It changes its resistance value in response to the amount of ambient light.

Here is your next question: *Which of the following is less likely to be used as an active transducer?*

(1) The piezoelectric method of generating a voltage. Go to Block 8.

(2) The chemical method of generating a voltage. Go to Block 25.

BLOCK 12

The correct answer to the question in Block 18 is choice (2). The waveform indicates underdamping because oscillation is occurring immediately after the input step voltage. There is an immediate overshoot, then undershoot.

When you get this kind of output from an amplifier, it means that the gain is too high.

When you get this kind of response in a power supply, it means that the feedback circuitry is too "stiff" and the whole power supply acts as an oscillating amplifier.

When you get this kind of response in a motor speed control, the condition is known as *hunting*. The motor speed will oscillate back and forth above and below the desired speed.

As a technician, you will not be required to design circuits, but you should recognize that if overshoot or oscillation occurs, it usually means something went wrong with the design. Start by looking at the feedback circuit and investigate those parts that control the gain of the closed loop.

Here is your next question: *The setup in this block is used for controlling motor speed. A voltage (V) is generated every time the permanent magnets pass the coil. The voltage is being generated in accordance with:*

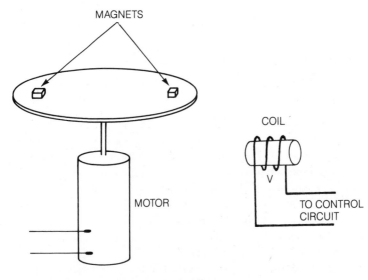

(1) Lenz's law. Go to Block 19.
(2) Faraday's law. Go to Block 7.

BLOCK 13

Your answer to the question in Block 1 is not correct. Go back and read the question again and select another answer.

BLOCK 14

The correct answer to the question in Block 2 is choice (1). For the bridge illustrated the bridge is balanced when R1 ÷ R2 = R3 ÷ R4. This is a ratio. In algebra you learn to solve ratios by *cross multiplying*. Mathematicians prefer to say *set the product of means equal to the product of the extremes*. Regardless of what terminology you use it boils down to this: R1 × R4 = R2 × R3.

Remember, this is for the bridge in Block 2. The letters may be a different value. Use this relationship: 27K divided by 50K equals 68K divided by X. Therefore,

$$X = [(68 \times 50)/27]K$$

The calculator gives a value of 125.9, or about 126K.

Here is your next question: *Usually, but not always, a transducer is:*

(1) An electronic circuit. Go to Block 23.
(2) An electric component. Go to Block 17.

BLOCK 15

The correct answer to the question in Block 1 is choice (2). Electrical and electronic sensors do the same thing for industrial electronic systems that your sensors (eyes, ears, nose, etc.) do for you. Virtually every human sensor has been mimicked by an industrial electronic equivalent. There are even sensors that can smell and feel.

Sensors are especially important in feedback loops. They are used to determine the condition that exists. That way, feedback circuitry can be used to make the necessary correction between what is happening and what should happen.

Sensors or transducers are not only important for industrial electronic controls but they are also essential for making measurements. Usually, the measurand is converted to an electrical signal of some type that can be measured with electronic equipment. For example, pressure is transferred into an electrical signal by a *load cell*. As another example, temperatures convert to an electrical signal by the use of a *thermocouple*.

When you are first entering the field of industrial electronics, it would be a good practice to read the catalogs available for each type of sensor. They tell the important parameters upon which the sensors are based and often show circuits (or, as they are called, applications) for each particular type of transducer.

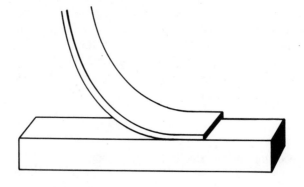

Here is your next question: *The figure in this block shows two:*

(1) Facing surfaces. Go to Block 16.
(2) Faying surfaces. Go to Block 10.

BLOCK 16

Your answer to the question in Block 15 is not correct. Go back and read the question again and select another answer.

BLOCK 17

The correct answer to the question in Block 14 is (2). The term *electronics* usually means a device that operates by controlling electrons in some specific way. An *electric* component, however, produces electricity or controls electricity by use of a circuit parameter. From that standpoint, transducers are electric components.

You would not call a thermocouple or a thermistor an electronic device in the normal use of the word.

There are some electronic components that can be used as transducers, but that is not usually their primary purpose.

Here is your next question: *Which of the following is an example of an active transducer?*

(1) Thermocouple. Go to Block 11.
(2) LDR. Go to Block 27.

BLOCK 18

The correct answer to the question in Block 6 is choice (2). As a Journeyman technician you should know that an operational amplifier has a differential input. For that reason an op amp can be connected in a wide variety of circuit types.

When you connect the inputs together the difference between the two inputs should produce a zero output. Unfortunately, that is not always exactly true. It can only happen if the input, or differential, amplifiers are exactly balanced. If one-half of the differential amplifier conducts slightly more than the other half there will be a dc output voltage when a common mode input is applied. This is an important way of rating operational amplifiers or any differential circuit. It is not a practical method of operating an operational amplifier.

Here is your next question: *The waveform in this block indicates:*

(1) Overdamping. Go to Block 3.
(2) Slight underdamping. Go to Block 12.
(3) Critical damping. Go to Block 26.

BLOCK 19

Your answer to the question in Block 12 is not correct. Go back and read the question again and select another answer.

BLOCK 20

Your answer to the question in Block 7 is not correct. Go back and read the question again and select another answer.

BLOCK 21

The correct answer to the question in Block 25 is choice (2). Electrostatic generators are not, in general, suited for use as transducers. Electrostatic voltages can be highly destructive in some types of equipment. An example is in the printing industry. It is said that the limit of the speed for which printing can occur is how fast you can move the paper. That, in turn, is limited by the amount of electrostatic voltage generated as the paper moves through the press.

Many techniques have been applied to remove that voltage but none of them can be considered to be highly effective. Bombarding the region with ions, use of atomic radiation, strips of foil and non-electrostatic (conductive) paper have all been used. This is definitely an area in industry that is waiting for a breakthrough.

Here is your next question: *A metal bar is twisted when there is an applied force. The amount of twist is a measure of the amount of:*

(1) Stress. Go to Block 30.
(2) Strain. Go to Block 31.

BLOCK 22

Your answer to the question in Block 2 is not correct. Go back and read the question again and select another answer.

BLOCK 23

Your answer to the question in Block 14 is not correct. Go back and read the question again and select another answer.

BLOCK 24

Your answer to the question in Block 7 is not correct. Go back and read the question again and select another answer.

BLOCK 25

The correct answer to the question in Block 11 is choice (2). Note that the question does not say that the chemical method of generating a voltage cannot be used as a transducer. It simply asks which of the two is less likely, the piezoelectric method or the chemical.

The piezoelectric method is used extensively for sensing pressure. It produces a voltage that is directly related to the amount of pressure exerted.

The chemical method is sometimes used to sense the presence of dampness or liquid. When the dampness or liquid is present, chemicals produce a generated voltage.

Here is your next question: *Which of the following is less likely to be used in an active transducer?*

(1) The photoelectric method of generating a voltage. Go to Block 4.
(2) The electrostatic method of generating a voltage. Go to Block 21.

BLOCK 26

Your answer to the question in Block 18 is not correct. Go back and read the question again and select another answer.

BLOCK 27

Your answer to the question in Block 17 is not correct. Go back and read the question again and select another answer.

BLOCK 28

The correct answer to the question in Block 10 is choice (2). Manual controls (which was choice (1)) are used as open-loop controls. They are set but not monitored.

In a closed-loop control there is a continuous monitoring and corrections are continually made to get the desired results.

Closed-loop controls are used extensively in industry. As mentioned previously, they utilize the output of some type of transducer to determine the condition that exists. If the condition that exists, such as motor speed, is not correct, the closed-loop system will take corrective action.

Here is your next question: *The time constant of a transducer measurement is important when that measurement is made:*

(1) Once a day. Go to Block 29.
(2) 300 times per second. Go to Block 6.

BLOCK 29

Your answer to the question in Block 28 is not correct. Go back and read the question again and select another answer.

BLOCK 30

Your answer to the question in Block 21 is not correct. Go back and read the question again and select another answer.

BLOCK 31

The correct answer to the question in Block 21 is choice (2). Strain is the deformation produced by the stress. The twisting *force* is the stress in this example.

Here is your next question: *The thing that you choose in a circuit in order to get the results that you want is called a* _____. Go to Block 32.

BLOCK 32

The answer to the question in Block 31 is *parameter*.

You have now completed Programmed Review No. 1

PROGRAMMED REVIEW NO. 2

Start with Block number 1. Pick the answer that you think is correct. If you select choice number 1, go to Block 13. If you select choice number 2, go to Block 15. Proceed as directed. There is only one correct answer for each question.

BLOCK 1

In transducer circuits the quantity being measured is called the:

(1) Measurand. Go to Block 13.
(2) Parameter. Go to Block 15.

BLOCK 2

The correct answer to the question in Block 8 is choice (1). In a piezoelectric transducer the voltage is produced in response to a pressure. In most cases the piezoelectric device is a crystalline material made with barium titanate, tourmaline, or roschell salts. Quartz is also a very popular piezoelectric material.

Piezoelectric devices work in two ways. If you exert a pressure on one it produces a voltage. However, if you place a voltage across a piezoelectric device it distorts its shape.

Both of these effects are utilized in piezoelectric devices. There are some materials that are not crystalline which will also produce a voltage under pressure. These materials are now being considered for specialized applications.

The disadvantages of most of the crystalline piezoelectric materials is that they are soluble. In other words they are completely destroyed by moisture or liquids. That renders them unsuitable for certain applications unless they are hermetically sealed.

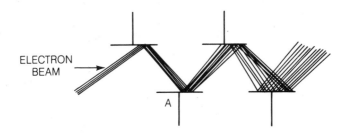

Here is your next question: *For the photomultiplier shown in this block, electron emission from electrode A is by:*

(1) Thermonic emission. Go to Block 16.
(2) Secondary emission. Go to Block 33.
(3) Photoemission. Go to Block 30.
(4) Field emission. Go to Block 24.

BLOCK 3

Your answer to the question in Block 13 is not correct. Go back and read the question again and select another answer.

BLOCK 4

The correct answer to the question in Block 17 is choice (1). Telemetering is a very important part of industrial electronics. It does not matter whether the measurand is being transmitted over a short distance on telephone wires or long distance on transmission lines or a very long distance over radio waves. All of these telemetering techniques come under the heading of industrial electronics.

It is because of telemetering that industrial electronics technicians must be familiar with communications systems. Specifically, the methods of modulating carrier waves and methods of transmitting energy over transmission lines.

In newer devices the transmission lines may be fiberoptic cables instead of copper conductors. In either case it is a popular technique to send a *modulated* wave over the line. In fact, that technique makes it possible to send several different signals simultaneously.

You may encounter questions on communications in the industrial electronics CET test.

Here is your next question: *A transducer must have an output that is:*

(1) Voltage related to the energy or quantity sensed. Go to Block 25.
(2) Value related to the energy or quantity sensed. Go to Block 20.

BLOCK 5

The correct answer to the question in Block 33 is choice (3). Provided the neon lamp is operated within certain limitations set by the manufacturer, the voltage across it will be a constant value.

In earlier days neon lamps were used instead of zener diodes to produce voltage regulation. They have also been used for other applications in the past, but today they are generally replaced by zener diodes.

One difference between the neon lamp and zener diode is that the neon lamp requires a voltage of about 65 volts to cause it to conduct. This voltage is too high for many modern semiconductor circuits.

You might read that the neon lamp has been replaced by the zener because the neon lamp is too noisy. This is not exactly correct. The zener diode is also a very noisy device, but it operates at voltages well within the range of applied voltages in semiconductor devices.

Here is your next question: *A strain gauge operates directly by:*

(1) Pressure. Go to Block 28.
(2) Force. Go to Block 21.
(3) Deformation. Go to Block 26.
(4) Retraction. Go to Block 23.

BLOCK 6

The correct answer to the question in Block 22 is choice (3). Most thermistors have a negative temperature coefficient. In other words, as the temperature goes up the resistance of the thermistor goes down. However, there are thermistors with positive temperature coefficients that are used in some systems.

Here is your next question: *Another name for transducer is:*

(1) Generator. Go to Block 37.
(2) Sensor. Go to Block 32.

BLOCK 7

Your answer to the question in Block 22 is not correct. Go back and read the question again and select another answer.

BLOCK 8

The correct answer to the question in Block 27 is choice (2). The term *optoelectronics* has come to mean devices that produce light, or are activated by light in electronic circuits. While it is true that the photocell is activated by light, its purpose is to *control* rather than to produce or sense light. Light activated devices (LADs) and light emitting devices (LEDs) are optoelectronic.

For example, a LAD is a light activated diode. It conducts readily in the presence of light and does not conduct (in the forward direction) in the absence of light.

A LACR is another example of an optoelectronic component. It is a light activated SCR. In that device light turns the SCR ON and permits a high current flow.

You can see from these applications of light activated devices that they are primarily used as *sensors* rather than producers of voltage.

Light emitting diodes (LEDs) produce a light when a *forward* current flows through the diode.

Here is your next question: *A weight presses against a transducer. The output of the transducer is a voltage that is directly related to the force exerted by the weight. The active transducer operates by the:*

(1) Piezoelectric effect. Go to Block 2.
(2) Faraday's law. Go to Block 36.

BLOCK 9

The correct answer to the question in Block 26 is choice (1). Again, the question relates to the difference between stress and strain, stress being the force and strain being the deformation.

Here is your next question: *In order to obtain a very precise control, it would be best to use:*

(1) Closed-loop control. Go to Block 17.
(2) Open-loop control. Go to Block 12.

BLOCK 10

Your answer to the question in Block 33 is not correct. Go back and read the question again and select another answer.

BLOCK 11

Your answer to the question in Block 22 is not correct. Go back and read the question again and select another answer.

BLOCK 12

Your answer to the question in Block 9 is not correct. Go back and read the question again and select another answer.

BLOCK 13

The correct answer to the question in Block 1 is choice (1). The word measurand is used more extensively in the fields of test and measurements than in the field of control. When you are asked a question about a measurand, think about a quantity that is being measured or sensed.

Here is your next question: *The voltage across a VDR is:*

(1) High when the voltage across it is high. Go to Block 3.
(2) Low when the voltage across it is high. Go to Block 35.

BLOCK 14

Your answer to the question in Block 27 is not correct. Go back and read the question again and select another answer.

BLOCK 15

Your answer to the question in Block 1 is not correct. Go back and read the question again and select another answer.

BLOCK 16

Your answer to the question in Block 2 is not correct. Go back and read the question again and select another answer.

BLOCK 17

The correct answer to the question in Block 9 is choice (1). Closed-loop systems make it possible to very accurately control activity in an industrial electronics system.

You may be controlling motor speed, mixing chemicals, limiting the level of a liquid, or controlling the position of a robot.

There is an almost endless list of controls that are used in industrial electronics. All of them become more precise by the use of feedback circuitry.

This is not to say that only feedback controls are used. Many open-loop control systems also exist. Manual controls are examples of open-loop controls.

Here is your next question: *Measuring at a distance is called:*

(1) Telemetering. Go to Block 4.
(2) Radio control. Go to Block 38.

BLOCK 18

Your answer to the question in Block 33 is not correct. Go back and read the question again and select another answer.

BLOCK 19

Your answer to the question in Block 32 is not correct. Go back and read the question again and select another answer.

BLOCK 20

The correct answer to the question in Block 4 is choice (2). It is not necessary that a transducer produce an output voltage. That is only true of active transducers. The output of a transducer may not be directly proportional to the energy being sensed. Many transducers such as a thermistor are nonlinear devices. But, there must be some relationship between the output of the transducer whether it be active or passive, and the amount of energy being sensed.

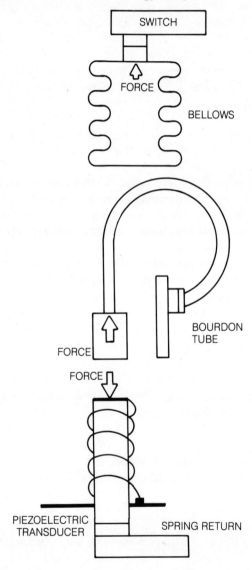

Here is your next question: *Which of the devices in the illustration in this block is used for sensing the pressure of a gas or fluid?*

_____. Go to Block 39.

BLOCK 21

Your answer to the question in Block 5 is not correct. Go back and read the question again and select another answer.

BLOCK 22

The correct answer to the question in Block 3 is choice (2). At the trailing edge of the positive pulse the NPN transistor turns OFF. The inductive kickback will produce a high voltage in series with the power supply voltage. That will destroy the transistor.

If the inductance value is high the kickback voltage can be measured in thousands of volts!!

Here is your next question: *Thermistors:*

(1) Always have a positive temperature coefficient. Go to Block 7.
(2) Always have a negative temperature coefficient. Go to Block 11.
(3) Can be made with a positive or negative temperature coefficient. Go to Block 6.

BLOCK 23

Your answer to the question in Block 5 is not correct. Go back and read the question again and select another answer.

BLOCK 24

Your answer to the question in Block 2 is not correct. Go back and read the question again and select another answer.

BLOCK 25

Your answer to the question in Block 4 is not correct. Go back and read the question again and select another answer.

BLOCK 26

The correct answer to the question in Block 5 is choice (3). The question is difficult to answer because it would appear that pressure would be the logical choice. However, remember that strain refers to the deformation of a body when it is under stress. The pressure would be the stress. Likewise, the force would be the stress. Strain gauges come in many different sizes and they can be very delicate devices that are used for sensing very small amounts of pressure or stress.

Here is your next question: *Which of the following is correct?*

(1) Stress produces strain. Go to Block 9.
(2) Strain produces stress. Go to Block 31.

BLOCK 27

The correct answer to the question in Block 32 is choice (1). When used for making measurements a transducer produces a change in a circuit parameter or, produces a voltage that is directly related to the quantity being measured. That quantity being measured is the measurand.

Complete books have been written on transducers and their use. As an industrial electronics technician you should be thoroughly acquainted with all types of transducers and their applications.

Here is your next question: *Is the following statement correct? A photocell is an example of an optoelectronic device.*

(1) Correct. Go to Block 14.
(2) Not correct. Go to Block 8.

BLOCK 28

Your answer to the question in Block 5 is not correct. Go back and read the question again and select another answer.

BLOCK 29

Your answer to the question in Block 35 is not correct. Go back and read the question again and select another answer.

BLOCK 30

Your answer to the question in Block 2 is not correct. Go back and read the question again and select another answer.

BLOCK 31

Your answer to the question in Block 26 is not correct. Go back and read the question again and select another answer.

BLOCK 32

The correct answer to the question in Block 6 is choice (2). The word sensor is used interchangeably with the word transducer in most technical literature.

Here is your next question: *Two major areas of transducer applications are sensing for the purpose of control, and:*

(1) Making measurements. Go to Block 27.
(2) Amplification. Go to Block 19.

BLOCK 33

The correct answer to the question in Block 2 is choice (2). The detractors in Block 2 are all methods of emitting electrons. For the photomultiplier, emission occurs when electrons bombard the surface at a high speed knocking other electrons loose.

Most vacuum tubes such as triodes, tetrodes, and pentodes operate by thermionic emission. The cathode was heated and it emitted electrons that came under the control of the tube electrodes.

Photoemission is utilized in some photocells. Light directed onto some materials, like selenium, causes electrons to be emitted from the surface. Field emission occurs when a positive voltage is brought near the surface of a material. This is the method of emission that occurs inside a neon lamp and some other types of gas discharge tubes.

When electrons are emitted from materials it leaves those materials positively charged. Therefore, a voltage is produced between the material and an anode that collects the emitted electrons.

Here is your next question: *Which of the following has a nearly constant voltage across it when in the operating mode?*

(1) JFET in a Class A amplifier. Go to Block 18.
(2) Hall devices. Go to Block 10.
(3) Neon lamp. Go to Block 5.
(4) Varistor. Go to Block 34.

BLOCK 34

Your answer to the question in Block 33 is not correct. Go back and read the question again and select another answer.

BLOCK 35

The correct answer to the question in Block 13 is choice (2). You will often see VDRs connected across inductors in solid-state equipment. They are used to prevent inductive kickback voltages from destroying components. A good example is a relay coil in the collector circuit of a bipolar transistor shown in this block. The transistor is used to turn the relay ON and OFF.

When the transistor stops conduction quickly, the relay should turn OFF immediately. However, the counter voltage across the inductor will try to keep the current going. This produces a voltage in series with the power supply voltage that can be destructive to the transistor. The VDR across the coil conducts when the kickback voltage is high and, therefore, shorts out the induced voltage. That, in turn, prevents it from destroying the transistor.

There are other components that you will see used instead of the VDR. Capacitors are sometimes used but they produce a danger of oscillation and that can be as destructive as the kickback voltage. Neon lamps and junction diodes are also used for the same purpose. The diode conducts only during the kickback voltage period and therefore produces a short circuit across the inductor.

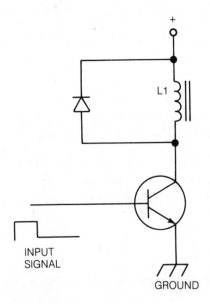

VDRs are also used to take the spikes off the line voltage that is being used for operating electronic equipment. Those spikes can get through the power supply and destroy components. The VDR circuit is designed to offer a minimum amount of opposition to the spikes but a maximum amount of opposition to the normal line voltages.

Here is your next question: *Refer to the illustration in this block. In order for the diode to be effective in protecting the transistor, it will conduct at:*

(1) The leading edge of the pulse. Go to Block 29.
(2) The trailing edge of the pulse. Go to Block 22.

BLOCK 36

Your answer to the question in Block 8 is not correct. Go back and read the question again and select another answer.

BLOCK 37

Your answer to the question in Block 6 is not correct. Go back and read the question again and select another answer.

BLOCK 38

Your answer to the question in Block 17 is not correct. Go back and read the question again and select another answer.

BLOCK 39

All of the devices can be used for sensing pneumatic (gas) or hydraulic (liquid) pressure.

You have now completed Programmed Review No. 2

KEY WORDS

Absolute values
Active and passive
Active arm
Active leg
Analog/Digital
Bridge
Closed-loop controls
Common mode input

Creep
Critical damping
Damping
Dynamic vs static
Hunting (or oscillating)
Load cell
Measurand
Open-loop controls

Optoelectronics
Parameters
Relative measurements
Sensors
Slewing rate
Strain
Stress

Tachometer
Telemetering
Thermocouple
Transducer
Transient (also transient response)
Wheatstone bridge

PRACTICE TEST

1. RPM is measured with:

   (A) A tachometer.
   (B) A speedometer.

2. Which of the following methods of generating a voltage might be used for producing the very high voltage used in an X-ray machine?

   (A) The chemical method of generating a voltage.
   (B) The electrostatic method of generating a voltage.

3. A TE generator can be made on the basis of Seebeck's law. It will be:

   (A) An active transducer.
   (B) A passive transducer.

4. In a passive transducer circuit, the transducer changes a:

   (A) Circuit parameter in response to a change in input energy.
   (B) Circuit voltage in response to a change in input resistance.

5. Two identical strips of copper are inserted into a fresh lemon. Which of the following is correct?

   (A) A voltage will be generated across the ends of the copper.
   (B) No voltage will be generated.

6. The resistance of a VDR changes over a wide range of values when there is a relatively small change in voltage across it. It is an example of:

   (A) An active transducer.
   (B) A passive transducer.

7. A transducer that changes resistance when the amount of ambient light changes is called a:

(A) Photoresistor.
(B) Photocell.

8. A closed-loop system is being used to control the temperature of an oven to a very exact value. The measurand in the system is:

(A) Electricity.
(B) Heat.

9. Is the following statement technically accurate? A transducer converts energy from one form to another.

(A) It is technically accurate.
(B) It is not technically accurate.

10. Which of the following is another name for feedback control?

(A) Closed-loop control.
(B) Rework control.

ANSWERS TO PRACTICE TEST

1. (A)   A tachometer may be in different forms. For example, one type of tachometer has a shaft that is pressed against a rotating wheel. That turns a generator inside the tachometer. The generated voltage produces an upscale reading on the display. This type of tachometer utilizes the electromechanical method of generating a voltage.

Tachometers in cars often use pulses from the distributor or spark plug. The pulses are counted electronically and, using simple electronic calculations, converted, to RPM for the display.

Another type of tachometer uses a stroboscopic effect. It produces a flashing light. You shine the light on the rotating wheel and adjust the flashing frequency until the wheel appears to be stopped. What really happens is that the light flashes in synchronization with the rotating wheel. Every time a mark on the wheel comes to a certain point, the stroboscope light flashes. That makes the point on the wheel appear to be stopped. The frequency of the stroboscope flashes is converted to RPM.

2. (B)   Examples of electrostatic generators made commercially are the *Van de Graaff* generator and the *Wimshurst* generator. Both are capable of generating very high voltages that can be utilized for making X-rays. Remember that any device that accelerates electrons and then stops them very quickly is capable of producing X-rays, even though that is not their primary purpose.

3. (A)   According to the Seebeck effect a *voltage* is generated whenever two dissimilar metals are attached to each other and heated. This principle is the basis of thermocouple operation and other TE (thermoelectric) devices.

4. (A)   Passive transducers work by changing resistance, capacitance, or inductance in a circuit. For example, a capacitive transducer changes the circuit capacitance in response to the measurand.

5. (B)   In order to generate a voltage by the chemical method it is necessary to use two *dissimilar* metals immersed in an acid or alkali solution.

6. (B)   The VDR is a passive transducer because it changes circuit resistance. It does not generate a voltage.

7. (A)   Don't confuse the *photoresistor* and the *photocell*. A photoresistor changes resistance in response to the amount of light falling on it. A photocell produces a voltage in response to the amount of light falling on it.

8. (B)   Heat is the measurand. That is the end product of the oven and must be measured in order to make an effective closed-loop system.

9. (B)   Transducers permit the energy of one system to control the energy of another system. Although energy cannot be created or destroyed it can be changed from one form to another as in the case of the atomic bomb or X-ray tube. But that is not the way a transducer works.

10. (A)   Feedback controls are also called closed-loop controls or servo controls.

2
Electronic
Circuit Components

YOU ARE OBVIOUSLY trained and experienced in electronics, so you do not need a full-blown course in basic electronics. However, it is a good idea to review the components and their characteristics before taking a CET test.

This is not the only chapter that reviews components. Chapter 1 was mostly a review of electric components—especially transducers. Chapter 3 gives a review of nonlinear components. Throughout the book there will be some questions that require a knowledge of components.

Diodes are an important part of the review in this chapter. At one time rectifiers and detectors were the extent of diode use. Today, there are special diodes—such as lasers and magnetrons—that provide a wide range of applications.

Three-terminal linear amplifying components are also reviewed here. A very important thing to know is the polarities of dc voltages needed for getting the three-terminal components into operation. It is necessary to know those polarities in order to be effective in troubleshooting. When troubleshooting systems you need to know signal paths as well as dc operating voltages.

There are three configurations that are possible with three-terminal devices. The type of configuration is determined by the input and output signal paths. Since there are only two signal paths (input and output) it follows that the third electrode will be common to the two. The configurations are not necessarily related to the dc connections.

A common emitter circuit has the emitter at signal ground but may, at the same time, have the emitter converted to the positive output of the dc supply. The three amplifier configurations are discussed in Table 2-1.

Table 2-1. Configurations of Three-Terminal Devices.

Common Electrode	Input Signal Goes To	Output Signal Comes From	Characteristics
Plate, Collector, or Drain	Control Grid, Base, or Gate	Cathode, Emitter, or Source	Circuit is called a follower. Voltage gain less than 1.0. May have power gain. Matches high impedance to low impedance.
Control Grid, Base, or Gate	Cathode, Emitter, or Source	Plate, Collector, or Drain	Common-connected control electrode acts as a Faraday shield between the input and output signal connections. Good for high-frequency operation. Matches low impedance to high impedance.
Cathode, Emitter, or Source	Control Grid, Base, or Gate	Plate, Collector, or Drain	Most common connection. Best compromise for both voltage and power gain. Input and output impedances are reasonably high.

Although the three-terminal devices in this chapter are linear they can be operated at two distinct levels: *cutoff* and *saturation*. So, they can be used for binary (digital) applications.

The term *linear*, as applied to three-terminal amplifying devices, means there is a continuous change in the output signal whenever there is a continuous change in the input signal. They are not always operated that way. However, the fact that they can be operated that way means they are linear devices. The term *analog* is also used to mean linear.

Occasionally a technician will feel that only digital electronics is of interest. Even so, the digital systems are interfaced with the world through analog devices. It is not a good idea to become so specialized that you do not understand concepts that are outside your main interest.

When you answer multiple-choice questions be sure to read all of the choices. Consider this question—*Diodes have:*

    (1) Forward resistance.
    (2) Reverse resistance.
    (3) Both choices are correct.
    (4) Neither choice is correct.

You will recognize choice (1) as being correct. If you select choice (1) and disregard the other choices you will miss correct choice (3).

Read all of the choices before you make a selection!

You may have learned electronics on the basis of electron flow. On the other hand, you may have learned on the basis of conventional current flow. Both methods of describing current are correct!!

Instead of limiting your understanding to one method of describing current, it would be better to think of charge carriers—electrons for negative-to-positive current and holes for positive-to-negative current. Learn to be comfortable with both current directions because you will find both being used in technical literature.

Remember that industrial electronics is a very broad subject. Included are the specialties of other fields. Examples are microwave energy, communications, and radio control. You should expect to find questions on *all* subjects related to industrial electronics.

PROGRAMMED REVIEW NO. 1

Start with Block number 1. Pick the answer that you think is correct. If you select choice number 1, go to Block 13. If you select choice number 2, go to Block 15. Proceed as directed. There is only one correct answer for each question.

BLOCK 1

To get a higher forward current rating, diodes can be connected in:

    (1) Parallel. Go to Block 13.
    (2) Series. Go to Block 15.

BLOCK 2

Your answer to the question in Block 33 is not correct. Go back and read the question again and select another answer.

BLOCK 3

Your answer to the question in Block 10 is not correct. Go back and read the question again and select another answer.

BLOCK 4

Your answer to the question in Block 28 is not correct. Go back and read the question again and select another answer.

BLOCK 5

Your answer to the question in Block 33 is not correct. Go back and read the question again and select another answer.

BLOCK 6

Your answer to the question in Block 25 is not correct. Go back and read the question again and select another answer.

BLOCK 7

The correct answer to the question in Block 16 is choice (1). Without a forward bias the depletion reaches all of the way through the channel. So, there is no current path through that channel unless a forward bias decreases the depletion region (or enhances the conduction path).

Here is your next question: *Another name for linear amplifier is:*

(1) Analog amplifier. Go to Block 10.
(2) BIFET amplifier. Go to Block 24.

BLOCK 8

The correct answer to the question in Block 21 is choice (2). Secondary electrons from the screen of the CRT are attracted by the positive second anode. That anode is made from a conductive coating on the inside of the tube. The coating material, in its simplest form, is a mixture of graphite and water called *aquadag*.

Here is your next question: *Which of the following is a characteristic in common with triodes, JFETs, and MOSFETs?*

(1) They are all very popular in modern circuit design. Go to Block 29.
(2) They cannot be destroyed by an improper voltage. Go to Block 14.
(3) All have high input impedances. Go to Block 33.
(4) All have low input impedances. Go to Block 26.

BLOCK 9

Your answer to the question in Block 18 is not correct. Go back and read the question again and select another answer.

BLOCK 10

The correct answer to the question in Block 7 is choice (1). Remember that the word linear is used in different ways when applied to resistors and amplifiers. A *linear resistor* follows Ohm's law. Double the voltage across it and the current through it will double. (This assumes the resistor is not operated beyond its power rating.)

For a *linear amplifier* there is a continuous change in its output signal whenever there is a continuous change in its input signal.

An ideal linear amplifier has an output waveform that is identical to the input signal waveform. The term linear amplifier is often used to mean an amplifier that has very nearly identical waveforms at its input and output terminals.

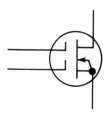

Here is your next question: *The device illustrated in this block has:*

(1) Two cathodes. Go to Block 3.
(2) Two plates. Go to Block 30.
(3) Two sources. Go to Block 35.
(4) Two gates. Go to Block 36.

BLOCK 11

Your answer to the question in Block 33 is not correct. Go back and read the question again and select another answer.

BLOCK 12

Your answer to the question in Block 27 is not correct. Go back and read the question again and select another answer.

BLOCK 13

The correct answer to the question in Block 1 is choice (1). Diodes in parallel, like resistors in parallel, have more paths for current flow.

Here is your next question: *A voltage-operated device has the advantage of not requiring input signal* power *(volts × amps). Which of the following devices requires input signal power?*

(1) JFET. Go to Block 17.
(2) PNP transistor. Go to Block 21.

BLOCK 14

Your answer to the question in Block 8 is not correct. Go back and read the question again and select another answer.

BLOCK 15

Your answer to the question in Block 1 is not correct. Go back and read the question again and select another answer.

BLOCK 16

The correct answer to the question in Block 27 is choice (3). The point that supplies charge carriers is considered to be zero volts with respect to the other electrodes.

Here is your next question: *Which type of MOSFET will not conduct a source-to-drain current unless it is forward biased?*

(1) Enhancement. Go to Block 7.
(2) Depletion. Go to Block 22.

BLOCK 17

Your answer to the question in Block 13 is not correct. Go back and read the question again and select another answer.

BLOCK 18

The correct answer to the question in Block 23 is choice (2). Manufacturers make different versions of these V-type MOSFETs with different names and different identifying numbers. However, most of the identifying numbers include the letter V.

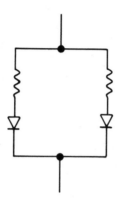

Here is your next question: *As shown in the illustration for this block, parallel-connected diodes have series-connected resistors. They are used to prevent:*

(1) Excessive PIV across any of the diodes. Go to Block 9.
(2) Current hogging. Go to Block 32.

BLOCK 19

Your answer to the question in Block 32 is not correct. Go back and read the question again and select another answer.

BLOCK 20

Your answer to the question in Block 27 is not correct. Go back and read the question again and select another answer.

BLOCK 21

The correct answer to the question in Block 13 is choice (2). Bipolar transistors require both current and voltage at their base electrodes. Therefore, they require signal power (volts × amps). This is an important disadvantage of bipolar transistors.

Here is your next question: *In a CRT electrons are collected at the:*

(1) Plate. Go to Block 34.
(2) Second anode. Go to Block 8.

BLOCK 22

Your answer to the question in Block 16 is not correct. Go back and read the question again and select another answer.

BLOCK 23

The correct answer to the question in Block 33 is choice (3). They are not constructed like rectifier and detector diodes. However, if you identify a diode as a device that has a cathode and anode, then both are forms of diodes.

Here is your next question: *Which of the following would more likely be used as a power amplifier?*

(1) JFET. Go to Block 31.
(2) VFET. Go to Block 18.

BLOCK 24

Your answer to the question in Block 7 is not correct. Go back and read the question again and select another answer.

BLOCK 25

The correct answer to the question in Block 32 is choice (2). The symbol is for an N-channel JFET. It requires the following voltage polarities with respect to the source:

- negative gate (corresponding with the negative triode grid),
- positive drain (corresponding with the positive triode plate).

Here is your next question: *Which of the following requires a negative voltage on its gate (with respect to its source).*

(1) N-channel Enhancement MOSFET. Go to Block 6.
(2) P-channel Enhancement MOSFET. Go to Block 28.

BLOCK 26

Your answer to the question in Block 8 is not correct. Go back and read the question again and select another answer.

BLOCK 27

The correct answer to the question in Block 28 is choice (1). Remember, the enhancement MOSFETs must be forward biased.

Here is your next question: *Which of the electrodes on a JFET is considered to be at zero volts with respect to the others?*

(1) Drain. Go to Block 12.
(2) Gate. Go to Block 20.
(3) Source. Go to Block 16.

BLOCK 28

The correct answer to the question in Block 25 is choice (2). With the P-channel enhancement MOSFET a negative voltage is needed on the gate to forward bias the gate-source junction.

Here is your next question: *Which type of N-channel MOSFET normally operates with a positive voltage on its gate with respect to the voltage on its source?*

(1) Enhancement. Go to Block 27.
(2) Depletion. Go to Block 4.

BLOCK 29

Your answer to the question in Block 8 is not correct. Go back and read the question again and select another answer.

BLOCK 30

Your answer to the question in Block 10 is not correct. Go back and read the question again and select another answer.

BLOCK 31

Your answer to the question in Block 23 is not correct. Go back and read the question again and select another answer.

BLOCK 32

The correct answer to the question in Block 18 is choice (2). When all of the current flows through one of the diodes in parallel it is hogging the current. The series resistors have a voltage drop that adds to the diode drop. The voltages assure that there is enough voltage to start all diodes in parallel.

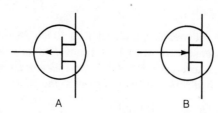

A   B

Here is your next question: *Which of the JFETs shown in this block has the same voltage polarities on its electrodes as a vacuum-tube triode?*

(1) The one marked A. Go to Block 19.
(2) The one marked B. Go to Block 25.

BLOCK 33

The correct answer to the question in Block 8 is choice(3). The devices require input signal *voltage* but zero *current*. Looking into the control terminal it appears that there is an extremely high resistance because the voltage does not produce any current flow.

Here is your next question: *Select the component that is an example of a vacuum tube diode.*

(1) Magnetron. Go to Block 5.
(2) X-ray tube. Go to Block 11.
(3) Both are vacuum tube diodes. Go to Block 23.
(4) Neither is a vacuum tube diode. Go to Block 2.

BLOCK 34

Your answer to the question in Block 21 is not correct. Go back and read the question again and select another answer.

BLOCK 35

Your answer to the question in Block 10 is not correct. Go back and read the question again and select another answer.

BLOCK 36

The correct answer to the question in Block 10 is choice (4). The symbol is for a *dual gate MOSFET*. It is very useful in applications where two signals are to be mixed or heterodyned.

You have now completed Programmed Review No. 1.

PROGRAMMED REVIEW NO. 2

Start with Block number 1. Pick the answer that you think is correct. If you select choice number 1, go to Block 13. If you select choice number 2, go to Block 15. Proceed as directed. There is only one correct answer for each question.

BLOCK 1.

Two things you need to know when you buy a diode are its PIV rating and its:

(1) Maximum forward current. Go to Block 13.
(2) Maximum forward breakover voltage. Go to Block 15.

BLOCK 2

Your answer to the question in Block 20 is not correct. Go back and read the question again and select another answer.

BLOCK 3

The correct answer to the question in Block 4 is choice (2). There is no gate electrode on a bipolar transistor. As far as the signal is concerned, one of the three electrodes on a tube, bipolar transistor, and field effect transistor must be common to the input and output signal. So, a bipolar transistor can be connected as a common emitter, common base, or common collector amplifier. This has nothing to do with the dc operating voltages.

It is important that you know the configurations, including their characteristics, although they are not usually subjects covered in a CET test.

Here is your next question: *In a vacuum tube device electrons are emitted by the:*

(1) Cathode. Go to Block 26.
(2) Anode. Go to Block 37.

BLOCK 4

The correct answer to the question in Block 14 is choice (4). There is no type of emission called optoelectronic. There is a type called photoemission. X-rays are electromagnetic emissions.

Here is your next question: *When the input signal is at the base of a bipolar transistor and the output signal is at the collector, it is called a common:*

    (1) Gate amplifier. Go to Block 24.
    (2) Emitter amplifier. Go to Block 3.

BLOCK 5

Your answer to the question in Block 14 is not correct. Go back and read the question again and select another answer.

BLOCK 6

Your answer to the question in Block 32 is not correct. Go back and read the question again and select another answer.

BLOCK 7

Your answer to the question in Block 26 is not correct. Go back and read the question again and select another answer.

BLOCK 8

Your answer to the question in Block 32 is not correct. Go back and read the question again and select another answer.

BLOCK 9

Your answer to the question in Block 10 is not correct. Go back and read the question again and select another answer.

BLOCK 10

The correct answer to the question in Block 18 is choice (2). For a bipolar transistor the control electrode is the base. It is the gate for MOSFETs and JFETs. For vacuum tube three-terminal devices it is the control grid.

Here is your next question: *Which of the following requires a forward bias for its operation?*

    (1) NPN transistor. Go to Block 25.
    (2) PNP transistor. Go to Block 16.
    (3) Both choices are correct. Go to Block 27.
    (4) Neither choice is correct. Go to Block 9.

BLOCK 11

The correct answer to the question in Block 21 is choice (2). The charge carriers (electrons and holes) are removed from the region during the manufacturing process. In order to get a charge carrier to move through the depletion region its energy level must be increased.

Here is your next question: *A voltmeter across a silicon diode that is out of the circuit should read:*

(1) Zero volts. Go to Block 32.
(2) About 0.6 volts. Go to Block 19.

BLOCK 12

The correct answer to the question in Block 20 is choice (2). In microwave systems inductance, capacitance, and resistance take on a completely different appearance than they have in lower-frequency circuits.

The *cavity resonators* in the magnetrons are hollow regions that behave like tuned circuits.

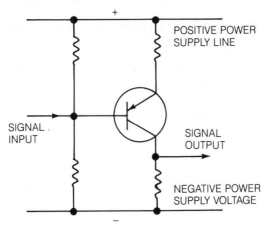

Here is your next question: *Consider the transistor amplifier in this block. Which of the following statements is correct?*

(1) The amplifier cannot operate because incorrect dc polarities are on the PNP transistor. Go to Block 33.
(2) The transistor has the correct voltage polarities for operation as an amplifier. Go to Block 14.

BLOCK 13

The correct answer to the question in Block 1 is choice (1). Technicians should spend some time studying specifications given in catalogs. Those specifications limit the operation of the components.

Here is your next question: *Increasing the base current of a bipolar transistor results in an increase in:*

(1) Collector voltage. Go to Block 28.
(2) Collector current. Go to Block 18.

BLOCK 14

The correct answer to the question in Block 12 is choice (2). In the PNP circuit of Block 12 the emitter is positive with respect to the base and collector. That is another way of saying that the base and collector are negative with respect to the emitter. So, the *polarities* of the voltages are correct.

In addition to having the correct polarities, it is also necessary to have the proper amounts of voltage. This is not apparent from the circuit in Block 12. The collector must be negative with respect to the base.

Here is your next question: *Which of the following types of electron emission is used to make a photocell?*

(1) Optoelectronic emission. Go to Block 5.
(2) X-rays. Go to Block 29.
(3) Both choices are correct. Go to Block 38.
(4) Neither choice is correct. Go to Block 4.

BLOCK 15

Your answer to the question in Block 1 is not correct. Go back and read the question again and select another answer.

BLOCK 16

Your answer to the question in Block 10 is not correct. Go back and read the question again and select another answer.

BLOCK 17

Your answer to the question in Block 31 is not correct. Go back and read the question again and select another answer.

BLOCK 18

The correct answer to the question in Block 13 is choice (2). The action of bipolar transistors in circuits is sometimes described in terms of voltages. However, you should always keep in mind the fact that they are current-operated devices.

Here is your next question: *Which electrode of a bipolar transistor is usually used for signal input or control?*

(1) Collector. Go to Block 34.
(2) Base. Go to Block 10.

BLOCK 19

Your answer to the question in Block 11 is not correct. Go back and read the question again and select another answer.

BLOCK 20

The correct answer to the question in Block 27 is choice (1). Avalanching also occurs in semiconductors. In fact, one type of semiconductor diode is called the *avalanche diode*. It has characteristics that are similar to zener diodes, but the zener diode mechanism is slightly different. You will review zener diodes in the chapter on power supplies.

Here is your next question: *You can think of the cavities in a magnetron as being:*

(1) RC circuits. Go to Block 2.
(2) RL circuits. Go to Block 12.

BLOCK 21

The correct answer to the question in Block 26 is choice (1). Electron current is always from cathode to anode. Conventional current flows from anode to cathode.

Here is your next question: *The nonconducting region between the N and P sections of a diode is called the:*

(1) Depression region. Go to Block 30.
(2) Depletion region. Go to Block 11.

BLOCK 22

The correct answer to the question in Block 31 is choice (4). There is no method of obtaining electron emission called piezoelectric emission.

Here is your next question: *Which of the following is not a method of getting electron emission from the surface of a material?*

(1) Field emission. Go to Block 40.
(2) Electromagnetic emission. Go to Block 41.

BLOCK 23

Your answer to the question in Block 32 is not correct. Go back and read the question again and select another answer.

BLOCK 24

Your answer to the question in Block 4 is not correct. Go back and read the question again and select another answer.

BLOCK 25

Your answer to the question in Block 10 is not correct. Go back and read the question again and select another answer.

BLOCK 26

The correct answer to the question in Block 3 is choice (1). In some types of tubes electron emission is from the filament. In that case the filament is the cathode.

Here is your next question: *A vacuum tube diode is* unilateral *meaning that electron current flows only from:*

(1) Cathode to anode. Go to Block 21.
(2) Anode to cathode. Go to Block 7.

BLOCK 27

The correct answer to the question in Block 10 is choice (3). Compare the polarities of voltages on bipolar transistor with the polarities of voltages on enhancement MOSFETs.

Here is your next question: *Avalanching occurs in:*

(1) Gas tubes. Go to Block 20.
(2) Vacuum tubes. Go to Block 39.

BLOCK 28

Your answer to the question in Block 13 is not correct. Go back and read the question again and select another answer.

BLOCK 29

Your answer to the question in Block 14 is not correct. Go back and read the question again and select another answer.

BLOCK 30

Your answer to the question in Block 21 is not correct. Go back and read the question again and select another answer.

BLOCK 31

The correct answer to the question in Block 32 is choice (3). They are not constructed like other diodes, but they are simply reduced to cathode and anode in a vacuum.

Here is your next question: *Electron emission is not obtained by:*

(1) The photoelectric emission. Go to Block 35.
(2) The thermionic emission. Go to Block 17.
(3) Secondary emission. Go to Block 36.
(4) Piezoelectric emission. Go to Block 22.

BLOCK 32

The correct answer to the question in Block 11 is choice (1). In the absence of any circuit connections the voltage across the diode is zero volts. Try this for yourself. It is contrary to statements sometimes made about diodes.

Here is your next question: *Which of the following is not a form of vacuum tube diode?*

(1) Magnetron. Go to Block 6.
(2) X-ray tube. Go to Block 23.
(3) Both are forms of a vacuum-tube diode. Go to Block 31.
(4) None of the choices is correct. Go to Block 8.

BLOCK 33

Your answer to the question in Block 12 is not correct. Go back and read the question again and select another answer.

BLOCK 34

Your answer to the question in Block 18 is not correct. Go back and read the question again and select another answer.

BLOCK 35

Your answer to the question in Block 31 is not correct. Go back and read the question again and select another answer.

BLOCK 36

Your answer to the question in Block 31 is not correct. Go back and read the question again and select another answer.

BLOCK 37

Your answer to the question in Block 3 is not correct. Go back and read the question again and select another answer.

BLOCK 38

Your answer to the question in Block 14 is not correct. Go back and read the question again and select another answer.

BLOCK 39

Your answer to the question in Block 27 is not correct. Go back and read the question again and select another answer.

BLOCK 40

Your answer to the question in Block 22 is not correct. Go back and read the question again and select another answer.

BLOCK 41

The correct answer to the question in Block 22 is choice (2). There is no method of electron emission called electromagnetic.

You have now completed the Programmed Review No. 2.

KEY WORDS

Analog	LED
Aquadag	Linear
Avalanching	Magnatron
Cavity resonator	Microwave
Cutoff	PIV
Depletion	Saturation
Dual gate	Space charge
Enhancement	Unilateral
LAD	VMOS

PRACTICE TEST

1. Increasing the reverse bias on a varactor diode will:

    (A) Increase its capacitance.
    (B) Decrease its capacitance.

2. Which of the following has the same voltage polarities on its electrodes?

    (A) NPN bipolar transistor and N-channel JFET.
    (B) PNP bipolar transistor and P-channel enhancement MOS-FET.

3. In a rectifier or detector vacuum tube diode there is a cloud of electrons around the cathode. It is called:

    (A) The cloud chamber.
    (B) The space charge.

4. To increase the drain current in a P-channel enhancement MOS-FET, make its gate voltage more:

    (A) Negative.
    (B) Positive.

5. Which of the following devices is current operated?

    (A) PNP transistor.
    (B) NPN transistor.
    (C) Both are voltage operated.
    (D) Neither is voltage operated.

6. To get a higher PIV rating, diodes can be connected in:

    (A) Series.
    (B) Parallel.

7. Which electrode of a MOSFET is used for dc input electron current?

    (A) Emitter.
    (B) Source.
    (C) Neither choice is correct.

8. Which of the following is more likely to be used as a power amplifier?

(A) P-channel JFET.
(B) VMOS transistor.

9. You can troubleshoot a system by following the signal with an oscilloscope, and by measuring:

(A) dc polarities and voltages.
(B) ac voltages.

10. A diode that has a low forward resistance when exposed to light is called a:

(A) LAD.
(B) LOD.

ANSWERS TO PRACTICE TEST

1. (B)   Increasing the reverse bias increases the size of the depletion region. That, in turn, moves the *plates* (N-type and P-type conductors) further apart and decreases the capacitance.

2. (B)   Memorize the polarities of voltages required for operating the devices.

3. (B)

4. (A)

5. (D)   Both require a base current for their operation.

6. (A)

7. (B)

8. (B)

9. (A)

10. (A)

3

Thyristors and Other Switching Devices

SWITCHES ARE NOT always simple ON and OFF devices. In electronics a switch may be a device that alternates between two distinct voltage levels.

Thyristors are the electronic switches of industrial electronics. They are also used in other fields of electronics. Thyristors are breakover devices. They will not conduct until the voltage across them, or the voltage applied to their gates, reaches a certain minimum predetermined level. That level is sometimes referred to as the *firing potential*, but more often it is referred to as the breakover voltage.

Relays are electromechanical switches. Newer types of relays are made very small. They can be built into an integrated circuit package, and they are still being used extensively in industrial electronics.

One advantage of the relay is its high fan-out capability. In other words, a single relay can drive a large number of individual circuits simultaneously. Another advantage of the relay is the very high isolation between contacts when the relay is not energized.

Disadvantages of relays and mechanical switches include *contact bounce* and mechanical *wear*. Contact bounce is especially troublesome in logic and computer circuits because the bouncing contacts produce pulses that can be interpreted as signals in a digital system. The moving part of the relay is called the *armature*. The electromagnetic field is created by the coil.

Thermal switches are sometimes called *thermal relays*. A bimetalic metal strip bends when it is heated. That motion is used to either make contact or break contact.

You should know the forms of switches and relay contacts. For example, Form A is a normally-open switch and Form B is a normally-closed switch. Form C has one normally-open contact and one normally-closed contact.

Losses in relays and other electromechanical devices are the same as for the losses in transformers. They include *eddy currents, copper losses*, and *hysteresis loss*. Eddy currents are reduced by laminating the magnetic material. Copper losses can sometimes be reduced by making the coils with larger wires. Hysteresis losses are reduced by proper selection of the magnetic core materials.

Unijunction transistors (UJTs) and programmable unijunction transistors (PUTs) have an *intrinsic standoff ratio* rating. It tells the decimal part of a power supply voltage that must be delivered to the operating electrode in order for the device to conduct.

On the UJT, the operating electrode is the emitter. The operating voltage applied is *across* a PUT. The output of a UJT or PUT can be positive short-term pulses or it can be a sawtooth waveform. The sawtooth waveform has a curved ramp because it depends on the charging of a capacitor. However, a constant current device can be placed in series with a charge path to linearize the ramp.

An SCR is usually considered to be a high-current switch. It is normally in the OFF condition until a positive gate pulse is applied. Once the SCR conducts it cannot be shut off with a gate voltage. Instead, it is necessary to open the anode-cathode circuit or to commutate the SCR OFF with a bipolar transistor (or with another SCR).

A silicon control switch (SCS) can be turned ON with one gate voltage and turned OFF with another gate voltage. Except for the fact that it can be turned ON and OFF, it is very similar in its operation to an SCR. The silicon bilateral switch (SBS) has only one gate electrode. It can be used to turn the device ON or OFF.

You should be able to calculate the frequency of a waveform if you know the time for one cycle. The time for one cycle is called the *period*. The frequency is equal to the reciprocal of the period.

In the earlier days of electronics, stepping switches were used to electromechanically select from different inputs. Today, *multiplexers* are made in integrated circuit packages and they accomplish the same thing. A multiplexer selects one of many inputs. A *demultiplexer* delivers an input to a selected output.

Triacs are components that are made with back-to-back SCRs. They are used in ac circuits, whereas the SCR is basically a dc component. In other words, it is unilateral in its operation. However, you can get full-cycle operation using an SCR and a full-wave rectifier at the input of the ac power. A bridge rectifier is commonly used for this purpose.

High voltage spikes can accidentally trigger an SCR into operation if the voltage is across the anode and the cathode. To prevent false triggering from noise pulses, a snubber circuit is connected across the SCR. It is made with a resistor and a capacitor in series.

One of the more recent SCRs is called MOS SCR. It triggers with a gate voltage, whereas a normal SCR triggers with a gate current. The MOS SCR is very useful because it can interface directly with low voltage, low current, logic systems. So, a computer or microprocessor or other logic system output can easily trigger the MOS SCR into operation.

You should have a basic understanding of *optoelectronic devices*, such as light emitting diodes and infrared diodes. Remember that these devices are made with gallium arsenide rather than with silicon. They light when current flows through them in the forward direction. Gallium arsenide is also used for high-speed switching transistors and very high frequency operation of bipolar transistors.

PROGRAMMED REVIEW NO. 1

Start with Block number 1. Pick the answer that you think is correct. If you select choice number 1, go to Block 13. If you select choice number 2, go to Block 15. Proceed as directed. There is only one correct answer for each question.

BLOCK 1

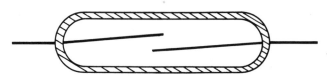

The contacts of the reed switch shown in this block are:

(1) Form A. Go to Block 13.
(2) Form B. Go to Block 15.

BLOCK 2

Your answer to the question in Block 12 is not correct. Go back and read the question again and select another answer.

BLOCK 3

Your answer to the question in Block 27 is not correct. Go back and read the question again and select another answer.

BLOCK 4

Your answer to the question in Block 25 is not correct. Go back and read the question again and select another answer.

BLOCK 5

Your answer to the question in Block 31 is not correct. Go back and read the question again and select another answer.

BLOCK 6

The correct answer to the question in Block 27 is choice (1). The silicon bilateral switch can be turned ON and OFF by the inputs to a single gate.

Among the other possibilities, STV stands for subscription television. It has no meaning in the world of thyristors.

Here is your next question: *A triac behaves like back-to-back _____.* Go to Block 33.

BLOCK 7

The correct answer to the question in Block 33 is choice (1). The word *armature* is used to designate the moving parts of relays, motors, and other electromechanical devices. When you see the word armature think of the words *moving parts*.

Here is your next question: *Why are the magnetic circuits of certain relays made with laminations, that is, thin slices of magnetic material?*

(1) To make them lighter. Go to Block 16.
(2) To reduce electromagnetic losses. Go to Block 25.

BLOCK 8

The correct answer to the question in Block 18 is choice (2). Start by dividing the total time displayed (or marked) by the number of complete cycles in that period. That will give you the time for one cycle. Then, use the equation

$$T = 1/f$$

When T is the time for one complete cycle it is called the period of the waveform; f is the frequency.

Since frequency is being requested, the equation is solved for f:

$$f = 1/T$$

Triggered sweep oscilloscopes have time bases calculated in seconds, milliseconds, and microseconds. The above equation is needed for converting the display to frequency.

Here is your next question: *The intrinsic standoff ratio of a PUT is set by:*

(1) The manufacturer. Go to Block 19.
(2) A voltage divider. Go to Block 27.

BLOCK 9

Your answer to the question in Block 28 is not correct. Go back and read the question again and select another answer.

BLOCK 10

Your answer to the question in Block 12 is not correct. Go back and read the question again and select another answer.

BLOCK 11

Your answer to the question in Block 27 is not correct. Go back and read the question again and select another answer.

BLOCK 12

The correct answer to the question in Block 25 is choice (2). Thermal relays are made by using two dissimilar metals banded together. When heated, the metals bend because they have different coefficients of expansion.

Contacts are used with the bimetal strip. They may close a circuit, or they may open a circuit when heated, depending upon how the device is designed.

The concept is used to make a thermal switch. It can also be used to make a circuit breaker or relay.

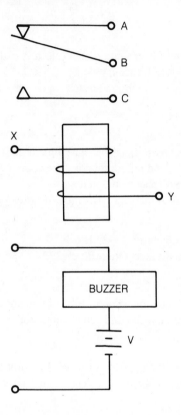

Here is your next question: *For the relay in the illustration in this block you want the buzzer to sound if the applied voltage (across X and Y) is lost. Connect the buzzer circuit terminals across:*

(1) Contacts A and B. Go to Block 28.
(2) Contacts A and C. Go to Block 10.
(3) Contacts B and C. Go to Block 2.

BLOCK 13

Your answer to the question in Block 1 is not correct. Go back and read the question again and select another answer.

BLOCK 14

Your answer to the question in Block 28 is not correct. Go back and read the question again and select another answer.

BLOCK 15

The correct answer to the question in Block 1 is choice (1). Relays and switch contacts are normally shown in their de-energized and not-activated positions. The contacts in the reed switch, or reed relay, like the contacts in the illustration of Block 1, are shown in their Normally Open (N.O.) position.

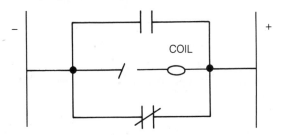

Here is your next question: *The illustration in this block shows a:*

(1) Form A contact arrangement. Go to Block 26.
(2) Form B contact arrangement. Go to Block 20.
(3) Form C contact arrangement. Go to Block 17.
(4) Useless arrangement of contacts. Go to Block 32.

BLOCK 16

Your answer to the question in Block 7 is not correct. Go back and read the question again and select another answer.

BLOCK 17

Your answer to the question in Block 15 is not correct. Go back and read the question again and select another answer.

BLOCK 18

The correct answer to the question in Block 21 is choice (1). Remember that a silicon controlled switch (SCS) has two gate electrodes. One is for turning the SCS ON and the other is for turning it OFF.

The problem with using an SCS is that you need two different signal sources—one for each gate. However, you need two different switches to turn an SCR ON and OFF.

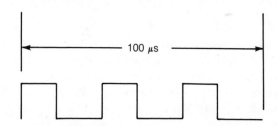

Here is your next question: *The output pulses of a UJT are shown in the illustration for this block. What is the output frequency?*

(1) 40 kilohertz. Go to Block 30.
(2) 30 kilohertz. Go to Block 8.

BLOCK 19

Your answer to the question in Block 8 is not correct. Go back and read the question again and select another answer.

BLOCK 20

Your answer to the question in Block 15 is not correct. Go back and read the question again and select another answer.

BLOCK 21

The correct answer to the question in Block 31 is choice (1). A stepping switch selects one of a number of inputs. Therefore, it is a form of multiplexer.

Stepping switches are electromechanical devices that have been replaced by integrated circuit multiplexers.

Here is your next question: *Which of the following devices can be turned ON and OFF by input signals?*

(1) SCS. Go to Block 18.
(2) SCR. Go to Block 24.

BLOCK 22

Your answer to the question in Block 28 is not correct. Go back and read the question again and select another answer.

BLOCK 23

Your answer to the question in Block 32 is not correct. Go back and read the question again and select another answer.

BLOCK 24

Your answer to the question in Block 21 is not correct. Go back and read the question again and select another answer.

BLOCK 25

The correct answer to the question in Block 7 is choice (2). There are three kinds of losses in electromechanical devices. You probably studied them when you were learning about transformers. However, these losses occur with any electromagnetic component. They are:

- Copper loss
- Hysteresis loss
- Eddy current loss

Copper loss occurs due to the resistance of the copper wire and connections of the electromagnet. This type of loss is also called the I^2R loss.

Hysteresis loss occurs because a certain amount of electromagnetic energy is needed to reverse the magnetism after each half cycle.

Eddy current loss occurs because of the expanding and contracting magnetic field around the coil due to ac current flow in the coil. That moving magnetic field induces circulating currents, called eddy currents, in the metal of the magnetic circuit.

You can reduce copper loss by using wire with a larger diameter.

You can reduce hysteresis loss by the proper selection of the magnetic materials in the magnetic circuit.

You can reduce eddy currents at lower frequencies by using thin slices of the magnetic material used for the core. Those slices are called *laminations*.

Here is your next question: *Thin strips of two different kinds of metals are clamped together. If they are free to move they will:*

(1) Bend when exposed to a fixed magnetic field. Go to Block 4.

(2) Bend when heated. Go to Block 12.

BLOCK 26

Your answer to the question in Block 15 is not correct. Go back and read the question again and select another answer.

BLOCK 27

The correct answer to the question in Block 8 is choice (2). The ratio of resistors in the voltage divider determines what decimal part of the power supply voltages must be obtained from anode-to-cathode in order for the PUT to conduct. The circuit is illustrated in this block.

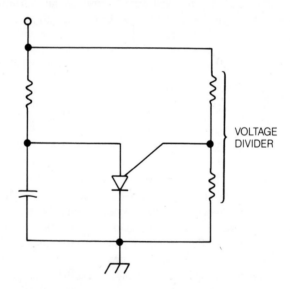

The output of the circuit is a series of pulses. A pulse occurs every time the PUT conducts.

A variable resistor or a transistor in one of the voltage divider legs can be used to vary the frequency of the oscillator.

A UJT has an intrinsic standoff ratio that is set during manufacture.

Here is your next question: *Which of the following is an example of a thyristor?*

(1) SBS. Go to Block 6.
(2) STV. Go to Block 11.
(3) Both are thyristors. Go to Block 3.
(4) Neither is a thyristor. Go to Block 29.

BLOCK 28

The correct answer to the question in Block 12 is choice (1). Remember that relays are always shown in their de-energized condition. When the voltage being sensed is connected to terminals X and Y the relay is energized and the buzzer should be OFF.

If the voltage is lost, the relay will be de-energized. That connects terminals A and B. When the buzzer is connected to those terminals it is ON when the voltage is lost.

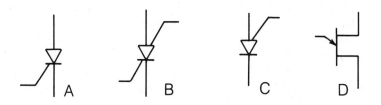

Here is your next question: *Refer to the symbols shown in this block. Which is for a PUT?*

(1) The one marked A. Go to Block 22.
(2) The one marked B. Go to Block 14.
(3) The one marked C. Go to Block 31.
(4) None of these choices is correct. Go to Block 9.

BLOCK 29

Your answer to the question in Block 27 is not correct. Go back and read the question again and select another answer.

BLOCK 30

Your answer to the question in Block 18 is not correct. Go back and read the question again and select another answer.

BLOCK 31

The correct answer to the question in Block 28 is choice (3). When you first studied electronics you learned some very important things. *Symbols* is an example. It isn't enough to know what a resistor does if you can't recognize it on a schematic diagram.

Another thing you learned was the *polarities of voltages* on important electronic devices. When you are troubleshooting you do not have time to stop and look up all of the voltage polarities you should encounter in the system.

Much of the information in this book concerns those two aspects of electronics. Also, you learned to trace dc paths and signal paths through a system. You must be able to do that if you are tracking down a problem.

Therefore, the PUT symbol is one of the basic things you should know. The PUT is a very important component in many industrial electronic systems.

Here is your next question: *Which of the following can be used as a multiplexer?*

(1) Stepping switch. Go to Block 21.
(2) SCR. Go to Block 5.

BLOCK 32

The correct answer to the question in Block 15 is choice (4). Note that current can flow from A to B or B to A regardless of whether or not the coil switch (SW) is closed. The contact arrangement could be replaced with a straight piece of wire.

Also, the switch contacts present a *short circuit* between the + and − terminals of the power supply! That is really a useless arrangement.

Remember, for answers to other questions, that the contact symbols shown in this block are used to represent both switch and relay contacts.

The relay (and switch) contact arrangements represented by those symbols are used in other applications. For example, a Programmable Controller is an industrial electronic system that can be used to control a wide variety of things like industrial chemical processes, movement of materials, speed control, automatic operations of a drill press, etc. Some programmable controllers have relay and switch contacts displayed to the programmer even though the system is made entirely of electronic components. This is especially true of early models—many of which are still being used.

Mechanical and electromechanical symbols were used to make it easier for programmers to make the transition to all-electronic systems, but the transition was not easy. Experienced controllers did not like the new electronic versions at first. Their complaint, among other things, was that *they didn't make any noise*! One manufacturer actually considered the idea of putting noise makers in the units to simulate the clattering and bumping noises!

Although the all-electronic systems are now firmly entrenched you will still see the relay symbols and the contact forms. You should take time to learn them.

Here is your next question: *The moving part of a relay is called the:*

(1) Armature. Go to Block 7.
(2) Rotor. Go to Block 23.

BLOCK 33

SCRs. In fact, you can use back-to-back SCRs to make a triac.
You have now completed Programmed Review No. 1.

PROGRAMMED REVIEW NO. 2

Start with Block number 1. Pick the answer that you think is correct. If you select choice number 1, go to Block 13. If you select choice number 2, go to Block 15. Proceed as directed. There is only one correct answer for each question.

BLOCK 1

A single output depends upon selecting one of many inputs in a:

(1) Multiplexer. Go to Block 13.
(2) Demultiplexer. Go to Block 15.

BLOCK 2

Your answer to the question in Block 13 is not correct. Go back and read the question again and select another answer.

BLOCK 3

The correct answer to the question in Block 10 is choice (1). Thyristors require an operating voltage across their terminals. However, they do not conduct until a certain minimum voltage (or current) is reached. The SCR, for example, requires a gate *current* to start it into conduction. A PUT, on the other hand, requires a dc voltage to start conduction.

Do not be confused by the fact that manufacturer's SCR specifications (may) list a trigger voltage to start conduction. Inside the device it is the gate current that results from the date trigger voltage that actually starts current through the device.

A MOS SCR is a different kind of component. Its symbol is shown in the illustration for this block. Observe that the gate is similar to the gate of a MOSFET. It is a voltage-operated SCR.

Unlike the conventional SCR, the MOSFET does not require a current to start conduction. It is ideally suited for use in integrated logic circuits.

Here is your next question: *Light-emitting diodes (LEDS) are made with:*

(1) Silicon. Go to Block 19.
(2) Gallium arsenide. Go to Block 6.

BLOCK 4

The correct answer to the question in Block 27 is choice (2). When a *negative* pulse is applied to the PNP transistor it conducts and short circuits the SCR. That in turn, shuts the SCR OFF.

Here is your next question: *What component can be used to get a linear sawtooth waveform from a UJT oscillator?*

_____. Go to Block 32.

BLOCK 5

Your answer to the question in Block 21 is not correct. Go back and read the question again and select another answer.

BLOCK 6

The correct answer to the question in Block 3 is choice (1). Gallium arsenide is not only used for making LEDs. Superior transistors for operating in the megahertz frequency ranges are made from gallium arsenide.

Here is your next question: *Which of the following is a unilateral device?*

(1) Four-layer diode. Go to Block 12.
(2) Three-layer diode. Go to Block 8.

BLOCK 7

The correct answer to the question in Block 16 is choice (1). It is easy to obtain a high fan-out design for an electromechanical relay. That is still one of its advantages.

Another advantage is in the fact that open contacts offer a very high impedance. By comparison, some of the electronic switches permit a leakage current to flow when they are *open*.

A disadvantage of electromechanical relays is that they are slow compared to electronic types.

Here is your next question: *Which of the following is an advantage of relays over mechanical switches?*

(1) No contact bounce. Go to Block 24.
(2) Remote turn ON and turn OFF of high-current switches. Go to Block 10.

BLOCK 8

Your answer to the question in Block 6 is not correct. Go back and read the question again and select another answer.

BLOCK 9

The correct answer to the question in Block 13 is choice (4). The proper circuit is shown in this block. Note that a resistor is connected in parallel with the lamp that has the lower current rating. The value of R is chosen so that the current through the lamp added to the current through the resistor equals the current through the lamp with the higher current rating.

Here is the calculation for the resistor value:

From the circuit you can see that $1/4$ amp ($= 0.25$A) must flow through R and the voltage across R must be 6V. By Ohm's law:

$$R = V/1 = 6/0.25 = 24 \text{ ohms}$$

The power dissipation of the resistor is calculated from Joule's law:

$$P = I^2R = (0.25)^2 \times 24 = 1.5 \text{ W}$$

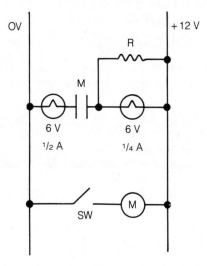

Here is your next question: *Refer to the circuit in this block. You have to add an LED to show that the switch is open. You will add the LED*

(1) In series with the switch. Go to Block 22.
(2) In parallel with the switch. Go to Block 16.
(3) Across a lamp. Go to Block 29.

BLOCK 10

The correct answer to the question in Block 7 is choice (2). You will encounter contact bounce in switches as well as with relay contacts. There are simple circuits that respond only to the first contact, then disregards all of the bounces.

The *one-shot multivibrator* is also called *monostable multivibrator*. When triggered, its output goes through a complete cycle before it goes back to its quiescent condition.

If the period of the cycle is longer than the time for bounces the effect of those bounces are then eliminated by the one shot.

Other bounceless switch circuits are available. Another example will be discussed later.

Here is your next question: *Which of the following are the electronic switching components called breakover devices?*

(1) Thyristors. Go to Block 3.
(2) Relays. Go to Block 25.

BLOCK 11

Your answer to the question in Block 13 is not correct. Go back and read the question again and select another answer.

BLOCK 12

The correct answer to the question in Block 6 is choice (1). As an industrial electronics technician you are expected to know how all of the thyristor devices work.

Here is your next question: *What is the name of the RC circuit used across an SCR to prevent false triggering by noise?*

_____. Go to Block 17.

BLOCK 13

The correct answer to the question in Block 1 is choice (1). A multiplexer has a number of inputs and one output. It selects one input at a time.

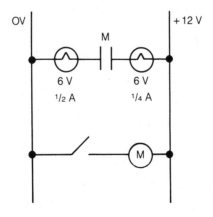

A demultiplexer has one input and a number of output. One output is selected at a time.

Multiplexers and demultiplexers are made in integrated circuit form. They are used in integrated circuit logic systems.

Here is your next question: *In the circuit for this block the lamps are to glow at their rated brightness when the relay is energized. It will be necessary to connect a resistor:*

(1) In series with the lamps. Go to Block 11.
(2) In parallel with the lamps. Go to Block 28.
(3) In series and another in parallel. Go to Block 2.
(4) None of these choices is correct. Go to Block 9.

BLOCK 14

The correct answer to the question in Block 21 is choice (1). For the dc circuit, once the SCR is ON the gate has no control over its operation. Therefore, the lamp will remain ON after the switch is opened.

Here is your next question: *Name three ways of shutting an SCR OFF when it is in a dc circuit.*

     ————————————.
     ————————————.
     ————————————. Go to Block 27.

BLOCK 15

Your answer to the question in Block 1 is not correct. Go back and read the question again and select another answer.

BLOCK 16

The correct answer to the question in Block 9 is choice (2). Of course, it would not make any sense to put the LED in series since the switch is to be open when the LED is ON.

You have to make sure that the 20 milliamperes or so drawn by the LED is very low compared to the current required for energizing the relay. If not, it might be possible to put the LED across the contacts in series with the lamps.

Always connect a resistor in series with the LED (if there is not one already built in). In a typical application the voltage across an LED is about 1.6 volts and the current through it is about 20 milliamperes.

That current is higher for the large (jumbo) LEDs.

Here is your next question: *The number of switch contacts a relay can operate simultaneously is called its:*

(1) Fan out. Go to Block 7.

(2) Multiplex. Go to Block 31.

BLOCK 17

The correct answer to the question in Block 12 is *snubber*. (Note: All questions in the CET test are multiple choice.)

Here is your next question: *To obtain full-wave operation with a single SCR, use:*

(1) A full-wave rectifier. Go to Block 21.

(2) A full-wave doubler. Go to Block 26.

(3) A half-wave doubler. Go to Block 30.

(4) A half-wave rectifier. Go to Block 23.

BLOCK 18

Your answer to the question in Block 4 is not correct. Go back and read the question again and select another answer.

BLOCK 19

Your answer to the question in Block 3 is not correct. Go back and read the question again and select another answer.

BLOCK 20

Your answer to the question in Block 27 is not correct. Go back and read the question again and select another answer.

BLOCK 21

The correct answer to the question in Block 17 is choice (1). For a complete sine wave cycle input there are two positive half cycles of output. Therefore, the SCR conducts on both half cycles of sine wave input.

Bridge rectifiers are often used for the full-wave rectifier because they can be used directly with the 120V ac input without a transformer.

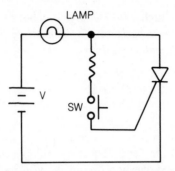

Here is your next question: *In the circuit shown in this block the switch is momentarily closed and then opened. The lamp will go:*

(1) ON and stay ON. Go to Block 14.
(2) ON and then OFF and stay OFF. Go to Block 5.

BLOCK 22

Your answer to the question in Block 9 is not correct. Go back and read the question again and select another answer.

BLOCK 23

Your answer to the question in Block 17 is not correct. Go back and read the question again and select another answer.

BLOCK 24

Your answer to the question in Block 7 is not correct. Go back and read the question again and select another answer.

BLOCK 25

Your answer to the question in Block 10 is not correct. Go back and read the question again and select another answer.

BLOCK 26

Your answer to the question in Block 17 is not correct. Go back and read the question again and select another answer.

BLOCK 27

The correct answers to the question in Block 14 are:

• Open the anode-cathode circuit.

- Connect a pulsed transistor across it.
- Commutate it off with another SCR.

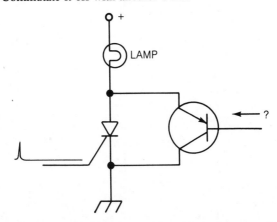

Here is your next question: *To shut off the lamp in the circuit shown in this block, apply a:*

(1) Negative base pulse to the transistor. Go to Block 4.
(2) Positive base pulse to the transistor. Go to Block 20.

BLOCK 28

Your answer to the question in Block 13 is not correct. Go back and read the question again and select another answer.

BLOCK 29

Your answer to the question in Block 9 is not correct. Go back and read the question again and select another answer.

BLOCK 30

Your answer to the question in Block 17 is not correct. Go back and read the question again and select another answer.

BLOCK 31

Your answer to the question in Block 16 is not correct. Go back and read the question again and select another answer.

BLOCK 32

The correct answer to the question in Block 4 is constant current diode. The illustration in this block shows the circuit.

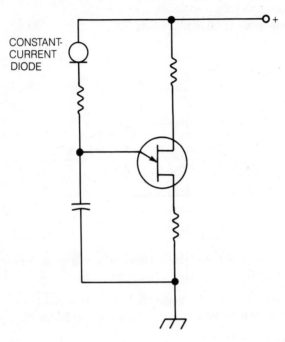

As the capacitor charge increases its charging current decreases. A constant-current diode is used to get a constant charging current.

You have now completed Programmed Review No. 2.

KEY WORDS

Breakover device	MOS
Breakover voltage	Multiplexer
Contact bounce	Optoelectronics
Contact form	PUT
Copper loss	Relay armature
Diac	SBS
Eddy currents	SCR
Firing potential	SCS
Gallium arsenide	Thyristors
Hysteresis loss	Triac
Intrinsic standoff ratio	UJT
Laminations	

PRACTICE TEST

1. You can set the intrinsic standoff ratio of a

    (A) PUT.
    (B) UJT.
    (C) SCS.
    (D) SBS.

2. Relays may be preferred in some circuits because of:

    (A) Their high resistance isolation between open contacts.
    (B) High fan-out capability.
    (C) Both choices are correct.
    (D) Neither choice is correct.

3. An SCR can be used for full-cycle operation from an ac power input provided they are connected to the output of:

    (A) A triac.
    (B) A LED.
    (C) A bridge rectifier.
    (D) A constant-current diode.

4. Which of the following is likely to prevent the use of relays in integrated circuit logic systems?

    (A) Contact bounce.
    (B) Relatively slow speed.
    (C) Inductive kickback from the coil.
    (D) All of these choices are correct.

5. Which of the following is the term for normally-closed contacts?

    (A) Form A.
    (B) Form B.
    (C) Form C.
    (D) Form D.

6. The normally curved ramp of a UJT emitter signal can be made linear by using a:

    (A) Zener diode.
    (B) SCS.

(C) SBS.
(D) Constant-current diode.

7. To be technically accurate, an SCR is started into conduction with a:

(A) Gate current.
(B) Gate voltage.

8. What type of component is associated with a snubber?

(A) SCR.
(B) VDR.
(C) LAD.
(D) LED.

9. A triggered-sweep oscilloscope shows that the period between the rise times of pulses is 0.114 microseconds. The frequency of the pulses is about _____.

10. A triac can be made with two back-to-back _____.

ANSWERS TO PRACTICE TEST

1. (A)   The intrinsic standoff ratio is set with a resistive voltage divider between the power supply and common.

2. (C)   Modern relays have a very high reliability and long life. They are often rated by the number of millions of cycles of operation they can perform without replacement.

3. (C)   The bridge rectifier delivers a positive output pulsation for every half cycle of input. Those positive pulsations are delivered to the anode of the SCR.

4. (D)   In older systems relays were used in relay logic configurations. They did the same types of jobs that integrated circuit logic does today.

5. **(B)**   The form identification of relay contacts is also used for other mechanical and electromechanical switches.

6. **(D)**   Constant-current diodes can be made with JFETS that have their gate and source electrodes connected together.

7. **(A)**   The MOS SCR is started with a gate voltage.

8. **(A)**   The snubber is connected *across* the SCR. It is an RC circuit used to prevent false triggering by noise pulses.

9. 8.77 Kilohertz. The equation $T = 1/f$ is used.

10. SCRs.

4

Digital Logic Gates and Microprocessors

THE USE OF digital logic and microprocessors has greatly changed the electronics in the industrial electronics field. Some of the older equipment, with thyratrons, ignatrons, and relay logic systems, still exist, but the newer equipment is microprocessor controlled. You may be asked a question about older equipment in a CET test.

Microprocessor interfaces, with digital logic systems and mass memories, and a host of newer electronic circuits make up the large part of the test. In this chapter you will review some of the important features of logic circuit and microprocessor theory.

Be sure to note those places where you are uncertain of the answer. Remember, if you had to guess the answer it is probably a subject that you need to review.

As with the other subjects, symbols in this book are very important. Remember that this is not a textbook! So, you will not get a complete range of study on symbols.

As far as logic circuitry is concerned, you should know the following symbols.

- Mill or standard symbol—Military;
- NEMA symbol—National Electrical Manufacturers Association; and
- ANSI symbol—American National Standards Institute.

There are companies that use industrial symbols which are not seen every day. One example is the symbol for a *timer*. As an industrial electronics technician you are expected to know these symbols when you take the Journeyman CET Test.

You can be sure of getting questions involving an understanding of the basic gates. The gates are listed here: AND, OR, NOT (INVERTER), NAND, NOR, EXCLUSIVE OR, and LOGIC COMPARATOR.

Be sure you know the truth table for each gate, and be able to identify input and output logic levels.

There are four logic families that may be the subject of questions. Important characteristics to remember about these families are *stand-by power*, speed (propagation delay), power supply operating voltages, and the special characteristics of each system.

An important thing to understand is the speed/voltage or speed/power trade-off for each family. For example, in CMOS the speed is slower as the applied voltage is reduced.

You can expect some questions on counters. Be sure you understand the difference between *synchronous* and *asynchronous counters*. Also, you should know how *ring counters* work and the special case called *Johnson counters*.

You should understand how a counter is *jammed*. The term *jam* refers to a method of stopping a count or starting a recount at some specific number in the counting sequence. For example, you may have a modulo 16 counter. That is, a counter that can perform 16 counts. It may be desirable to stop that count at 10. With a TTL counter, which triggers on the trailing edge, you have to stop it after the 10th count. With CMOS, which triggers on the leading edge, you have to stop it at the beginning of the 11th count.

Jamming is usually accomplished by using one of the gates to sense the count and then deliver a logic 0 to the J and K of the input (least significant bit).

Counters are not only used for counting, they are also used for dividing. For example, a divide-by-six counter can be accomplished by three flip flops; that is, either jammed or reset at the number 6.

A very important part of industrial electronics is the timer. The industry standard for integrated circuit timers is the 555. The 3909 timer is also very popular.

In the tradition of the CET test you will not be asked about specific component numbers such as 555. However, because of the very wide popularity of that particular integrated circuit, there have been questions on it on both the Associate and Journeyman tests.

You should have a very good understanding of how microprocessors are constructed. For example, knowing their bus architecture is important if you are to understand how the microprocessor works.

You should know that *registers* are sometimes called *accumulators*. They accomplish the same purpose. They are used for temporary storage of information.

Counters are used in the microprocessors. For example, the *program counter* keeps track of the step-by-step procedure through a stored program.

A microprocessor has an internal *arithmetic logic unit* (ALU) that does the number crunching and the logic operations.

All microprocessor systems work with memories. Be sure you know the difference between RAMS, ROMS, EPROMS, EEROMS, and BUBBLE MEMORY.

You are likely to be asked some questions about basic digital theory. For example, how to count numbers in binary. You may even be asked to convert from binary to decimal numbers or to octal and hexidecimal systems. These questions are not a major part of the CET test.

The laws of Boolean algebra are very important. They make it possible to reduce the complexity of logic systems. Also, they make it possible for a technician to interpret circuits in logic systems. You might be asked some questions on the basic Boolean algebra or Boolean laws. Examples are shown here:

$$A \times A = A$$
$$B + B = B$$

By far, the greatest concentration of questions is in the hardware of the logic and microprocessor systems, but there are occasional excursions into pure theory. The addition of binary numbers, for example, and the Boolean algebra equation for the output of a simple combination of gates are often used for questions.

PROGRAMMED REVIEW NO. 1

Start with Block number 1. Pick the answer that you think is correct. If you select choice number 1, go to Block 13. If you select choice number 2, go to Block 15. Proceed as directed. There is only one correct answer for each question.

BLOCK 1

Is the following statement correct? The symbol in this block matches the truth table shown in this block.

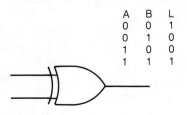

```
A   B   L
0   0   1
0   1   0
1   0   0
1   1   1
```

(1) Yes. Go to Block 13.
(2) No. Go to Block 15.

BLOCK 2

The correct answer to the question in Block 43 is choice (1). The D flip flop is also called a *Data* flip flop. Its output is the same as the last input.

Here is your next question: *Is the following statement correct? Data flip flops are easily toggled and are often used in counting circuits.*

(1) Not correct. Go to Block 21.
(2) Correct. Go to Block 48.

BLOCK 3

Your answer to the question in Block 12 is not correct. Go back and read the question again and select another answer.

BLOCK 4

Your answer to the question in Block 20 is not correct. Go back and read the question again and select another answer.

BLOCK 5

The correct answer to the question in Block 54 is choice (1). You need five flip flops to count to the number 16. However, to make 16 counts you only need four. Remember that 0 is a count.

Here is your next question: *In binary addition, the sum of 10011 and 11 is:*

(1) 10101. Go to Block 24.
(2) 10110. Go to Block 40.
(3) 10100. Go to Block 8.

BLOCK 6

The correct answer to the question in Block 14 is choice (2). Only zeros and ones are allowed in the logic families.

Here is your next question: *Compared to CMOS, ECL is (very fast or very slow).* Go to Block 51.

BLOCK 7

Your answer to the question in Block 27 is not correct. Go back and read the question again and select another answer.

BLOCK 8

Your answer to the question in Block 5 is not correct. Go back and read the question again and select another answer.

BLOCK 9

The correct answer to the question in Block 51 is choice (3). The inputs are always 1 and 0. An EXCLUSIVE OR gate gives a logic 1 output when the inputs are not identical. (It could also be an OR or a NAND.)

Here is your next question: *The time that it takes for a pulse to go from 10% to 90% of its maximum value is called its* _____. Go to Block 46.

BLOCK 10

Your answer to the question in Block 52 is not correct. Go back and read the question again and select another answer.

BLOCK 11

Your answer to the question in Block 40 is not correct. Go back and read the question again and select another answer.

BLOCK 12

The correct answer to the question in Block 23 is choice (1). The output of the NOR gate is $\overline{A + B}$. According to the laws of Boolean algebra, that is the same as $\overline{A}\,\overline{B}$. This is called *DeMorgan's theorem*.

Technicians use the following rule for converting terms with overbars:

Break the bar and change the sign.

Examples of DeMorgan's theorems:

$$\overline{AB} = \overline{A} + \overline{B}$$
$$\overline{A+B} = \overline{A}\overline{B}$$

A double overbar can be disregarded.

Example:

$$\overline{\overline{A+B}} = A + B$$

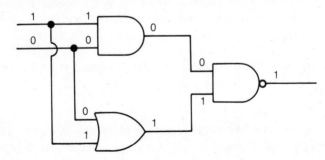

Here is your next question: *The circuit shown in this block is equivalent to:*

(1) A NAND gate. Go to Block 3.

(2) An AND gate. Go to Block 20.

BLOCK 13

Your answer to the question in Block 1 is not correct. Go back and read the question again and select another answer.

BLOCK 14

The correct answer to the question in Block 16 is choice (1). The inputs and outputs of the circuit are shown in the illustration for this block.

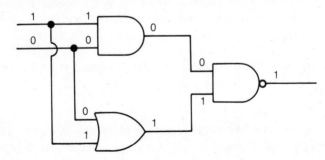

If you know the truth tables for the gates you can easily answer questions like the one in Block 44.

Here is your next question: *In a certain I.C. logic family logic 0 is any voltage between 0 V and 0.8 V. Logic 1 is any voltage between 2 V and 5 V. What binary number is represented by 1.6 V?*

(1) About 1.5. Go to Block 47.
(2) No number. The voltage is not allowed. Go to Block 6.

BLOCK 15

The correct answer to the question in Block 1 is choice (2). The truth table is for a LOGIC COMPARATOR. It is sometimes called an EXCLUSIVE NOR because of the way it is made.

The symbol in Block 1 is for an EXCLUSIVE OR.

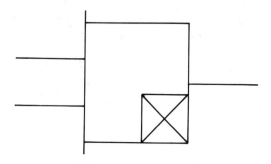

Here is your next question: *The symbol shown in this block is sometimes used in industrial electronics schematics. The symbol represents an:*

(1) AND gate. Go to Block 17.
(2) OR gate. Go to Block 31.
(3) Neither choice is correct. Go to Block 52.

BLOCK 16

The correct answer to the question in Block 27 is choice (1). A *demultiplexer* has one input and a number of outputs.

Here is your next question: *What is the logic output of the circuit shown in this block?*

(1) 1. Go to Block 14.
(2) 0. Go to Block 39.

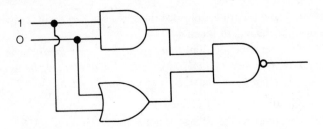

BLOCK 17

Your answer to the question in Block 15 is not correct. Go back and read the question again and select another answer.

BLOCK 18

The correct answer to the question in Block 20 is choice (2). You do not often see the symbol in writing because it is not as easy to print as $A\overline{B} + \overline{A}B$. However, the symbol in the question for Block 20 is used on drawings.

Here is your next question: *An R-S flip flop is made with NOR gates. Which of the following is a* not-allowed *input?*

(1) R = 0, S = 0. Go to Block 22.
(2) R = 1, S = 1. Go to Block 55.

BLOCK 19

The correct answer to the question in Block 46 is:

(1) 1
(2) 1
(3) A
(4) 0

You should know all of the laws of Boolean algebra.
Here is your next question: *What is the value of L in the Boolean equation?*

$$A + \overline{A}B = L$$

(1) 0. Go to Block 32.
(2) 1. Go to Block 53.
(3) L = A + B. Go to Block 23.

BLOCK 20

The correct answer to the question in Block 12 is choice (2). It is sometimes easier to redraw this with equivalent separate gates as is done in the illustration for this block.

BREAK THE BAR & CHANGE THE SIGN

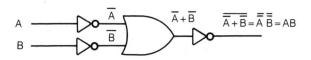

Here is your next question: *The expression of A ⊕ B is another way of writing:*

(1) NOR. Go to Block 42.
(2) EXCLUSIVE OR. Go to Block 18.
(3) Logic comparator (EXCLUSIVE NOR). Go to Block 4.

BLOCK 21

The correct answer to the question in Block 2 is choice (1). The J-K flip flop is easily toggled and is often used in counting circuits.

Here is your next question: *Which of the following families of logic gates is faster?*

(1) CMOS. Go to Block 34.
(2) TTL. Go to Block 50.

BLOCK 22

Your answer to the question in Block 18 is not correct. Go back and read the question again and select another answer.

BLOCK 23

The correct answer to the question in Block 19 is choice (3). The equation $(A + \overline{A}B = A + B)$ is one of the fundamental laws of Boolean algebra. There are a number of ways to demonstrate that the equation is true.

Here is an interesting example:

Write all possible combinations of A and B. Add A by inverting the $\overline{A}$ column.

TABLE A

A	B	$\overline{A}$
0	0	1
0	1	1
1	0	0
1	1	0

Add an A + B column by ORing the first and second columns of Table A.

TABLE B

A	B	$\overline{A}$	A+B
0	0	1	0
0	1	1	1
1	0	0	1
1	1	0	1

Make a $\overline{A}B$ column by ANDing the two right-hand columns of Table A.

TABLE C

A	B	$\overline{A}$	A+B	$\overline{A}B$
0	0	1		0
0	1	1		1
1	0	0		0
1	1	0		0

OR the first and last column to get A + AB.

TABLE D

A	B	$\overline{A}$	A+B	$\overline{A}B$	A+$\overline{A}B$
0	0	1	0	0	0
0	1	1	1	1	1
1	0	0	1	0	1
1	1	0	1	0	1

Note that the A + B column in Table B is the same as the A + $\overline{A}B$ column in Table D. So,

$$A + \overline{A}B = A + B$$

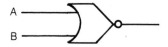

Here is your next question: *Is the output of the gate shown in this block equal to $\overline{A}\overline{B}$?*

(1) Yes. Go to Block 12.
(2) No. Go to Block 38.

BLOCK 24

Your answer to the question in Block 5 is not correct. Go back and read the question again and select another answer.

BLOCK 25

Your answer to the question in Block 16 is not correct. Go back and read the question again and select another answer.

BLOCK 26

Your answer to the question in Block 51 is not correct. Go back and read the question again and select another answer.

BLOCK 27

The correct answer to the question in Block 50 is choice (1). An active low circuit requires a logic 0 input to make it work. To select the IC shown in Block 50 it is necessary to deliver a logic 0 to the $\overline{CS}$ terminal.

Here is your next question: *Which of the following is a* multiplexer?

(1) 10 inputs and 1 output. Go to Block 16.
(2) 1 input and 10 outputs. Go to Block 7.

BLOCK 28

Your answer to the question in Block 54 is not correct. Go back and read the question again and select another answer.

BLOCK 29

Your answer to the question in Block 35 is not correct. Go back and read the question again and select another answer.

BLOCK 30

Your answer to the question in Block 52 is not correct. Go back and read the question again and select another answer.

BLOCK 31

Your answer to the question in Block 15 is not correct. Go back and read the question again and select another answer.

BLOCK 32

Your answer to the question in Block 19 is not correct. Go back and read the question again and select another answer.

BLOCK 33

Your answer to the question in Block 51 is not correct. Go back and read the question again and select another answer.

BLOCK 34

Your answer to the question in Block 21 is not correct. Go back and read the question again and select another answer.

BLOCK 35

The correct answer to the question in Block 40 is choice (1). Refer again to the circuit in Block 40. The most significant bit is at FF4 and the least significant bit is at FF1. The first time the flip flops deliver two ones to the NAND occurs at 0101. That is decimal 5.

Note that a zero to either J or K would stop the count, but the zero is often delivered to both J and K as shown.

Here is your next question: *Which of the following is an advantage of synchronous counters over ripple counters?*

(1) Low power supply demand. Go to Block 29.
(2) Speed. Go to Block 45.

BLOCK 36

Your answer to the question in Block 54 is not correct. Go back and read the question again and select another answer.

BLOCK 37

Your answer to the question in Block 50 is not correct. Go back and read the question again and select another answer.

BLOCK 38

Your answer to the question in Block 23 is not correct. Go back and read the question again and select another answer.

BLOCK 39

Your answer to the question in Block 51 is not correct. Go back and read the question again and select another answer.

BLOCK 40

The correct answer to the question in Block 5 is choice (2). Here are the important binary sums:

$$0 + 0 = 0$$
$$0 + 1 = 1$$
$$1 + 0 = 1$$
$$1 + 1 = 0 \text{ and carry } 1$$

The problem is solved here:

column	5 4 3 2 1
augend	1 0 0 1 1
addend	1 1
sum	1 0 1 1 0

Explanation

Starting with *column 1*: 1 + 1   = 0 (Carry 1 to column 2)
                column 2: 1 + 1   = 0 + carry = 1
                                         (Carry 1 to column 3)
            column 3: 0 + carry = 1
            column 4: 0 + 0   = 0
            column 5: 1 + 0   = 1

So,

$$10011 + 11 = 10110 \text{ (answer)}$$

Here is your next question: *The counter shown in this block will stop at decimal number:*

(1) 15. Go to Block 35.

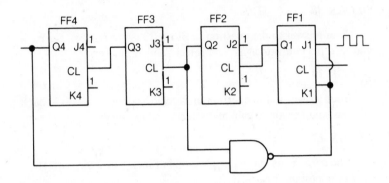

(2) 10. Go to Block 41.

(3) Neither choice is correct. Go to Block 11.

BLOCK 41

Your answer to the question in Block 40 is not correct. Go back and read the question again and select another answer.

BLOCK 42

Your answer to the question in Block 20 is not correct. Go back and read the question again and select another answer.

BLOCK 43

The correct answer to the question in Block 52 is choice (4). The correct Boolean equation for EXCLUSIVE OR is:

$$\overline{A}\,\overline{B} + \overline{A}\,\overline{B} = L$$

Here is your next question: *Which of the following might be used as a memory unit in a RAM?*

(1) D flip flop. Go to Block 2.

(2) RS flip flop. Go to Block 56.

BLOCK 44

Your answer to the question in Block 50 is not correct. Go back and read the question again and select another answer.

BLOCK 45

The correct answer to the question in Block 35 is choice (2). All of the flip flops change at the same time in a synchronous counter and that causes a great demand on the power supply. However, the count changes very rapidly.

Here is your next question: *Name the three busses in a microprocessor.* Go to Block 57.

(1) _____.
(2) _____.
(3) _____.

BLOCK 46

The correct answer to the question in Block 9 is *rise time*. The time that it takes to go from 90% to 10% of maximum is called its *fall time*, or decay time.

Here is your next question: *A few basic laws of Boolean algebra are given here. Write the outputs of each.*

(1) $A + \overline{A}$ = _____.
(2) $A + 1$ = _____.
(3) $A \cdot A$ = _____.
(4) $A \cdot 0$ = _____. Go to Block 19.

BLOCK 47

Your answer to the question in Block 14 is not correct. Go back and read the question again and select another answer.

BLOCK 48

Your answer to the question in Block 2 is not correct. Go back and read the question again and select another answer.

BLOCK 49

Your answer to the question in Block 52 is not correct. Go back and read the question again and select another answer.

BLOCK 50

The correct answer to the question in Block 21 is choice (2). The term *fast*, when applied to logic gates, means *short propagation delay*. Propagation delay means the time it takes the output of a gate to reflect a change in its input.

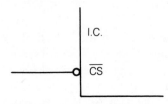

Here is your next question: *The chip select in the illustration for this block is:*

(1) Active low. Go to Block 27.
(2) Active high. Go to Block 44.
(3) Temporarily not connected. Go to Block 37.

BLOCK 51

The correct answer to the question in Block 6 is *very fast*. Since ECL operates with negative voltages it is not easily interfaced with logic families that use positive voltages. Also, the fact that it is very fast (low value of propagation delay) means that timing problems can occur.

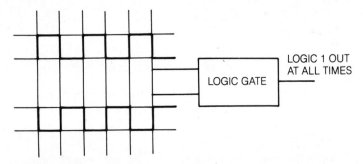

Here is your next question: *The logic gate in the illustration for this block must be a:*

(1) AND. Go to Block 26.
(2) NOR. Go to Block 33.
(3) Neither choice is correct. Go to Block 9.

BLOCK 52

The correct answer to the question in Block 15 is choice (3). The symbol represents a NAND. It is a NEMA symbol. Some manufacturers prefer this type to the type shown in Block 1.

Here is your next question: *Which of the following Boolean equations represents EXCLUSIVE OR?*

(1) $A\overline{B} \times \overline{A}B = L$. Go to Block 49.
(2) $\overline{AB} + AB = L$. Go to Block 10.
(3) Both choices are correct. Go to Block 30.
(4) Neither choice is correct. Go to Block 43.

BLOCK 53

Your answer to the question in Block 19 is not correct. Go back and read the question again and select another answer.

BLOCK 54

The correct answer to the question in Block 16 is choice (1). The J-K flip flops are toggled by the clock signal.

Here is your next question: *How many flip flops are needed to make 16 counts?*

(1) Four. Go to Block 5.
(2) Five. Go to Block 28.
(3) Six. Go to Block 36.

BLOCK 55

The correct answer to the question in Block 18 is choice (2). The circuit for the NOR flip flop is shown in this block. An undetermined state exists by applying a logic 1 to R and a logic 1 to S.

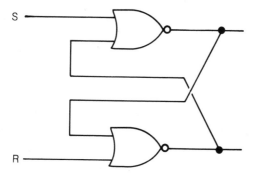

Here is your next question: *Which of the following can be used as a divide-by-two device?*

(1) Toggled J-K flip flop. Go to Block 54.
(2) Clocked R-S flip flop. Go to Block 25.

BLOCK 56

Your answer to the question in Block 43 is not correct. Go back and read the question again and select another answer.

BLOCK 57

The correct answer to the question in Block 45 is:

Address bus.
Data bus.
Control bus.

You have now completed Programmed Review No. 1.

PROGRAMMED REVIEW NO. 2

Start with Block number 1. Pick the answer that you think is correct. If you select choice number 1, go to Block 13. If you select choice number 2, go to Block 15. Proceed as directed. There is only one correct answer for each question.

BLOCK 1

In digital systems, a byte *is:*

(1) Two bits. Go to Block 13.
(2) Eight bits. Go to Block 15.

BLOCK 2

Your answer to the question in Block 40 is not correct. Go back and read the question again and select another answer.

BLOCK 3

The correct answer to the question in Block 55 is choice (2). In fact, the I^2L family of logic has a very good speed/power trade-off.

Here is your next question: *Which of the following is needed for converting the stroke of a key on the keyboard to a binary number code in a microprocessor system?*

(1) Encoder. Go to Block 59.
(2) Decoder. Go to Block 12.

BLOCK 4

The correct answer to the question in Block 36 is choice (4). Logic gates can sink more current than they can source (deliver).

Here is your next question: *Which of the following can be used to produce fast rise times and fall times regardless of the rise and fall times of the input signal?*

(1) Logic reliner. Go to Block 38.
(2) Schmitt trigger. Go to Block 61.
(3) Both answers are correct. Go to Block 11.

BLOCK 5

Your answer to the question in Block 35 is not correct. Go back and read the question again and select another answer.

BLOCK 6

Your answer to the question in Block 47 is not correct. Go back and read the question again and select another answer.

BLOCK 7

Your answer to the question in Block 56 is not correct. Go back and read the question again and select another answer.

BLOCK 8

Your answer to the question in Block 46 is not correct. Go back and read the question again and select another answer.

BLOCK 9

Your answer to the question in Block 27 is not correct. Go back and read the question again and select another answer.

BLOCK 10

Your answer to the question in Block 45 is not correct. Go back and read the question again and select another answer.

BLOCK 11

Your answer to the question in Block 4 is not correct. Go back and read the question again and select another answer.

BLOCK 12

Your answer to the question in Block 3 is not correct. Go back and read the question again and select another answer.

BLOCK 13

Your answer to the question in Block 1 is not correct. Go back and read the question again and select another answer.

BLOCK 14

Your answer to the question in Block 50 is not correct. Go back and read the question again and select another answer.

BLOCK 15

The correct answer to the question in Block 1 is choice (2). A bit is a *binary digit*. A *nibble* is four bits. A *byte* is eight bits. Sixteen bits is two bytes.

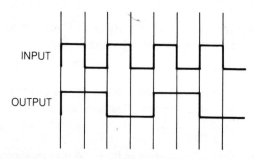

Here is your next question: *Refer to the illustration in this block. What type of flip flop can produce the output signal shown for the given input signal?*

(1) Toggled J-K flip flop. Go to Block 25.
(2) Quad NAND. Go to Block 58.

BLOCK 16

Your answer to the question in Block 25 is not correct. Go back and read the question again and select another answer.

BLOCK 17

Your answer to the question in Block 60 is not correct. Go back and read the question again and select another answer.

BLOCK 18

Your answer to the question in Block 39 is not correct. Go back and read the question again and select another answer.

BLOCK 19

The correct answer to the question in Block 47 is choice (2). Two examples of counters made with D flip flops are *Johnson counters* and *Ring counters*. Johnson counters are also called twisted ring counters.

Here is your next question: *A* modulo 60 *counter can be used to:*

(1) Divide by 60. Go to Block 36.
(2) Multiply by 60. Go to Block 41.

BLOCK 20

Your answer to the question in Block 35 is not correct. Go back and read the question again and select another answer.

BLOCK 21

Your answer to the question in Block 34 is not correct. Go back and read the question again and select another answer.

BLOCK 22

Your answer to the question in Block 36 is not correct. Go back and read the question again and select another answer.

BLOCK 23

Your answer to the question in Block 59 is not correct. Go back and read the question again and select another answer.

BLOCK 24

Your answer to the question in Block 27 is not correct. Go back and read the question again and select another answer.

BLOCK 25

The correct answer to the question in Block 15 is choice (1). A toggled J-K flip flop is also called a divide-by-two device.

Here is your next question: *In this block the signals into A and B are shown with the logic circuit of interest. What output signal is obtained?*

(1) (Answer: see illustration for this block). Go to Block 16.
(2) (Answer: see illustration for this block). Go to Block 39.
(3) (Answer: see illustration for this block). Go to Block 31.

BLOCK 26

Your answer to the question in Block 43 is not correct. Go back and read the question again and select another answer.

BLOCK 27

The correct answer to the question in Block 60 is choice (1). The illustration in this block represents a greatly enlarged view of a bubble. Viewed from the top (as they usually are) they look like bubbles. Actually, they are cylindrically shaped regions of magnetic intensity.

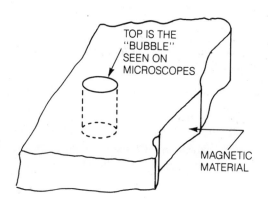

Here is your next question: *Which of the following ROMs can you program in the field as opposed to being programmed during the manufacturing process?*

(1) PROM. Go to Block 24.
(2) EPROM. Go to Block 44.
(3) EEROM. Go to Block 9.
(4) All choices are correct. Go to Block 56.

BLOCK 28

Your answer to the question in Block 61 is not correct. Go back and read the question again and select another answer.

BLOCK 29

Your answer to the question in Block 48 is not correct. Go back and read the question again and select another answer.

BLOCK 30

Your answer to the question in Block 45 is not correct. Go back and read the question again and select another answer.

BLOCK 31

Your answer to the question in Block 25 is not correct. Go back and read the question again and select another answer.

BLOCK 32

Your answer to the question in Block 59 is not correct. Go back and read the question again and select another answer.

BLOCK 33

Your answer to the question in Block 36 is not correct. Go back and read the question again and select another answer.

BLOCK 34

The correct answer to the question in Block 56 is choice (2). There is no code called BODOT. The ASCII code is used for displaying alphanumeric characters on CRT screens and dot matrix displays.

Here is your next question: *An advantage of a DRAM over a RAM is:*

(1) Greater speed. Go to Block 48.
(2) Circuit simplicity. Go to Block 21.

BLOCK 35

The correct answer to the question in Block 61 is choice (1). When the switch is closed a logic 1 is delivered to the input. When the signal on input A is at logic 1 there is a logic 1 output. When the signal at A is at logic 0 the output is at logic 0. That is not the same as the action of the three-state device.

Here is your next question: *One family of logic is called I^2L. That stands for:*

(1) Integrated injection logic. Go to Block 55.
(2) Integrated inverter. Go to Block 5.
(3) Power logic. Go to Block 20.

BLOCK 36

The correct answer to the question in Block 19 is choice (1). A modulo 60 counter makes 60 counts. In clock systems there is one output for every 60 counts. That gives one count per second for a 60 Hz input signal from the ac power line.

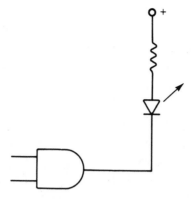

Here is your next question: *When there is a logic 0 input, a certain gate connects an LED from power supply to common* (see the illustration in this block). This is an example of:

(1) Power driven action. Go to Block 33.
(2) Common voltage. Go to Block 54.
(3) Inverse feedback. Go to Block 22.
(4) Current sinking. Go to Block 4.

BLOCK 37

Your answer to the question in Block 50 is not correct. Go back and read the question again and select another answer.

BLOCK 38

Your answer to the question in Block 4 is not correct. Go back and read the question again and select another answer.

BLOCK 39

The correct answer to the question in Block 25 is choice (2). The related signals are shown in this block.

When both signals are at a logic 1 level there is a logic 1 output from the AND gate.

When either input is at logic level 1 the output of the OR gate is at logic level 1.

The only time there is a logic 0 out of the NAND gate is when both inputs are at a logic 1 level.

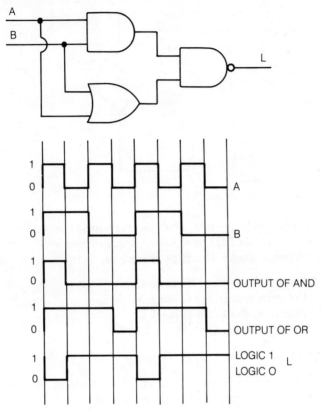

Here is your next question: *Is the following statement correct? An electrolytic capacitor should be used to eliminate a glitch at some point in a logic circuit.*

(1) Correct. Go to Block 18.
(2) Not correct. Go to Block 45.

BLOCK 40

The correct answer to the question in Block 46 is choice (2). The letters FIFO mean *first in—first out*. With this type of shift register the first digit stored is the first digit that comes out of the register. Other types are:

LIFO—last in, first out;
FILO—first in, last out;
LILO—last in, last out.

Here is your next question: *When you* jam *a counter you*

(1) Destroy it. Go to Block 52.
(2) Get all of the counts piled together in one spot. Go to Block 2.
(3) Neither choice is correct. Go to Block 47.

BLOCK 41

Your answer to the question in Block 19 is not correct. Go back and read the question again and select another answer.

BLOCK 42

Your answer to the question in Block 48 is not correct. Go back and read the question again and select another answer.

BLOCK 43

The correct answer to the question in Block 59 is choice (3). To convert the binary decimal number into a decimal number you start by writing the bits in groups of four. Write the decimal value under each group.

$$0\ 1\ 1\ 1 \qquad 1\ 0\ 0\ 0 \qquad 0\ 1\ 0\ 1$$
$$7 \qquad\qquad 8 \qquad\qquad 5$$

The value is 785.

Here is your next question: *Which of the following might have a sine wave input?*

(1) DAC (D/A). Go to Block 26.
(2) ADC (A/D). Go to Block 60.

BLOCK 44

Your answer to the question in Block 27 is not correct. Go back and read the question again and select another answer.

BLOCK 45

The correct answer to the question in Block 39 is choice (2). Never connect a capacitor into a logic circuit for the purposes of eliminating undesired spike voltages (called glitches).

Capacitors will:

- Change waveshapes,
- Introduce a delay,
- Overload circuits due to the charging current.

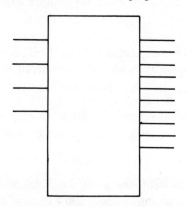

Here is your next question: *Consider the device shown in this block. For each binary count at the input there is one—and only one—output at logic level 1. What is the name of the device?*

(1) Divide-by-ten decoder. Go to Block 30.
(2) One-of-ten decoder. Go to Block 50.
(3) Neither choice is correct. Go to Block 10.

BLOCK 46

The correct answer to the question in Block 50 is choice (4). Registers and accumulators are both used for storage in microprocessors. Different manufacturers use the terms interchangeably.

Here is your next question: *Which of the following is an example of a shift register?*

(1) LOFO. Go to Block 8.
(2) FIFO. Go to Block 40.

BLOCK 47

The correct answer to the question in Block 40 is choice (3). Presettable counters use a *jam entry* to determine the number of counts to be used. Jam signals go to the set and clear terminals of the flip flops in the counter.

Here is your next question: *Is the following statement correct? D flip flops are NEVER used in counters.*

(1) Correct. Go to Block 6.
(2) Not correct. Go to Block 19.

BLOCK 48

The correct answer to the question in Block 34 is choice (1). Dynamic random access memory (DRAM) requires a refresh signal to recharge the capacitor storage levels. A separate IC is usually used for this process and the circuitry is not simple.

Speed is the advantage of DRAMS. In other words, you can get information in and out rapidly.

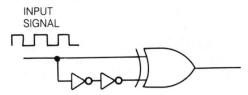

Here is your next question: *The output of the circuit in this block is:*

(1) Logic 1. Go to Block 42.
(2) Logic 0. Go to Block 29.
(3) A glitch. Go to Block 53.

BLOCK 49

Your answer to the question in Block 60 is not correct. Go back and read the question again and select another answer.

BLOCK 50

The correct answer to the question in Block 45 is choice (2). One application of this type of decoder is to stroke a display.

Here is your next question: *A short-term memory that stores a byte of information in a microprocessor is called:*

(1) A register. Go to Block 14.
(2) An accumulator. Go to Block 51.
(3) Neither choice is correct. Go to Block 37.
(4) Both choices are correct. Go to Block 46.

BLOCK 51

Your answer to the question in Block 50 is not correct. Go back and read the question again and select another answer.

BLOCK 52

Your answer to the question in Block 40 is not correct. Go back and read the question again and select another answer.

BLOCK 53

The correct answer to the question in Block 48 is choice (3). If the input signals were identical the output would always be logic 0. However, due to the propagation delay of the inverters there is an instant of time where the signals on the EXCLUSIVE OR input are at levels of 1 and 0. That occurs every time the input signal is in transition. During that instant of time there is a very short-duration spike—called a *glitch*—in the output.

You need an oscilloscope with a wide bandwidth to see the glitch. A good logic probe will display evidence of the glitch.

BLOCK 54

Your answer to the question in Block 36 is not correct. Go back and read the question again and select another answer.

You have now completed the programmed review.

BLOCK 55

The correct answer to the question in Block 35 is choice (1). An advantage of I^2L is that high component density is possible in an integrated circuit.

Here is your next question: *Another advantage of* I^2L *is that it:*

(1) Can deliver a very high current. Go to Block 57.
(2) Dissipates very low power when operated at slow speeds. Go to Block 3.

BLOCK 56

The correct answer to the question in Block 27 is choice (4). One way to distinguish between the ROMs is by the way they are erased in preparation for a new storage.

PROM—Programmable read-only memory Cannot be erased.
EEPROM—Electrically erasable pro-   Erased by
                grammable read-only memory electrical signal.

EEPROM—Electrically erasable pro-   Erased by
        grammable read-only memory   electrical signal.

Here is your next question: *Which of the following is a code that converts a binary number to a code for displaying alphanumeric characters?*

(1) BODOT. Go to Block 7.
(2) ASCII. Go to Block 34.

BLOCK 57

Your answer to the question in Block 55 is not correct. Go back and read the question again and select another answer.

BLOCK 58

Your answer to the question in Block 15 is not correct. Go back and read the question again and select another answer.

BLOCK 59

The correct answer to the question in Block 3 is choice (1). Encoders convert *into* binary numbers. Decoders convert binary numbers into other types of signals.

Here is your next question: *Convert binary decimal code 011110000101 into a decimal number.*

(1) Cannot be done. Go to Block 23.
(2) 85. Go to Block 32.
(3) Neither choice is correct. Go to Block 43.

BLOCK 60

The correct answer to the question in Block 43 is choice (2). A sine wave is an analog (continuously variable) input signal. To convert the sine wave to a digital signal you need an analog-to-digital (A/D) converter.

Here is your next question: *The bubbles in a bubble memory are actually shaped like:*

(1) Cylinders. Go to Block 27.
(2) Cubes. Go to Block 49.
(3) Spheres. Go to Block 17.

BLOCK 61

The correct answer to the question in Block 4 is choice (2). There is no circuit called *logic reliner*.

An important characteristic of Schmitt triggers is their ability to convert sine waves into pulses.

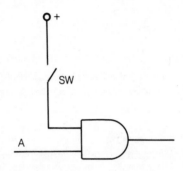

Here is your next question: *The connection shown in this block works as:*

(1) An ENABLE. Go to Block 35.
(2) Three-state (tristate) device. Go to Block 28.

KEY WORDS

Accumulator
ADC
Address bus
Addressing
ALU
ANDing
ASCII
Bit
Bit slice
Boolean algebra
Bridge rectifier
Bubble memory
Byte
CMOS
Constant-current diode

Contact bounce
Control bus
Current sinking
Current sourcing
DAC
Data bus
Data flip flop
Decay time
Decoder
Demorgan's theorem
Demultiplexer
Dot matrix
DRAM
Eccles Jordan flip flop
ECL

Encoder
EPROM
EEROM
ENABLE
EXCLUSIVE OR
Fan in
Fan out
Fall time
FIFO, LIFO, FILO, and LILO
Four-layer diode
Full-wave doubler
Gate
Half-wave doubler
I^2L
INCLUSIVE OR
JAM
Flip flop
Johnson counters
Logic comparator
Modem
Modulo

Multiplexer
Nibble
ORing
PROM
Propagation delay
Registers
Ring counters
Rise time
RS flip flop
Schmitt trigger
Schockley diode
Shift register
Schottky diode
Three-layer diode
Three state
Toggled
Triggered sweep snubber
TTL
Twisted ring counters
Tristate
VMOS

PRACTICE TEST

1. An 8-bit microprocessor has an:

    (A) 8-bit address bus.
    (B) 8-bit control bus.
    (C) 8-bit data bus.
    (D) 8-bit memory address.

2. Which of the logic gates has a truth table like this:

    A B L
    0 0 1
    0 1 0
    1 0 0
    1 1 0

    (A) NAND
    (B) NOR
    (C) AND
    (D) OR

3. Which of the following logic families uses a negative power supply?

    (A) TTL
    (B) ECL
    (C) CMOS
    (D) RTL

4. An accumulator in a microprocessor is:

    (A) A capacitor that stores a bit.
    (B) A temporary memory.
    (C) A method of selecting a memory address.
    (D) Another name for a DRAM.

5. Instead of using a single-chip microprocessor, one system puts the individual sections of the microprocessor together using individual integrated circuits. Which of the following is an important advantage of bit slice technology?

    (A) Simple programming procedures.
    (B) High speed.
    (C) 32 bit busses.
    (D) Fewer ICs required than a microprocessor system.

6. A memory cell:

    (A) Supplies voltage to the memory system.
    (B) Is an internal power supply in a RAM. It prevents loss of memory when power to the system is lost.
    (C) Is a supply that is totally ripple free.
    (D) None of these choices is correct.

7. $D_{16} =$

    (A) 13_{10}
    (B) 1101_2
    (C) Both choices are correct.
    (D) Neither choice is correct.

8. Modems utilize:

    (A) Serial transmission.
    (B) Parallel transmission.

(C) Single sideband transmission.

(D) Pulse amplitude modulation (PAM).

9. Which of the following is a use of the *index register* in a microprocessor?

(A) Put data in numerical address.

(B) Put data and address in proper order.

(C) Store index to the system memory.

(D) Provide an addressing mode.

10. Making measurements at a distance may require digital data transmission. Which of the following is a remote measuring *system*?

(A) DAC.

(B) ADC.

(C) Telemetering.

(D) Convoluted transmission.

ANSWERS TO PRACTICE TEST

1. (C)

2. (B)

3. (B)

4. (B)

5. (B)

6. (D)

7. (C)

8. (A)

9. (D)

10. (C)

5
Control of Power

WHEN YOU ARE troubleshooting a power supply it is a good idea to (mentally) divide the supply into various sections and isolate the trouble into one of those sections. The divisions are arbitrary, but a good example is given in the list below.

- Input
- Rectifier
- Regulator
- Filter
- Output

The input part of the supply starts with the power source. That can be from a battery, or it can be from the power company.

As a technician you should have a basic understanding of the work. They have the advantage of being much faster than fuses and their added cost is justified when an overvoltage or overcurrent can cause an expensive repair problem.

Standby power is a very important feature of today's system. Usually the standby power is obtained from a battery. *Inverters* convert dc to ac and *converters* convert dc to a higher value of dc. *Transformers* are used for increasing and decreasing the value of ac. *Voltage dividers* are used for reducing the dc to a lower voltage.

The output of a power supply may have a voltage divider to deliver various voltage values. Calculation of voltage dividers is a simple Ohm's law problem. You are more likely to run across it in the Associate Level Test than in the Industrial Electronics Systems.

Following the regulator there may be one or more stages of filtering. With very sophisticated regulators a simple capacitor can be used for filtering because the regulator itself takes out most of the ripple from the rectifier.

In *brute force* supplies, that is supplies that have no regulator, the filter may become more complicated. You should understand the characteristics of filters. In its simplest form, a filter can be either choke input or capacitive input. The choke input filter gives better regulation but the capacitive input gives a higher output voltage.

Constant K and M derived filters are still being used very extensively. By using computers, the design of the more complicated filters has been greatly simplified.

The output of the power supply is usually monitored for *overvoltage* and/or *overcurrent*. This is especially true when the power supply is being used for logic or microprocessor systems.

The switching regulators utilize an oscillator and some type of pulse-width modulation control. In many cases it is necessary to have a start-up circuit with this type of regulator since it requires a dc output voltage for the operation of the oscillator and control circuitry.

Reference voltages and regulators are often obtained from shunt regulators utilizing a zener diode. In the commercial laboratory type, regulated power supplies a separate power supply that may be used to obtain the reference voltage.

Some type of sense circuit is necessary in a regulator circuit. For example, a voltage divider may be used to sense the output voltage to determine if a regulator correction is necessary. On the other hand, a bipolar transistor in series with a power supply load can be used to sense the output current. Remember that in a power supply the *load* is the current. Do not confuse the term with load resistance.

You should be able to identify the basic rectifiers including the doublers. You should know how rectifier circuits can be used for regulating power output. An example is the SCR regulators that are utilized in a closed-loop feedback system.

Connection of diodes in series and parallel may be necessary to get the desired current or voltage rating for the supply.

You must have a basic understanding of the types of three-phase operation. In this chapter you will encounter three-phase rectifiers and three-phase power transformer operation.

Following the rectifier circuit you will likely have some type of electronic regulator. For example, in digital logic systems it may be necessary to have a very stiff regulator.

Regulators are in two versions, *analog* and *switching*. Analog regulators are cheaper to make and they are simple in their construction, but they are not as efficient as switching regulators.

If the input is from the power company there may be filters on the power line to remove transients and noise.

An important part of the input circuit to the power supply is the power transformer. Be sure you understand how the *Faraday shield* prevents electrostatic coupling from the primary to the secondary. While on the subject of transformers be sure that you understand the *dot notation* for identifying points that have the same phase.

There are several kinds of regulating transformers you should understand. Some are manually adjustable, others are *self-saturating* or *ferroresonant*. In these cases the transformers are considered to be preregulators and they may perform a sufficient amount of regulation for the complete system. In other words, it may not be necessary to employ electronic regulators if these regulating transformers are used.

PROGRAMMED REVIEW NO. 1

Start with Block number 1. Pick the answer that you think is correct. If you select choice number 1, go to Block 13. If you select choice number 2, go to Block 15. Proceed as directed. There is only one correct answer for each question.

BLOCK 1

A measure of how quickly a regulated power supply can recover from a step voltage input is called its:

(1) Slewing rate. Go to Block 13.
(2) Transient index. Go to Block 15.

BLOCK 2

The correct answer to the question in Block 31 is choice (2). The switching regulator gets its power from the output of the supply. However, if there is no output from the supply the regulator cannot work. To get around this problem, there is usually a start-up circuit to get things going.

Here is your next question: *Rectifier diodes may be connected in parallel to get:*

(1) A higher current rating. Go to Block 55.
(2) A higher voltage rating. Go to Block 11.
(3) A higher resistance. Go to Block 10.

BLOCK 3

The correct answer to the question in Block 7 is choice (1). With the full-wave doubler you cannot have the same common connection as the input power source. It is also difficult to get a proper common connection to the circuitry being operated by the full-wave supply.

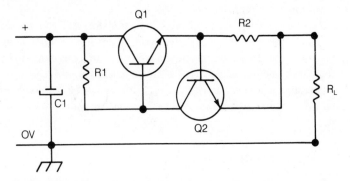

Here is your next question: *The circuit shown in this block is for:*

(1) Regulating current. Go to Block 43.
(2) Regulating voltage. Go to Block 25.

BLOCK 4

Your answer to the question in Block 43 is not correct. Go back and read the question again and select another answer.

BLOCK 5

Your answer to the question in Block 49 is not correct. Go back and read the question again and select another answer.

BLOCK 6

Your answer to the question in Block 38 is not correct. Go back and read the question again and select another answer.

BLOCK 7

The correct answer to the question in Block 22 is choice (1). The input capacitor (next to the rectifier) charges to the peak value of input voltage. That gives capacitor-input filters a higher output voltage compared to the output of choke-input filters.

Here is your next question: *Half-wave doublers require the same number of components as full-wave doublers. Why are half-wave regulators often preferred?*

(1) Common power connection. Go to Block 3.
(2) Better control. Go to Block 35.

BLOCK 8

Your answer to the question in Block 32 is not correct. Go back and read the question again and select another answer.

BLOCK 9

Your answer to the question in Block 27 is not correct. Go back and read the question again and select another answer.

BLOCK 10

Your answer to the question in Block 2 is not correct. Go back and read the question again and select another answer.

BLOCK 11

Your answer to the question in Block 2 is not correct. Go back and read the question again and select another answer.

BLOCK 12

Your answer to the question in Block 36 is not correct. Go back and read the question again and select another answer.

BLOCK 13

The correct answer to the question in Block 1 is choice (1). Slewing rate is also a measure of how fast an operational amplifier can respond to a step voltage input.

It should be no surprise that regulators and operational amplifiers are evaluated by the same parameters. Analog regulators can be used as operational amplifiers under certain circumstances.

Here is your next question: *You would expect to find an oscillator in:*

(1) An analog regulator circuit. Go to Block 42.
(2) A switching regulator circuit. Go to Block 27.

BLOCK 14

The correct answer to the question in Block 32 is choice (2). The illustration in this block shows a typical zener regulator. It is an example of an open-loop regulator. At least 10% of the total current (zener $+R_L$ currents) must flow through the zener diode to assure good regulation.

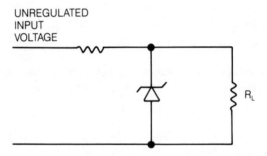

Here is your next question: *A certain adjustable power supply delivers a stiffly regulated positive and negative voltage. If the positive voltage is adjusted to a voltage output the negative supply immediately adjusts to a negative voltage with the same numeric value. This is a:*

(1) Tracking supply. Go to Block 48.
(2) Voltage foldback supply. Go to Block 20.

BLOCK 15

Your answer to the question in Block 1 is not correct. Go back and read the question again and select another answer.

BLOCK 16

Your answer to the question in Block 24 is not correct. Go back and read the question again and select another answer.

BLOCK 17

The correct answer to the question in Block 48 is choice (4). You have to reverse the diode *and* the electrolytic capacitors in order to get a negative output from the supply shown in Block 48.

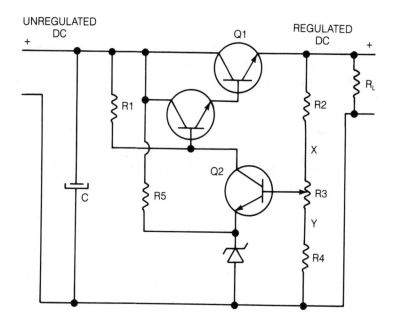

Here is your next question: *Consider the simple analog supply regulator shown in this block. To increase the output voltage, move the arm of variable resistor R₃ toward:*

(1) X. Go to Block 46.
(2) Y. Go to Block 18.

BLOCK 18

The correct answer to the question in Block 17 is choice (2). Moving the arm toward Y reduces the forward bias of Q_2. That reduces the current through Q_2. The base of Q_1 becomes more positive and more current flows through the load resistance. That, in turn, results in a more positive output voltage.

Here is your next question: *Refer again to the power supply circuit in Block 17. The series-pass transistor connection is called:*

(1) Darlington. Go to Block 51.
(2) Parallel. Go to Block 29.
(3) Series-parallel. Go to Block 52.

BLOCK 19

The correct answer to the question in Block 47 is choice (2). The LC circuit is resonant with the power input frequency. That causes a flywheel current that saturates the transformer core on each half cycle.

Here is your next question: *Which is more desirable in a non-regulated supply?*

(1) Low percent regulation value. Go to Block 24.
(2) High percent regulation value. Go to Block 41.

BLOCK 20

Your answer to the question in Block 14 is not correct. Go back and read the question again and select another answer.

BLOCK 21

Your answer to the question in Block 48 is not correct. Go back and read the question again and select another answer.

BLOCK 22

The correct answer to the question in Block 40 is choice (1). Thevenin generators are not possible in the real world. They have no internal resistance, so they are constant-voltage generators. Thevein generators are used for simplifying networks in design problems.

Because Thevenin generators have a constant-voltage output, regulated supplies are sometimes (erroneously) called Thevenin generators.

Here is your next question: *Which of the following gives better regulation in an unregulated supply?*

(1) Choke-input filter. Go to Block 7.
(2) Capacitor-input filter. Go to Block 57.

BLOCK 23

The correct answer to the question in Block 37 is choice (1). When the output voltage of the supply changes the voltage amplifier amplifies the sensed change. It delivers a correctional voltage to the series-pass power amplifier to correct the change.

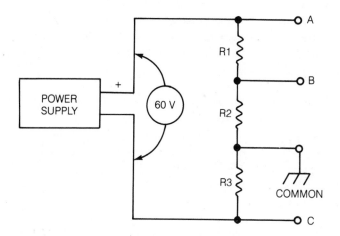

Here is your next question: *All of the resistors shown in the circuit for this block have a resistance of 2.7K. The voltages at A, B, and C are measured, in the traditional manner, with respect to common. Calculate the following voltages:*

(1) A _____ volts.
(2) B _____ volts.
(3) C _____ volts.
Go to Block 60.

BLOCK 24

The correct answer to the question in Block 19 is choice (1). The equation for percent regulation is

$$\% \ REGULATION = \frac{(V_{NO \ LOAD}) - (V_{FULL \ LOAD})}{(V_{FULL \ LOAD})} \times 100$$

The best possible condition is that the full-load voltage equals the no-load voltage. That makes the numerator and % regulation equal to zero.

Here is your next question: *Which of the following diodes is usually operated with a reverse voltage across it?*

(1) Varactor diode. Go to Block 16.
(2) Zener diode. Go to Block 54.
(3) Both choices are correct. Go to Block 38.
(4) Neither choice is correct. Go to Block 26.

BLOCK 25

Your answer to the question in Block 3 is not correct. Go back and read the question again and select another answer.

BLOCK 26

Your answer to the question in Block 24 is not correct. Go back and read the question again and select another answer.

BLOCK 27

The correct answer to the question in Block 13 is choice (2). The oscillator provides high-frequency pulses to the system. The width of the pulses is controlled to determine the output power.

Here is your next question: *LeClanche cells are also called:*

(1) Zinc-carbon (or carbon-zinc) cells. Go to Block 36.
(2) Mercury cells. Go to Block 9.

BLOCK 28

Your answer to the question in Block 51 is not correct. Go back and read the question again and select another answer.

BLOCK 29

Your answer to the question in Block 18 is not correct. Go back and read the question again and select another answer.

BLOCK 30

Your answer to the question in Block 48 is not correct. Go back and read the question again and select another answer.

BLOCK 31

The correct answer to the question in Block 43 is choice (2). With foldback current limiting, the power output of the supply decreases when the demand is too great. The power output is lowered by decreasing the current and voltage.

A crowbar circuit is used to protect against an overvoltage or overcurrent. However, the crowbar instantly stops all power supply output.

Here is your next question: *Which of the following uses a start-up circuit?*

(1) Analog regulator. Go to Block 58.
(2) Switching regulator. Go to Block 2.

BLOCK 32

The correct answer to the question in Block 56 is choice (1). As a rule, circuits that operate continuously (as with analog regulators) are not as efficient as circuits that are pulsed (as with switching regulators).

Here is your next question: *Zener diodes are usually used as:*

(1) Series regulators. Go to Block 8.
(2) Shunt regulators. Go to Block 14.

BLOCK 33

Your answer to the question in Block 55 is not correct. Go back and read the question again and select another answer.

BLOCK 34

Your answer to the question in Block 40 is not correct. Go back and read the question again and select another answer.

BLOCK 35

Your answer to the question in Block 7 is not correct. Go back and read the question again and select another answer.

BLOCK 36

The correct answer to the question in Block 27 is choice (1). The LeClanche cell is not as good as other types of cells when you compare their ability to deliver a steady current over a long period of time. However, they are less expensive and, therefore, still popular.

Here is your next question: *What type of device is represented by the symbol shown in this block?*

(1) Silicon bilateral switch. Go to Block 50.
(2) Four-layer diode. Go to Block 12.
(3) Neither choice is correct. Go to Block 40.

BLOCK 37

The correct answer to the question in Block 38 is choice (1). Phanatrons are gas-filled rectifier tubes. The high forward current is due to avalanching. The forward voltage drop is relatively low (about 15 V) and is constant over a range of current values. (Refer again to the question in Block 17.)

Here is your next question: *The sense amplifier in an analog regulated voltage supply is a:*

(1) Voltage amplifier. Go to Block 23.
(2) Power amplifier. Go to Block 59.

BLOCK 38

The correct answer to the question in Block 24 is choice (3). The varactor diode and zener diode both require a reverse voltage. The zener diode also requires a reverse current.

Here is your next question: *Phanatrons have:*

(1) High forward current. Go to Block 37.
(2) High forward voltage drop. Go to Block 6.

BLOCK 39

Your answer to the question in Block 47 is not correct. Go back and read the question again and select another answer.

BLOCK 40

The correct answer to the question in Block 36 is choice (3). You will sometimes see the symbol shown in Block 36 on industrial electronic diagrams. It represents a zener diode.

Here is your next question: *Another name for a constant-voltage generator is:*

(1) Thevenin generator. Go to Block 22.
(2) Norton generator. Go to Block 34.

BLOCK 41

Your answer to the question in Block 19 is not correct. Go back and read the question again and select another answer.

BLOCK 42

Your answer to the question in Block 13 is not correct. Go back and read the question again and select another answer.

BLOCK 43

The correct answer to the question in Block 3 is choice (1). Load current flows through R_2 and forward biases Q_2. Due to the phase inversion at the collector of Q_2, any increase in load current will result in a decrease of current through Q_1.

Conversely, if the load current tries to decrease, the conduction of Q_1 increases and restores the current to the desired value.

Here is your next question: *A certain power supply delivers voltage and current to a variable load resistance. If the power supply output requirement exceeds a predetermined power level, the output current starts to decrease. This is a:*

(1) Crowbar circuit. Go to Block 4.
(2) Foldback current limiter. Go to Block 31.

BLOCK 44

Your answer to the question in Block 55 is not correct. Go back and read the question again and select another answer.

BLOCK 45

Your answer to the question in Block 48 is not correct. Go back and read the question again and select another answer.

BLOCK 46

Your answer to the question in Block 17 is not correct. Go back and read the question again and select another answer.

BLOCK 47

The correct answer to the question in Block 51 is choice (2). Without a diode in series with each battery, the stronger one will try to charge the weaker one.

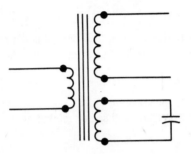

Here is your next question: *The transformer represented by the symbol in this block is:*

(1) Self-saturating. Go to Block 39.
(2) Ferroresonant. Go to Block 19.

BLOCK 48

The correct answer to the question in Block 14 is choice (1). There is no supply called a voltage feedback supply, but there are supplies that use voltage feedback.

Tracking supplies are very useful in applications where identical positive and negative voltage values are desired. Many operational amplifiers have this requirement.

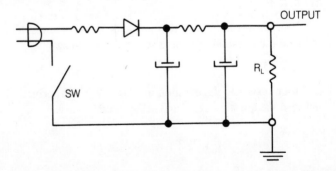

Here is your next question: *Consider the simple half-wave rectifier in the circuit in this block. To get a negative output voltage, simply:*

(1) Reverse the ac plug. Go to Block 30.
(2) Reverse the diode. Go to Block 45.
(3) Either choice is correct. Go to Block 21.
(4) Neither choice is correct. Go to Block 17.

BLOCK 49

The correct answer to the question in Block 55 is choice (1). In the earliest days of radio, batteries were the only supplies in many rural areas. The batteries were identified as follows:

A Battery—Filaments
B Battery—Plates
C Battery—Grids

Today you can still find places where those letters are used. This is especially true for *B+ supplies*.

Here is your next question: *Surge limiting resistors are used to protect a rectifier:*

(1) Diode. Go to Block 56.
(2) Filter capacitor. Go to Block 5.

BLOCK 50

Your answer to the question in Block 36 is not correct. Go back and read the question again and select another answer.

BLOCK 51

The correct answer to the question in Block 18 is choice (1). Although Q_I is shown as two separate transistors, they are usually in the same case. The disadvantage of Darlingtons is their higher internal heat. The advantage is that they have a high current gain.

Here is your next question: *Which of the following battery connections requires diodes?*

(1) Series. Go to Block 28.
(2) Parallel. Go to Block 47.

BLOCK 52

Your answer to the question in Block 18 is not correct. Go back and read the question again and select another answer.

BLOCK 53

Your answer to the question in Block 56 is not correct. Go back and read the question again and select another answer.

BLOCK 54

Your answer to the question in Block 24 is not correct. Go back and read the question again and select another answer.

BLOCK 55

The correct answer to the question in Block 2 is choice (1). Two diodes in parallel can conduct more current than one diode. The greater the number of diodes in parallel the higher the current.

Here is your next question: *Which of the following batteries is used to supply filament voltage?*

(1) A battery. Go to Block 49.
(2) B battery. Go to Block 33.
(3) C battery. Go to Block 44.

BLOCK 56

The correct answer to the question in Block 40 is choice (1). The surge limiting resistor is shown in this block. The partial schematic of a half-wave rectifier shows the resistor in series with the diode.

On the first positive half cycle the filter capacitor is charged as shown by the electron path. The resistor limits that charging current to protect the diode.

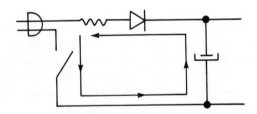

Here is your next question: *Which of the following is an advantage of a switching regulator over an analog regulator?*

(1) Efficiency. Go to Block 32.
(2) Simplicity. Go to Block 53.

BLOCK 57

Your answer to the question in Block 22 is not correct. Go back and read the question again and select another answer.

BLOCK 58

Your answer to the question in Block 31 is not correct. Go back and read the question again and select another answer.

BLOCK 59

Your answer to the question in Block 37 is not correct. Go back and read the question again and select another answer.

BLOCK 60

The 60 V is equally divided between the three points because the resistors are equal. So, voltage at A = 40 V, voltage at B = 20 V, and voltage at C = −20 V.

No output current is taken into consideration because none is included in the problem.

You have now completed Programmed Review No. 1.

PROGRAMMED REVIEW NO. 2

Start with Block number 1. Pick the answer that you think is correct. If you select choice number 1, go to Block 13. If you select choice number 2, go to Block 15. Proceed as directed. There is only one correct answer for each question.

BLOCK 1

Which of the following is measured in siemens?

(1) Susceptance. Go to Block 13.
(2) VARS. Go to Block 15.

BLOCK 2

The correct answer to the question in Block 16 is choice (1). The capacitor short-circuits high frequencies across the line. So, high frequencies cannot be delivered to the output terminals.

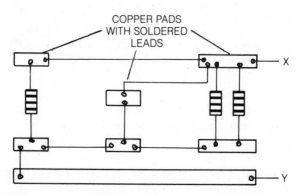

COPPER PADS
WITH SOLDERED
LEADS

X

Y

Here is your next question: *Each resistor in the illustration for this block is 270 ohms. What is the resistance between X and Y?*

_____ ohms. Go to Block 40.

BLOCK 3

The correct answer to the question in Block 27 is choice (2). *Inverters* convert dc to ac. *Converters* convert a lower value of dc to a higher value of dc. *Voltage dividers* convert a higher dc voltage to a lower value of dc.

Here is your next question: *A hot carrier diode is used in:*

(1) Low voltage circuits. Go to Block 35.
(2) High voltage circuits. Go to Block 11.

BLOCK 4

Your answer to the question in Block 28 is not correct. Go back and read the question again and select another answer.

BLOCK 5

The correct answer to the question in Block 26 is choice (3). One of the important things you must know is the schematic symbols of components. Do not take a CET test or a test for employment in industrial electronics without knowing all of the symbols.

Here is your next question: *The current delivered by a power supply is called the:*

(1) Load. Go to Block 27.
(2) Conversion factor. Go to Block 9.
(3) VR. Go to Block 30.

BLOCK 6

Your answer to the question in Block 8 is not correct. Go back and read the question again and select another answer.

BLOCK 7

Your answer to the question in Block 35 is not correct. Go back and read the question again and select another answer.

BLOCK 8

The correct answer to the question in Block 29 is choice (2). The two examples shown in this block are examples of how conjugate loads are used to get maximum power from ac generators.

Think of it this way. The resistance values must be equal. The reactive values must be in resonance—that is, they must cancel.

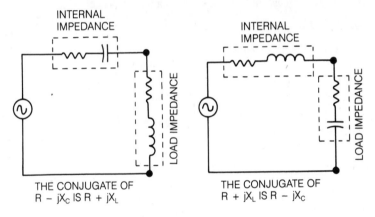

THE CONJUGATE OF $R - jX_C$ IS $R + jX_L$

THE CONJUGATE OF $R + jX_L$ IS $R - jX_C$

Here is your next question: *Which of the following is correct for efficiency?*

(1) % Efficiency $= \dfrac{\text{Output Voltage} - \text{Input Voltage}}{\text{Input Voltage}} \times 100$

Go to Block 24.

(2) % Efficiency $= \dfrac{\text{Output Voltage} + \text{Input Voltage}}{\text{Output Voltage}} \times 100$

Go to Block 6.

(3) Neither choice is correct. Go to Block 16.

BLOCK 9

Your answer to the question in Block 5 is not correct. Go back and read the question again and select another answer.

BLOCK 10

Your answer to the question in Block 26 is not correct. Go back and read the question again and select another answer.

BLOCK 11

Your answer to the question in Block 3 is not correct. Go back and read the question again and select another answer.

BLOCK 12

Your answer to the question in Block 16 is not correct. Go back and read the question again and select another answer.

BLOCK 13

The correct answer to the question in Block 1 is choice (1). Susceptance is the reciprocal of reactance and it is represented by the letter B.

$$B_L = \frac{1}{X_L} \text{ siemens}$$

$$B_C = \frac{1}{X_C} \text{ siemens}$$

(At one time this was measured in mhos.)

Susceptance is a measure of how easily ac current can flow through a reactance. This subject is beyond the requirements of the CET test, but as a technician you should know about ac circuits.

Here is your next question: *Which of the following is rechargeable?*

(1) Nicad batteries. Go to Block 31.
(2) LeClanche batteries. Go to Block 19.

BLOCK 14

The correct answer to the question in Block 25 is choice (2). This subject was covered in Block 3.

Here is your next question: *Which of the following is used to convert dc to ac?*

(1) Inverter. Go to Block 22.
(2) Converter. Go to Block 34.

BLOCK 15

Your answer to the question in Block 1 is not correct. Go back and read the question again and select another answer.

BLOCK 16

The correct answer to the question in Block 8 is choice (3). The efficiency can always be calculated as follows: % Efficiency = $\dfrac{P_{OUT}}{P_{IN}} \times 100$ The input power is the total input power required by the generator and the load resistance.

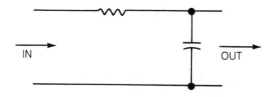

Here is your next question: *The circuit in this block can be used as:*

(1) A low-pass filter. Go to Block 2.
(2) A high-pass filter. Go to Block 12.

BLOCK 17

Your answer to the question in Block 38 is not correct. Go back and read the question again and select another answer.

BLOCK 18

Your answer to the question in Block 29 is not correct. Go back and read the question again and select another answer.

BLOCK 19

Your answer to the question in Block 13 is not correct. Go back and read the question again and select another answer.

BLOCK 20

Your answer to the question in Block 39 is not correct. Go back and read the question again and select another answer.

BLOCK 21

Your answer to the question in Block 22 is not correct. Go back and read the question again and select another answer.

BLOCK 22

The correct answer to the question in Block 14 is choice (1). The terms *inverter* and *converter* should be used correctly:

conversion of dc to ac—Inverter,

conversion of dc to dc—Converter.

Here is your next question: *Which of the following gives a higher output voltage when used with a full-wave rectifier?*

(1) Choke input filter. Go to Block 21.

(2) Capacitive input filter. Go to Block 38.

BLOCK 23

Your answer to the question in Block 27 is not correct. Go back and read the question again and select another answer.

BLOCK 24

Your answer to the question in Block 8 is not correct. Go back and read the question again and select another answer.

BLOCK 25

The correct answer to the question in Block 35 is choice (3). In the first place, it is not a voltage doubler. Also, the circuit cannot work.

Note that the diodes are connected back-to-back. It is not possible for current to pass through the diodes in either direction.

A half-wave doubler circuit that works is shown in this block.

Here is your next question: *To convert a high dc voltage to a low dc voltage, use a:*

(1) Converter. Go to Block 32.

(2) Divider. Go to Block 14.

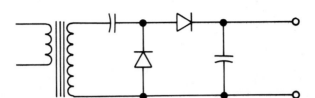

BLOCK 26

The correct answer to the question in Block 31 is $2.08+$ watts. Maximum power is dissipated in the dc circuit when the load resistance (R_L) equals the battery internal resistance $(R_L = R_i)$. That makes the total circuit resistance equal to 2400 ohms. The power for the total circuit is:

$$P = \frac{V^2}{R}$$
$$= \frac{(100)^2}{2400}$$
$$P = 4.167 \text{ watts}$$

This is the total power dissipated in the circuit. Only half of this is dissipated by the load resistance.

$$\frac{P}{2} = P_L = \frac{4.167}{2} = 2.08^+ \text{ watts}$$

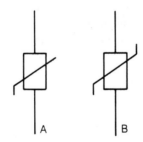

Here is your next question: *Which of the symbols shown in this block represents a* varistor?

(1) The one marked A. Go to Block 10.
(2) The one marked B. Go to Block 37.
(3) Either symbol is correct. Go to Block 5.
(4) Neither symbol is correct. Go to Block 33.

BLOCK 27

The correct answer to the question in Block 5 is choice (1). Do not confuse the terms load current and load resistance. *Load current* is usually shortened to *load*.

Here is your next question: *To change a low value of dc voltage to a high value of dc voltage, use:*

   (1) An inverter. Go to Block 23.
   (2) A converter. Go to Block 3.

BLOCK 28

The correct answer to the question in Block 38 is choice (2). Crowbar circuits that act like a crowbar jammed across the output terminals whenever the output voltage rises above the predetermined value.

Here is your next question: *Which of the following is used for a series-pass regulator?*

   (1) Voltage amplifier. Go to Block 4.
   (2) Power amplifier. Go to Block 39.

BLOCK 29

The correct answer to the question in Block 39 is choice (2). Norton generators are imaginary current suppliers. They deliver the same amount of current regardless of the load resistance.

Since constant current supplies can be obtained over a limited range by using electronic circuitry they are sometimes (erroneously) called Norton generators.

Here is your next question: *In an ac supply the maximum amount of power that can be delivered to a load impedance occurs when the load impedance is:*

   (1) Identical to the generator internal impedance. Go to Block 18.
   (2) The conjugate of the internal impedance. Go to Block 8.

BLOCK 30

Your answer to the question in Block 5 is not correct. Go back and read the question again and select another answer.

BLOCK 31

The correct answer to the question in Block 13 is choice (1). *LeClanche cells* are also known as carbon-zinc (or zinc-carbon) batteries. They can be rejuvenated by heating, but they cannot be recharged.

Recharging involves reversing the chemical process of producing a voltage.

Nickel-cadmium batteries are truly rechargeable.

Warning: Cadmium is poison *to humans! Do not get curious and take one apart.* Never *throw them in the fire! The fumes can kill you!!!*

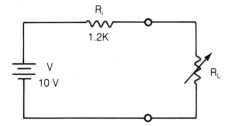

Here is your next question: *The maximum amount of output power from the simple supply shown in this block is* _____ *watts*. Go to Block 26.

BLOCK 32

Your answer to the question in Block 25 is not correct. Go back and read the question again and select another answer.

BLOCK 33

Your answer to the question in Block 26 is not correct. Go back and read the question again and select another answer.

BLOCK 34

Your answer to the question in Block 14 is not correct. Go back and read the question again and select another answer.

BLOCK 35

The correct answer to the question in Block 3 is choice (1). One example of a hot carrier diode is the point contact type. The first illustration in this block shows a model for the construction of hot carrier diodes. Hot carrier diodes are also called Schottky diodes, or Schottky barrier diodes.

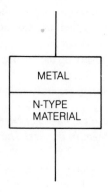

Here is your next question: *The following voltage doubler:*

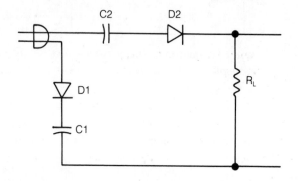

(1) Is a half-wave doubler. Go to Block 7.
(2) Is a full-wave doubler. Go to Block 36.
(3) Will not work. Go to Block 25.

BLOCK 36

Your answer to the question in Block 35 is not correct. Go back and read the question again and select another answer.

BLOCK 37

Your answer to the question in Block 26 is not correct. Go back and read the question again and select another answer.

BLOCK 38

The correct answer to the question in Block 22 is choice (2). The input capacitor of a capacitive input filter charges to the peak of the input ac power. So, its output voltage is higher than the output voltage of a choke (inductor) input filter.

Here is your next question: *A crowbar circuit is used for:*

(1) Raising the output voltage of regulated supply. Go to Block 17.
(2) Protection of components from an overvoltage. Go to Block 28.

BLOCK 39

The correct answer to the question in Block 28 is choice (2). All of the load current passes through the series-pass regulator. Also, the sense current passes through that amplifier. So, a power amplifier is needed.

When you see the term *power amplifier* think of an amplifier that can control high current.

Here is your next question: *A generator that delivers the same amount of current to a load resistor as the load resistance is varied is called a:*

(1) Thevenin generator. Go to Block 20.
(2) Norton generator. Go to Block 29.

BLOCK 40

The correct answer to the question in Block 2 is *zero*. There is a short circuit between X and Y.

You have now completed the Programmed Review No. 2.

KEY WORDS

'A' battery	Capacitive input filters
Admittance	Choke input filters
Analog regulators	Conjugate
'B' battery	Constant current supply
Brute force	Constant K filters
Cadmium	Converters
'C' battery	Crowbar circuit

Current avalanching
Darlington amplifier
Dot notation
Efficiency
Fullback current regulators
Ferroresonant
Foldback current regulators
High-pass filter
Inverters
LaClanche cell
Load
Load current
Load resistance
Low-pass filter
M-derived filters
Neon lamp
Nicad
Nickel Cadmium

Norton generator
Percent regulation
Self-saturating
Series regulators
  (also, series-pass regulators)
Shunt regulators
Siemens
Slewing rate
Surge-limiting resistors
Susceptance
Switching regulators
Thevenin generator
Thyratron
Tracking supplies
Varactor diode
Varistor
Vars
Zener diode

PRACTICE TEST

1. Which of the following is a combination of series resistance and leakage resistance for an electrolytic capacitor?

  (A) ESR.
  (B) E & R.

2. Assuming that both rectifiers operate from 60 Hertz power, which of the following has a higher ripple frequency?

  (A) Full-wave, single-phase rectifier.
  (B) Half-wave, three-phase rectifier.

3. The *load* of a power supply refers to its output:

  (A) Power.
  (B) Current.

4. Which of the following is used as a preregulator in a power supply?

  (A) Ferroresonant transformer.

(B) Self-resonating transformer.

(C) Neither choice is correct.

(D) Both choices are correct.

5. An advantage of a switching regulator over an analog regulator is:

(A) Its higher output voltage.

(B) Its lower cost.

(C) Neither choice is correct.

(D) Both choices are correct.

6. To get a higher PIV rating, rectifier diodes can be connected in:

(A) Series.

(B) Parallel.

7. Maximum power can be obtained from a battery when the load resistance is:

(A) Equal to the battery internal resistance.

(B) Five times the battery internal resistance.

8. Surge limiting resistors are used to:

(A) Protect the circuits connected to a power supply from an overload.

(B) Protect rectifier diodes.

9. Which of the following might be used as a reference in a regulated supply?

(A) Four-layer diode.

(B) Zener diode.

10. Why are small beads threaded onto the base lead of a transistor amplifier?

(A) They are ferrite beads and they act like chokes. They are used to prevent parasitic oscillations.

(B) They are actually spacers.

ANSWERS TO PRACTICE TEST

1. (A) ESR stands for *equivalent* series resistance. It includes series and leakage resistances.

2. (B) The single-phase rectifier has a ripple frequency of 120 hertz. The three-phase rectifier has a ripple frequency of 180 hertz.

3. (B)

4. (D)

5. (C) The advantage is higher efficiency.

6. (A)

7. (A) This is called the *Maximum Power Transfer Theorem.*

8. (B)

9. (B)

10. (A)

6

Motors, Generators, and Their Control

THE CONTROL APPLICATIONS of industrial electronics deal mostly with the methods of regulating motor speed, torque, power, etc. For that reason you would expect to find applications of motor *speed control* in the LET TEST. That includes the use of phase-locked loops, pulse width control, open-loop, and simple feedback control circuits.

Of course, you need to have some insight into how a motor operates before you can understand how its speed is controlled. This means that you need to have a feeling for series, shunt, and compound-wound dc motors, capacitive start ac motors, synchronous motors, basic induction motors, and stepping motors.

It is not possible to cover every single facet of motors and their operation in one single chapter of a CET review. In fact, you cannot cover it in a single chapter in any book.

After you have been tested on this section you will have a good idea if you need to do additional review on motor theory.

One advantage of dc motors is that their speed can be controlled easily when they are delivering a low torque or starting torque. Speed control for ac motors is not always that simple. (Exceptions are stepping motors and synchronous motors. Their speed is very easily controlled.)

For a given size of motor, a series-wound dc motor has the highest starting torque that you can get. But, it is a runaway speed device. In other words, if something is not done to regulate its speed it will continue to increase until it flies apart. There are two special cases.

In very small series-wound motors the speed may be automatically regulated by the friction of the bearings.

A series-wound motor can be driven with a pulse rather than with a continuous dc. By monitoring the width of the pulses it is possible to control the speed of a series-wound dc motor.

Two electronic components are especially important for controlling power to any device. They are the SCR and the triac. Their associated circuitry is also very important. Many of those subjects were covered earlier but some are reviewed in this section.

You will sometimes see a snubber circuit used with SCRs and triacs. This is nothing more complicated than a filter around a thyristor to prevent noise from falsely triggering it into operation.

Motors are sometimes given a volt × amp, or apparent power rating. The relationship between this and the true power, and also with a vars in a circuit, is important and will be reviewed in this chapter.

Speed control of ac motors is often accomplished mechanically with gears or pulleys. Although not electronic, you may encounter questions on those controls in a CET test.

You can expect questions on the theory of motor operation including the use of commutators and phase controls. Questions may be as basic as which way a conductor will move if current is flowing through it and it is exposed to a magnetic field.

Since phase-locked loops will be a subject for this chapter you can expect questions on frequency synthesizing.

You may be surprised to find some very basic questions that require mechanical knowledge. They are included in this study to let you know that these are possible questions on the CET test.

PROGRAMMED REVIEW NO. 1

Start with Block number 1. Pick the answer that you think is correct. If you select choice number 1, go to Block 13. If you select choice number 2, go to Block 15. Proceed as directed. There is only one correct answer for each question.

BLOCK 1

To protect an electric load from excessive dc voltage, use a:

(1) Crowbar circuit. Go to Block 13.
(2) Pulse code inverter. Go to Block 15.

BLOCK 2

Your answer to the question in Block 23 is not correct. Go back and read the question again and select another answer.

BLOCK 3

The correct answer to the question in Block 25 is choice (2). The waveform shown in Block 25 is a *full wave* rectified sine wave voltage. The bridge circuit can provide that waveform. The bridge circuit is sometimes used with SCR control to get operation on both half cycles of sine wave input.

Here is your next question: *Rotary converters are made with:*

(1) A motor/generator combination. Go to Block 18.
(2) A motor and 3ϕ rectifier. Go to Block 45.

BLOCK 4

Your answer to the question in Block 31 is not correct. Go back and read the question again and select another answer.

BLOCK 5

Your answer to the question in Block 34 is not correct. Go back and read the question again and select another answer.

BLOCK 6

Your answer to the question in Block 29 is not correct. Go back and read the question again and select another answer.

BLOCK 7

Your answer to the question in Block 12 is not correct. Go back and read the question again and select another answer.

BLOCK 8

Your answer to the question in Block 18 is not correct. Go back and read the question again and select another answer.

BLOCK 9

The correct answer to the question in Block 13 is choice (1). The device shown in Block 13 is called an *optical coupler*. It can be used for triggering, but it is not called by the name trigger.

Here is your next question: *Which of the following statements is correct?*

(1) A triac can be made with two diacs. Go to Block 55.
(2) A triac can be made with two SCRs. Go to Block 25.

BLOCK 10

Your answer to the question in Block 33 is not correct. Go back and read the question again and select another answer.

BLOCK 11

Your answer to the question in Block 46 is not correct. Go back and read the question again and select another answer.

BLOCK 12

The correct answer to the question in Block 28 is choice (2). A Hall device can be used in a circuit for controlling speed, but it works by sensing a magnetic field. The illustration in this block shows how the Hall device is used for sensing motor speed. Every time a magnet passes the Hall device it generates a voltage pulse. The pulses are used in different ways to regulate the speed of the motor.

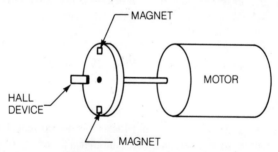

Here is your next question: *The equation for induced voltage is V = −N dφ/dt. Which part of the equation is due to Lenz' law?*

(1) The negative sign. Go to Block 41.
(2) N. Go to Block 7.
(3) dφ/dt. Go to Block 26.

BLOCK 13

The correct answer to the question in Block 1 is choice (1). There is no protection circuit called *pulse code inverter*.

Crowbar circuits are used to protect devices from excessive voltage or current. They are most often found in power supply systems, but they will also work for any device that can be destroyed by an excessive input.

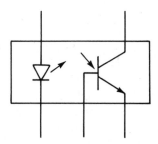

Here is your next question: *The device shown in this block is called:*

(1) An optical coupler. Go to Block 9.
(2) A one-shot trigger. Go to Block 17.

BLOCK 14

Your answer to the question in Block 31 is not correct. Go back and read the question again and select another answer.

BLOCK 15

Your answer to the question in Block 1 is not correct. Go back and read the question again and select another answer.

BLOCK 16

Your answer to the question in Block 38 is not correct. Go back and read the question again and select another answer.

BLOCK 17

Your answer to the question in Block 13 is not correct. Go back and read the question again and select another answer.

BLOCK 18

The correct answer to the question in Block 3 is choice (1). A converter changes a dc voltage from one level to a higher level. A rotary converter is a motor/generator combination. The motor operates at lower dc voltage and the generator delivers a higher voltage.

Here is your next question: *A capacitor start motor is used on:*

(1) 3-ϕ power. Go to Block 8.
(2) Single-phase power. Go to Block 31.

BLOCK 19

Your answer to the question in Block 20 is not correct. Go back and read the question again and select another answer.

BLOCK 20

The correct answer to the question in Block 33 is choice (1). Although the dc motor will produce an output voltage it will not be efficient because the brushes will not be in the current position. It is presumed that the dc motor has brushes and a commutator. Other types of dc generators—like the alternators used in cars—will not act as motors when their shaft is turned.

Here is your next question: *Which of the following types of motors is often used in electric drills?*

(1) Republic. Go to Block 35.
(2) Universal. Go to Block 53.
(3) Neither choice is correct. Go to Block 19.

BLOCK 21

Your answer to the question in Block 53 is not correct. Go back and read the question again and select another answer.

BLOCK 22

Your answer to the question in Block 41 is not correct. Go back and read the question again and select another answer.

BLOCK 23

The correct answer to the question in Block 36 is choice (2). The gate voltage lags the applied voltage. So, the SCR does not conduct for an instant of time. That reduces the power delivered to the load.

Here is your next question: *Whenever there is relative motion between a magnetic field and a conductor a voltage is produced. This is according to:*

(1) Faraday's law. Go to Block 44.
(2) Coulomb's law. Go to Block 2.

BLOCK 24

Your answer to the question in Block 49 is not correct. Go back and read the question again and select another answer.

BLOCK 25

The correct answer to the question in Block 9 is choice (2). Two SCRs can be connected back-to-back (and in parallel) to make a triac. The connection is shown in this block.

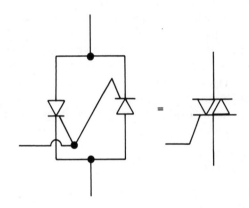

Triacs can be used to give full-cycle control of an ac input signal.

WAVEFORM

Here is your next question: *Assume that the input power is sinusoidal. Which of the following rectifier circuits can be used to give an output voltage with the* waveform *shown in this block?*

(1) A half-wave rectifier. Go to Block 43.
(2) A bridge rectifier. Go to Block 3.
(3) Neither choice is correct. Go to Block 32.

BLOCK 26

Your answer to the question in Block 12 is not correct. Go back and read the question again and select another answer.

BLOCK 27

Your answer to the question in Block 29 is not correct. Go back and read the question again and select another answer.

BLOCK 28

The correct answer to the question in Block 29 is choice (1). The disadvantage of the series-wound dc motor is that it must be connected to a mechanical load. If allowed to run without a mechanical load its speed will continue to increase until it self-destructs.

The advantage of the series-wound dc motor is that it has a very high starting torque.

Here is your next question: *In the normal operation of a Hall effect device, it is used to sense:*

(1) Speed. Go to Block 51.
(2) Magnetic fields. Go to Block 12.

BLOCK 29

The correct answer to the question in Block 44 is choice (2). *Power factor* is the true power divided by the apparent power. From the power triangle shown in this block, you can see that the power factor can also be written as the cosine of the phase angle (ϕ). When there is no phase angle between the current and voltage the best condition exists. From the equation:

$$\text{Power factor} = \text{Cos } \phi = \text{Cos } 0^\circ = 1.0$$

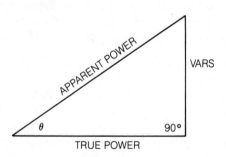

Here is your next question: *Which of the following can self-destruct when it has no mechanical load?*

(1) Series-wound dc motor. Go to Block 28.
(2) Shunt-wound dc motor. Go to Block 6.
(3) Neither choice is correct. Go to Block 40.
(4) Both choices are correct. Go to Block 27.

BLOCK 30

The correct answer to the question in Block 31 is choice (3). The equation

$$(\text{force} \times \text{diameter}) \div 2$$

is the same as

$$\text{force} \times \text{radius}$$

since

$$\text{radius} = \text{diameter} \div 2$$

Torque is the turning effect of a force. Motors are sometimes rated by the amount of torque (turning force) they can deliver.

Here is your next question: *Which of the following dc generators is seldom used?*

(1) Shunt wound. Go to Block 47.
(2) Series wound. Go to Block 33.

BLOCK 31

The correct answer to the question in Block 18 is choice (2). Three-phase motors are self-starting. Single-phase ac motors cannot start without help. The capacitor in a capacitor-start motor simulates two-phase operation with a rotating magnetic field.

Once the motor is started the capacitor can be switched out. A centrifugal switch is often used to switch out the capacitor. When the motor speed reaches a certain predetermined value the switch is activated.

Here is your next question: *Which of the following is the correct equation for torque?*

(1) (Diameter $\times$ radius) $\div$ 2. Go to Block 14.

(2) (Diameter × pressure). Go to Block 52.
(3) (Force × diameter) ÷ 2. Go to Block 30.
(4) None of these choices is correct. Go to Block 4.

BLOCK 32

Your answer to the question in Block 25 is not correct. Go back and read the question again and select another answer.

BLOCK 33

The correct answer to the question in Block 30 is choice (2). Series-wound generators are not often used because of their very poor regulation.

Here is your next question: *Is the following statement true? If you turn the shaft of a series-wound dc motor it will generate a voltage.*

(1) True. Go to Block 20.
(2) Not true. Go to Block 10.

BLOCK 34

The correct answer to the question in Block 53 is choice (4). All of the methods are used for sensing motor speed. You should go back to Block 53 and review those methods again.

Here is your next question: *Which of the following best describes a commutator?*

(1) Oscillator. Go to Block 5.
(2) Mechanical rectifier. Go to Block 38.

BLOCK 35

Your answer to the question in Block 20 is not correct. Go back and read the question again and select another answer.

BLOCK 36

The correct answer to the question in Block 49 is choice (2). You can use the *right-hand motor rule* (using conventional current flow) to determine the direction of motion. Remember that the direction of magnetic flux is presumed to be from the North pole to the South pole.

Here is your next question: *In an SCR-controlled power circuit the input voltage to the gate will:*

(1) Lead the applied power. Go to Block 42.
(2) Lag the applied power. Go to Block 23.

BLOCK 37

Your answer to the question in Block 53 is not correct. Go back and read the question again and select another answer.

BLOCK 38

The correct answer to the question in Block 34 is choice (2). For a dc generator, the commutator mechanically switches the voltage so that current flows only in one direction.

For a dc motor, the commutator mechanically switches the connection to the wires in the armature so that current flow produces rotation.

Here is your next question: *A disadvantage of dc motors (when compared to ac motors) is that they:*

(1) Cannot have their speed easily controlled. Go to Block 16.
(2) Have brushes that require periodic replacement. Go to Block 49.

BLOCK 39

Your answer to the question in Block 44 is not correct. Go back and read the question again and select another answer.

BLOCK 40

Your answer to the question in Block 29 is not correct. Go back and read the question again and select another answer.

BLOCK 41

The correct answer to the question in Block 12 is choice (1). In the equation, N is the number of conductors being moved through the magnetic field. A voltage is induced in each conductor. $d\phi/dt$ is the rate at which the conductor(s) move through the magnetic field.

The negative sign means that whenever a current flows as a result of the induced voltage (V) it will have a magnetic field that opposes the motion.

Here is your next question: *There is a rotating magnetic field in:*

(1) An induction motor. Go to Block 46.
(2) A compound-wound dc motor. Go to Block 22.

BLOCK 42

Your answer to the question in Block 36 is not correct. Go back and read the question again and select another answer.

BLOCK 43

Your answer to the question in Block 25 is not correct. Go back and read the question again and select another answer.

BLOCK 44

The correct answer to the question in Block 23 is choice (1). Coulomb's law describes the force of attraction and repulsion between electric charges. It has nothing to do with the voltage induced in a conductor.

Faraday's law describes how much voltage is induced in a conductor moving through a magnetic field.

It is a good idea to know the physical laws and effects. It will help you to understand many devices used in industrial electronics.

Here is your next question: *Ideally, the value of power factor in an industrial power system should be:*

(1) 0.0. Go to Block 39.
(2) 1.0. Go to Block 29.
(3) Neither choice is correct. Go to Block 50.

BLOCK 45

Your answer to the question in Block 3 is not correct. Go back and read the question again and select another answer.

BLOCK 46

The correct answer to the question in Block 41 is choice (1). You must understand the rotating magnetic field to understand the way the ac induction motor works.

Here is your next question: *Part of a motor speed control circuit is shown in this block. The RC circuit:*

(1) Assures that the motor will conduct on both half cycles. Go to Block 11.

(2) Prevents false triggering from transients on the line voltage. Go to Block 54.

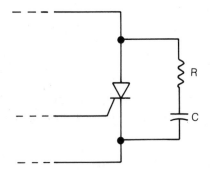

BLOCK 47

Your answer to the question in Block 30 is not correct. Go back and read the question again and select another answer.

BLOCK 48

Your answer to the question in Block 53 is not correct. Go back and read the question again and select another answer.

BLOCK 49

The correct answer to the question in Block 38 is choice (2). The speed of dc motors is more easily controlled than the speed of ac motors. Brushes wear down and must be replaced after a period of use. Therefore, maintenance of brushes is a requirement.

Here is your next question: *The conductor shown in this circuit has an electron current flowing in the direction of the arrow. (Only a section of the conductor is shown.) The conductor will move:*

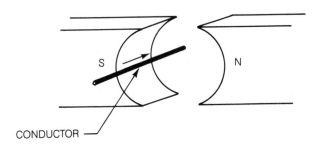

CONDUCTOR

(1) Up if free to do so. Go to Block 24.

(2) Down if free to do so. Go to Block 36.

BLOCK 50

Your answer to the question in Block 44 is not correct. Go back and read the question again and select another answer.

BLOCK 51

Your answer to the question in Block 28 is not correct. Go back and read the question again and select another answer.

BLOCK 52

Your answer to the question in Block 31 is not correct. Go back and read the question again and select another answer.

BLOCK 53

The correct answer to the question in Block 20 is choice (2). There is no motor type called Republic. (However, that could be a trade name. You will seldom find trade names in the CET test.)

Here is your next question: *Which of the following is used as a sensor for motor speed?*

(1) Hall effect devices. Go to Block 37.

(2) Coil/magnet combinations. Go to Block 48.

(3) Light source/LAD combinations. Go to Block 21.

(4) All are used as motor speed sensors. Go to Block 34.

BLOCK 54

The correct answer to the question in Block 46 is choice (2). The RC circuit is called a snubber. Without it, a voltage spike on the ac line can start an SCR, or a triac, into conduction regardless of the fact that there is no voltage on the gate.

Here is your next question: *Name two motors that have a speed which is dependent upon the* frequency *of the input power.* Go to Block 56.

BLOCK 55

Your answer to the question in Block 9 is not correct. Go back and read the question again and select another answer.

BLOCK 56

The correct answer to the question in Block 54 is stepping motor and synchronous motor.

You have now completed Programmed Review No. 1.

PROGRAMMED REVIEW NO. 2

Start with Block number 1. Pick the answer that you think is correct. If you select choice number 1, go to Block 13. If you select choice number 2, go to Block 15. Proceed as directed. There is only one correct answer for each question.

BLOCK 1

Which of the following is an advantage of an optical coupler?

(1) High-impedance isolation. Go to Block 13.
(2) Low-level output impedance when off. Go to Block 15.

BLOCK 2

Your answer to the question in Block 42 is not correct. Go back and read the question again and select another answer.

BLOCK 3

Your answer to the question in Block 53 is not correct. Go back and read the question again and select another answer.

BLOCK 4

The correct answer to the question in Block 56 is choice (2). Current must flow through the Hall device in order to get an output voltage that is related to the magnetic field. That means the Hall device is current dependent. Of course, the Hall device is also magnetic field dependent, but that was not one of the choices.

Voltage out of the Hall device depends upon its current and the presence of a magnetic field. Current is the independent variable. Voltage is the dependent variable.

Here is your next question: *Which of the following is the correct way of determining power factor?*

(1) Power factor = true power ÷ apparent power. Go to Block 45.

(2) Power factor = apparent power & true power. Go to Block
    40.

BLOCK 5

Your answer to the question in Block 13 is not correct. Go back
and read the question again and select another answer.

BLOCK 6

The correct answer to the question in Block 47 is choice (3). The
rotating field must turn faster than the rotor. If they are turning at the
same speed then there is no relative motion between the conductors
in the rotor and the magnetic field.

Induced current must flow in the rotor conductor so the force on
that magnetic field (due to the rotating field) can turn the rotor.

Here is your next question: *To minimize arcing at the brushes,
the brushes of a motor should be realigned with the:*

(1) Geometric center. Go to Block 37.
(2) Neutral field. Go to Block 19.

BLOCK 7

Your answer to the question in Block 54 is not correct. Go back
and read the question again and select another answer.

BLOCK 8

The correct answer to the question in Block 20 is choice (2). It is
assumed that Wheel 1 and Wheel 3 are the same size. Wheel 2 is an
idler. It does not affect the speed of Wheel 3—assuming Wheel 1 is
the driven wheel.

Here is your next question: *Is the following statement true? If
you supply a dc voltage to the terminals of a dc generator it will run
like a motor if free to do so.*

(1) True. Go to Block 24.
(2) False. Go to Block 39.

BLOCK 9

Your answer to the question in Block 33 is not correct. Go back
and read the question again and select another answer.

BLOCK 10

The correct answer to the question in Block 36 is choice (3). The waveform marked C causes current to be delivered to the motor for a longer period of time for each cycle. So, the motor receives more power.

Here is your next question: *The field winding of a shunt-wound motor that has no mechanical load is open. The motor will run:*

(1) Faster. Go to Block 52.
(2) Slower. Go to Block 50.

BLOCK 11

The correct answer to the question in Block 52 is choice (2). The alternator is a three-phase generator. Diodes are used to convert the ac output to dc.

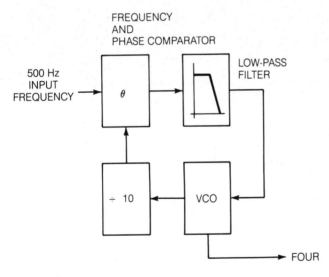

Here is your next question: *What is the VCO output frequency for the system in this block?* Go to Block 57.

BLOCK 12

Your answer to the question in Block 25 is not correct. Go back and read the question again and select another answer.

BLOCK 13

The correct answer to the question in Block 1 is choice (1). The input and output circuits in an optical coupler are completely isolated from each other. That means that the input and output circuits can each look into their characteristic impedances. Also, circuits with two different voltages and currents can be linked together by an optical coupler.

Here is your next question: *The magnetic field of an induced current always has a magnetic field that opposes the motion that produced it. This is a statement of:*

(1) Lenz's law. Go to Block 56.
(2) Faraday's law. Go to Block 41.
(3) Coulomb's law. Go to Block 5.

BLOCK 14

Your answer to the question in Block 52 is not correct. Go back and read the question again and select another answer.

BLOCK 15

Your answer to the question in Block 1 is not correct. Go back and read the question again and select another answer.

BLOCK 16

Your answer to the question in Block 51 is not correct. Go back and read the question again and select another answer.

BLOCK 17

Your answer to the question in Block 23 is not correct. Go back and read the question again and select another answer.

BLOCK 18

Your answer to the question in Block 42 is not correct. Go back and read the question again and select another answer.

BLOCK 19

The correct answer to the question in Block 6 is choice (2). The neutral field is due to rotation of the magnetic field in the motor. The first illustration in this block compares the geometric center and the neutral field.

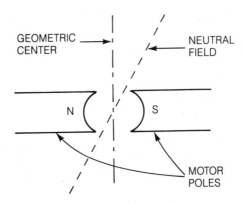

GEOMETRIC CENTER → | NEUTRAL FIELD

N (S

MOTOR POLES

Here is your next question: *The wheels in the following illustration have rubber tires and are pressed against each other. Wheel number 3 will turn:*

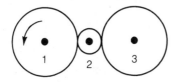

(1) Clockwise. Go to Block 30.
(2) Counterclockwise. Go to Block 8.

BLOCK 20

The correct answer to the question in Block 19 is choice (2). The question is typical for tests given for possible employment. It is often presumed that industrial electronics technicians have a basic mechanical aptitude.

Here is your next question: *Refer again to the illustration in Block 19. Wheel 3:*

(1) Turns faster than Wheel 1. Go to Block 29.
(2) Turns the same speed as Wheel 1. Go to Block 8.
(3) Turns slower than Wheel 1. Go to Block 49.

BLOCK 21

Your answer to the question in Block 36 is not correct. Go back and read the question again and select another answer.

BLOCK 22

Your answer to the question in Block 26 is not correct. Go back and read the question again and select another answer.

BLOCK 23

The correct answer to the question in Block 8 is choice (1). The generator will not run efficiently because its brushes will not be in the right position.

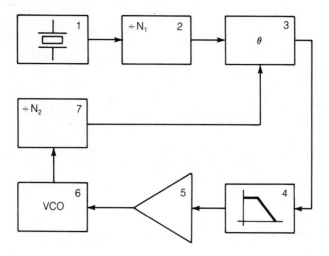

Here is your next question: *Refer to the illustration in this block. It is a block diagram of a:*

(1) Speed control. Go to Block 17.
(2) Phase-locked loop. Go to Block 33.

BLOCK 24

The correct answer to the question in Block 23 is choice (2). The phase-locked loop can be used to control motor speed. To do that, the output of the VCO is delivered through a power amplifier to a motor that has its speed controlled by the *frequency* of its input power.

In the illustration of Block 23, the phase-locked loop is used as a frequency synthesizer. Many accurately controlled frequencies can be obtained from a single crystal oscillator.

Here is your next question: *Refer again to the illustration in Block 23. The crystal oscillator frequency is 8 megahertz and N1 is a divide-by-ten circuit. If N2 is a divide-by-two circuit, the output frequency is:*

(1) 0.4 megahertz. Go to Block 44.
(2) 1.6 megahertz. Go to Block 33.

BLOCK 25

The correct answer to the question in Block 45 is choice (1). When the generator is delivering a load current, that current is flowing through the generator. Its magnetic field reacts with the internal magnetic field of the generator to oppose the motion. That is in compliance with Lenz's law.

Here is your next question: *Which of the following has the highest starting torque?*

(1) Compound-wound motor. Go to Block 12.
(2) Shunt-wound motor. Go to Block 31.
(3) Series-wound motor. Go to Block 26.

BLOCK 26

The correct answer to the question in Block 25 is choice (3). When voltage is first applied to the series-wound motor the only opposition to current flow is the inductive reactance of the motor coil. A high current flows with an accompanying strong magnetic field. That produces a high starting torque.

Here is your next question: *You would expect to find a commutator in a:*

(1) Synchronous motor. Go to Block 48.
(2) DC motor. Go to Block 54.
(3) Induction motor. Go to Block 22.

BLOCK 27

Your answer to the question in Block 43 is not correct. Go back and read the question again and select another answer.

BLOCK 28

Your answer to the question in Block 36 is not correct. Go back and read the question again and select another answer.

BLOCK 29

Your answer to the question in Block 20 is not correct. Go back and read the question again and select another answer.

BLOCK 30

Your answer to the question in Block 19 is not correct. Go back and read the question again and select another answer.

BLOCK 31

Your answer to the question in Block 25 is not correct. Go back and read the question again and select another answer.

BLOCK 32

Your answer to the question in Block 51 is not correct. Go back and read the question again and select another answer.

BLOCK 33

The correct answer to the question in Block 24 is choice (2). The output of N1 is 0.8 megahertz. That value is *multiplied* by 2 due to N2, (80 megahertz ÷ 10) × 2 = 1.6 megahertz.

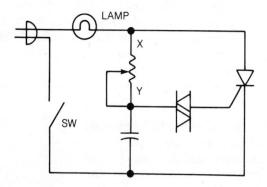

Here is your next question: *Consider the simple SCR circuit shown in this block. The lamp will be dimmer if you move the arm of the variable resistor:*

(1) Toward X. Go to Block 9.
(2) Toward Y. Go to Block 18.

BLOCK 34

Your answer to the question in Block 56 is not correct. Go back and read the question again and select another answer.

BLOCK 35

Your answer to the question in Block 47 is not correct. Go back and read the question again and select another answer.

BLOCK 36

The correct answer to the question in Block 42 is choice (2). The diac will not conduct until the voltage across it reaches a predetermined value that is set by the manufacturer.

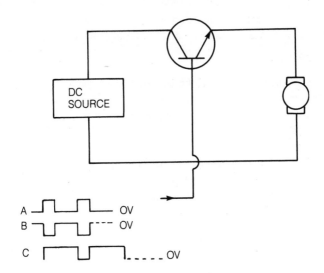

Here is your next question: *Which of the waveforms for the motor control circuit in this block will give the highest speed?*

(1) The one marked A. Go to Block 21.
(2) The one marked C. Go to Block 10.
(3) The one marked B. Go to Block 28.

BLOCK 37

Your answer to the question in Block 6 is not correct. Go back and read the question again and select another answer.

BLOCK 38

Your answer to the question in Block 51 is not correct. Go back and read the question again and select another answer.

BLOCK 39

Your answer to the question in Block 8 is not correct. Go back and read the question again and select another answer.

BLOCK 40

Your answer to the question in Block 4 is not correct. Go back and read the question again and select another answer.

BLOCK 41

Your answer to the question in Block 13 is not correct. Go back and read the question again and select another answer.

BLOCK 42

The correct answer to the question in Block 33 is choice (2). Think about this. If the arm is moved to point X, the voltage on the gate of the SCR will be approximately the same as the voltage on its anode. Without any delay, the SCR will conduct the maximum current through the lamp.

The maximum brightness of the lamp in the circuit of Block 33 is only one-half the maximum possible brightness because the SCR half-wave rectifies the ac input voltage.

Here is your next question: *Consider again the circuit in Block 33. The two-terminal device shown in the gate circuit of the SCR is a:*

(1) Triac. Go to Block 2.
(2) Diac. Go to Block 36.
(3) Neither choice is correct. Go to Block 18.

BLOCK 43

The correct answer to the question in Block 51 is choice (3). To change the output level it is necessary to change the input level. The RMS value of a sine wave does not change when the frequency is changed provided the amplitude remains the same. Likewise, changing the phase does not alter the RMS value of two equal-amplitude signals.

Changing the dc voltage, the RMS voltage, or half-cycle average changes the base current. That, in turn, changes the power to the load resistance.

Here is your next question: *Which of the following types of dc motors can run on dc or ac?*

(1) Series wound. Go to Block 53.
(2) Shunt wound. Go to Block 27.

BLOCK 44

Your answer to the question in Block 24 is not correct. Go back and read the question again and select another answer.

BLOCK 45

The correct answer to the question in Block 4 is choice (1). Power factor is equal to the cosine of the phase angle (ϕ) between the voltage and the current. The best condition exists when the voltage and current are in phase. (That means $\phi = 0$.) The cosine of zero degrees is 1.0 and that is the ideal power factor.

Here is your next question: *A dc generator turns more easily when:*

(1) It is not delivering current. Go to Block 25.
(2) It is delivering current. Go to Block 46.

BLOCK 46

Your answer to the question in Block 45 is not correct. Go back and read the question again and select another answer.

BLOCK 47

The correct answer to the question in Block 53 is choice (1). The belt and pulley method of changing speed is very effective and low in cost compared to some other methods.

When the motor-driven pulley turns 360° the load pulley must turn more than 360°. So, the number of revolutions per minute (rpm) of the load pulley must be greater than the rpm of the motor pulley.

Here is your next question: *In a nonsynchronous motor the rotor must turn:*

(1) Faster than the rotating field. Go to Block 35.
(2) At the same speed as the rotating field. Go to Block 55.
(3) Slower than the rotating field. Go to Block 6.

BLOCK 48

Your answer to the question in Block 26 is not correct. Go back and read the question again and select another answer.

BLOCK 49

Your answer to the question in Block 20 is not correct. Go back and read the question again and select another answer.

BLOCK 50

Your answer to the question in Block 10 is not correct. Go back and read the question again and select another answer.

BLOCK 51

The correct answer to the question in Block 54 is choice (2). By rotating the brushes the arcing (at the brushes) is stopped. That arcing is the source of electrical noise.

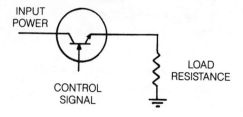

Here is your next question: *Consider the partial control circuit shown in this block. To exercise control of power to the load resistor, the control signal can be:*

(1) Varied in frequency. Go to Block 16.
(2) Varied in phase. Go to Block 38.
(3) Varied in dc voltage, RMS voltage, or average voltage. Go to Block 43.
(4) All of the choices are correct. Go to Block 32.

BLOCK 52

The correct answer to the question in Block 10 is choice (1). Without a mechanical load the motor will move faster and faster until it self-destructs. The weak remaining field is sufficient for motor operation. With the field winding open there is very little counter voltage and very little opposition to motor speed (except for friction).

Here is your next question: *The alternator used in cars is:*

(1) An ac 3φ motor/generator set. Go to Block 14.
(2) An ac 3φ alternator/rectifier set. Go to Block 11.

BLOCK 53

The correct answer to the question in Block 43 is choice (1). *Universal motors* are actually series-wound dc motors. However, their magnetic circuit is different from the dc motor because they are made of laminated material to reduce eddy current loss.

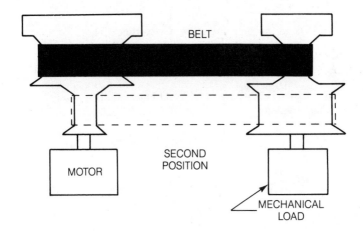

Here is your next question: *Refer to the illustration in this block. The load will be driven at the highest speed:*

(1) With the belt in the first position as shown. Go to Block 47.
(2) By moving the belt to the second position. Go to Block 3.

BLOCK 54

The correct answer to the question in Block 26 is choice (2). Synchronous motors and induction motors operate on ac power. Only dc motors have commutators.

Here is your next question: *Which of the following will likely reduce noise in the output of a dc generator?*

(1) Put a capacitor in series with the field. Go to Block 7.
(2) Rotate the brushes off dead center. Go to Block 51.

BLOCK 55

Your answer to the question in Block 47 is not correct. Go back and read the question again and select another answer.

BLOCK 56

The correct answer to the question in Block 13 is choice (1). An *induced current* can be defined as a current that flows as a result of an induced voltage. The magnetic field of the induced current will react with the magnetic field that produced it to oppose the generation of the voltage. That is Lenz's law.

Here is your next question: *Hall effect devices depend on:*

(1) Voltage for their operation. Go to Block 34.
(2) Current for their operation. Go to Block 4.

BLOCK 57

The answer is 5000 Hz. The VCO must oscillate at 5000 Hz so that, when divided by 10, it equals the 500 Hz reference input.

You have now completed Programmed Review No. 2.

KEY WORDS

Armature
Brushes
Capacitor-start motor
Centrifugal switch
Commutator
Compound-wound motor
Coulomb's law
dφ/dt
Divide-by-M
Electrical noise
Faraday's law
Field
Geometric center
Half-cycle average
Hall device
Impedance triangle
Induced current

Induction motor
Lead vs lag
Left-hand motor rule
Lenz's law
Mechanical load
Mechanical rectifier
Neutral field
Optical coupler
Phase-locked loop
Power factor
Power triangle
Pulse code modulation
Pulse width modulation
RMS voltage
Rotor
Rotary converter
RPM

Series-wound motor   Torque
Shunt-wound motor   Universal motor
Starting torque   VCO
Synchronous motor

PRACTICE TEST

1. From the following list, which dc motor meets all of these requirements?

- High starting torque.
- Will always be operated with a mechanical load.
- Will operate on dc power.
- Speed regulation is not a requirement.

(A) Series-wound motor.
(B) Shunt-wound motor.
(C) Compound-wound motor.
(D) Synchronous motor.

2. Which of the following types of motors can operate effectively on ac or dc power?

(A) Series-wound motor.
(B) Shunt-wound motor.
(C) Compound-wound motor.
(D) None of these choices is correct.

3. An induction motor:

(A) Has a speed that equates the speed of rotation of its internal magnetic field.
(B) Has a speed that is faster than the speed of rotation of its internal magnetic field.
(C) Has a speed that is slower than the speed of rotation of its internal magnetic field.
(D) Has a speed that is not related in any way to its internal magnetic field.

4. Which of the following components is often used to start a single-phase induction motor?

(A) Resistor.

(B) Capacitor.
(C) Inductor.
(D) SCR.

5. Phase-locked loops are used to control frequency. Which of the following motors is usually speed-controlled with a PLL?

(A) Induction motor.
(B) Series-wound motor.
(C) Shunt-wound motor.
(D) None of these choices is correct.

6. When a PLL is used to get a number of different crystal-stabilized frequencies from a single capital oscillator the circuit is called a:

(A) Synchronizer.
(B) Stabilizer.
(C) PLA.
(D) Synthesizer.

7. Which of the following statements is incorrect?

(A) The direction of rotation of a shunt-wound dc motor can be reversed by reversing the connection to its rotor.
(B) The direction of rotation of a series-wound dc motor cannot be reversed.
(C) The direction of rotation of a capacitor-start motor is reversed by reversing the power leads to the motor.
(D) Only synchronous motors can be reversed. All other motors have a direction of rotation that is set during manufacture.

8. It is easier to control the speed of:

(A) A dc motor.
(B) A capacitor-start motor.
(C) Both choices are correct.
(D) Neither choice is correct.

9. A very small series-wound dc motor may not self-destruct when operated without a load because of:

(A) Air currents.

(B) Internal dc resistance.
(C) Low field strength.
(D) Friction.

10. Which of the following is used as a sensor for motor speed?

(A) Accelerometer.
(B) Synchro.
(C) Electrometer.
(D) Hall effect device.

ANSWERS TO PRACTICE TEST

1. (A)

2. (A)   When designed to operate on ac or dc it is called a universal motor. Also, its magnetic circuit is made with laminated material.

3. (C)   The slower speed is due to the necessary *slip* in this kind of motor.

4. (B)   The capacitor is usually switched out of the circuit after the motor reaches a certain predetermined speed.

5. (D)   Synchronous motors and stepping motors are easily controlled with a frequency.

6. (D)

7. (A)   One of the advantages of dc motors is that their direction of rotation can be easily controlled with a switch.

8. (A)   Another advantage of dc motors is the ease of controlling their speed. (This does not include series-wound dc motors.)

9. (D)

10. (D)   Accelerometers are used to measure acceleration. Synchros are used for controlling direction of rotation. Electrometers are used to sense or measure electric field strength.

7

Numerical Control and Other Automation Techniques

THE SUBJECT MATTER in this chapter is not a major in the CET test. However, you will find a few questions related to the material presented. You will also find some additional questions on power supplies presented here.

Be sure to identify the definitions of terms. An example is *process control*.

As with other chapters, this one will serve as a guide to things you may want to study in greater depth.

PROGRAMMED REVIEW NO. 1

Start with Block number 1. Pick the answer that you think is correct. If you select choice number 1, go to Block number 2. If you select choice number 2, go to Block number 3. Proceed as directed. There is only one correct number for each question.

BLOCK 1

High current in a gas regulator tube is due to:

(1) High dc supply voltage. Go to Block 2.
(2) Avalanching. Go to Block 3.

BLOCK 2

Your answer to the question in Block 1 is not correct. Go back and read the question again and select another answer.

BLOCK 3

The correct answer to the question in Block 1 is choice (2). Avalanching is the result of electrons colliding with atoms of gas in the gas tube. The collisions knock other electrons loose and, therefore, add electrons to the current flow. Large currents are the result of avalanching.

Here is your next question: *An inductor in a filter circuit has an advantage over the resistor that often takes its place. The advantage is:*

(1) Lower cost. Go to Block 4.
(2) Higher output voltage. Go to Block 5.

BLOCK 4

Your answer to the question in Block 3 is not correct. Go back and read the question again and select another answer.

BLOCK 5

The correct answer to the question in Block 3 is choice (2). The higher voltage results from the fact that there is practically no voltage drop across the coil as there would be if a resistor was used.

Here is your next question: *A series-pass regulator is:*

(1) A power amplifier. Go to Block 7.
(2) A voltage amplifier. Go to Block 6.

BLOCK 6

Your answer to the question in Block 5 is not correct. Go back and read the question again and select another answer.

BLOCK 7

The correct answer to the question in Block 5 is choice (1). All of the power supply current flows through the series-pass regulator. Therefore, it must be a power amplifier.

Here is your next question: *Which of the following has a higher voltage gain?*

(1) A common emitter amplifier. Go to Block 9.
(2) A common collector amplifier. Go to Block 8.

BLOCK 8

Your answer to the question in Block 7 is not correct. Go back and read the question again and select another answer.

BLOCK 9

The correct answer to the question in Block 7 is choice (2). A common-collector amplifier is also known as an emitter follower. It has a voltage gain that is less than 1, but it may have a power gain.

Here is your next question: *An NPN transistor series-pass regulator in a positive output supply is connected as:*

(1) A common-emitter amplifier. Go to Block 10.
(2) A common-collector amplifier. Go to Block 11.

BLOCK 10

Your answer to the question in Block 9 is not correct. Go back and read the question again and select another answer.

BLOCK 11

The correct answer to the question in Block 9 is choice (2). The input signal is to the base and the output signal is at the emitter. This is characteristic of common-collector circuits. They are also called emitter followers.

Here is your next question: *If you have 16 lines on an address bus in a microprocessor, you can access:*

(1) 256 lines in a memory. Go to Block 12.
(2) 16K lines in a memory. Go to Block 13.
(3) 64K lines in a memory. Go to Block 14.

BLOCK 12

Your answer to the question in Block 11 is not correct. Go back and read the question again and select another answer.

BLOCK 13

Your answer to the question in Block 11 is not correct. Go back and read the question again and select another answer.

BLOCK 14

The correct answer to the question in Block 11 is choice (3). You can calculate the number of choices by raising two to a power equal to the number of lines in the bus. So, two raised to the 16th power is more than 64K, but it is traditionally called 64K.

Here is your next question: *In a software flow diagram, the diamond-shaped symbol shown in this block means:*

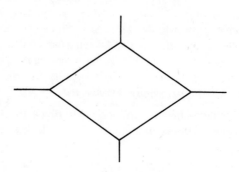

(1) Choose, or make a decision. Go to Block 15.
(2) Stop unless both inputs are at a logic 1 level. Go to Block 16.

BLOCK 15

The correct answer to the question in Block 14 is choice (1). The symbols used in flow charts are not only used for computer and microprocessor programs, but also for troubleshooting charts.

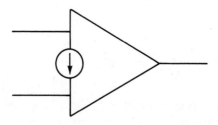

Here is your next question: *What type of device is shown in this block?*

_____. Go to Block 17.

BLOCK 16

Your answer to the question in Block 14 is not correct. Go back and read the question again and select another answer.

BLOCK 17

The correct answer to the question in Block 15 is *current differencing amplifier*.

Here is your next question: *In a certain computer-controlled industrial system the program can be loaded directly into memory instead of going through the computer. This is an example of:*

(1) MMD. Go to Block 18.
(2) DMA. Go to Block 19.

BLOCK 18

Your answer to the question in Block 17 is not correct. Go back and read the question again and select another answer.

BLOCK 19

The correct answer to the question in Block 17 is choice (2). Current differencing amplifiers are similar in their operation to op amps.

Here is your next question: *A programmable controller can be thought of as being:*

(1) A dedicated computer. Go to Block 20.
(2) A hand-held calculator. Go to Block 21.

BLOCK 20

The correct answer to the question in Block 19 is choice (1). The programmable controller has been in existence for many years. It has an advantage over the computer that it is easier to control. It is also less expensive.

Here is your next question: *Which of the following would be a step in machine language?*

(1) LDAA X. Go to Block 22.
(2) 10011011. Go to Block 23.

BLOCK 21

Your answer to the question in Block 19 is not correct. Go back and read the question again and select another answer.

BLOCK 22

Your answer to the question in Block 20 is not correct. Go back and read the question again and select another answer.

BLOCK 23

The correct answer to the question in Block 20 is choice (2). Machine language is cumbersome to work with, but it executes the program very quickly.

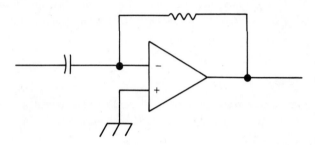

Here is your next question: *The op amp in this block is:*

(1) A differentiator. Go to Block 24.
(2) A integrator. Go to Block 25.

BLOCK 24

Your answer to the question in Block 23 is not correct. Go back and read the question again and select another answer.

BLOCK 25

The correct answer to the question in Block 23 is choice (2). The illustration shows an integrator. The differentiator has an output that is related to the rate of change of the input signal.

Here is your next question: *Which is faster?*

(1) Fast-acting fuse. Go to Block 26.
(2) Crowbar circuit. Go to Block 27.

BLOCK 26

Your answer to the question in Block 25 is not correct. Go back and read the question again and select another answer.

BLOCK 27

The correct answer to the question in Block 25 is choice (2). Crowbar circuits require less than a half cycle of input power to completely shut down a power supply. Fuses are not that fast.

Here is your next question: *Which is better?*

(1) Low percent regulation. Go to Block 28.
(2) High percent regulation. Go to Block 29.

BLOCK 28

The correct answer to the question in Block 27 is choice (1). If a power supply is perfect, the output voltage will not change when going from no-load to a full-load voltage. This is only possible in a stiffly-regulated supply.

Here is your next question: *Which gives a higher output voltage?*

(1) Capacitive input filter. Go to Block 30.
(2) Inductive input filter. Go to Block 31.

BLOCK 29

Your answer to the question in Block 27 is not correct. Go back and read the question again and select another answer.

BLOCK 30

The correct answer to the question in Block 28 is choice (1). The input capacitor charges to the peak value of the input voltage.

Here is your next question: *Which gives better regulation?*

(1) Capacitive input filter. Go to Block 32.
(2) Choke input filter. Go to Block 33.

BLOCK 31

Your answer to the question in Block 28 is not correct. Go back and read the question again and select another answer.

BLOCK 32

Your answer to the question in Block 30 is not correct. Go back and read the question again and select another answer.

BLOCK 33

The correct answer to the question in Block 30 is choice (2). Choke input filters must be used with gaseous rectifiers. Since their output voltage is lower, they are not often used in brute force power supplies that use conventional tube or semiconductor diodes.

Here is your next question: *When there is a sine wave input (at the required voltage) to a ferroresonant transformer you would expect the output to be:*

(1) A sine wave clipped at the top and bottom. Go to Block 34.
(2) A square wave. Go to Block 35.

BLOCK 34

The correct answer to the question in Block 33 is choice (1). The magnetic circuit in the transformer becomes saturated at the peaks, so the output voltage cannot change once saturation occurs. Anything beyond the saturation point is clipped off and does not appear across the secondary winding.

Here is your next question: *If the surge-limiting resistor is open, check the:*

(1) Filter choke. Go to Block 36.
(2) Electrolytic capacitors. Go to Block 37.

BLOCK 35

Your answer to the question in Block 33 is not correct. Go back and read the question again and select another answer.

BLOCK 36

Your answer to the question in Block 34 is not correct. Go back and read the question again and select another answer.

BLOCK 37

The correct answer to the question in Block 34 is choice (2). If the electrolytic capacitors are leaky the current through the rectifier and surge-limiting resistor will be excessive. Very often the surge-limiting resistor is chosen with a power rating that will result in it burning out before the diode is destroyed.

Here is your next question: *AC motor speed may be controlled by:*

(1) A transmission with gears. Go to Block 38.
(2) A rheostat controlling the field current. Go to Block 39.

BLOCK 38

The correct answer to the question in Block 37 is choice (1). You will also see arrangements with pulleys and belts. This method of speed control is not necessary with dc motors. That is why they are so popular in control systems.

Here is your next question: *When the field current is lost, a shunt-wound motor without a load will:*

(1) Race faster and faster until it is destroyed. Go to Block 40.

(2) Stop. Go to Block 41.

BLOCK 39

Your answer to the question in Block 37 is not correct. Go back and read the question again and select another answer.

BLOCK 40

The correct answer to the question in Block 38 is choice (1). Without the field current the magnetic field is very weak and no countervoltage is generated. There is virtually no opposition to armature speed.

Here is your next question: *In a microprocessor system you would expect a chip select signal to be on the:*

(1) Data bus. Go to Block 42.

(2) Control bus. Go to Block 43.

BLOCK 41

Your answer to the question in Block 38 is not correct. Go back and read the question again and select another answer.

BLOCK 42

Your answer to the question in Block 40 is not correct. Go back and read the question again and select another answer.

BLOCK 43

The correct answer to the question in Block 40 is choice (2). The control bus has signals that select the various sections of the microprocessor as they are needed for a program; for example, it selects the desired memory for a given step.

Here is your next question: *A certain microprocessor is not made as one integrated circuit. Instead, it is made with individual integrated circuits. It is:*

(1) A bit slice. Go to Block 44.

(2) A dedicated microprocessor. Go to Block 45.

BLOCK 44

The correct answer to the question in Block 43 is choice (1). The reason for the high speed of a bit slice is the fact that the operation does not have to follow internal programming steps as in the case of a microprocessor.

Here is your next question: *Which of the following is a disadvantage of a bit slice?*

(1) Timing problems. Go to Block 47.
(2) Speed. Go to Block 46.

BLOCK 45

Your answer to the question in Block 43 is not correct. Go back and read the question again and select another answer.

BLOCK 46

Your answer to the question in Block 44 is not correct. Go back and read the question again and select another answer.

BLOCK 47

The correct answer to the question in Block 44 is choice (1). Timing problems are inherent in bit slice technology. That is one of its biggest disadvantages.

Here is your next question: *After the manufacturing plant closes for the day a computer takes part in the burglar alarm system. It checks each gate, door and window, one at a time. This is called:*

(1) Single stepping. Go to Block 48.
(2) Polling. Go to Block 49.

BLOCK 48

Your answer to the question in Block 47 is not correct. Go back and read the question again and select another answer.

BLOCK 49

The correct answer to the question in Block 47 is choice (2). An alternative to programming is to go to preferred gates first and then to less likely gates and windows. With this method it is possible to signal a break-in of the most likely places more quickly. The less likely places do not have to be polled each time.

Here is your next question: *A PLA cannot be:*

(1) Programmed. Go to Block 50.
(2) Erased. Go to Block 51.

BLOCK 50

Your answer to the question in Block 49 is not correct. Go back and read the question again and select another answer.

BLOCK 51

The correct answer to the question in Block 49 is choice (2). Field programmable PLAs, as their name implies, can be programmed in the field, but no PLA is erasable.

You have now completed Programmed Review No. 1.

PROGRAMMED REVIEW NO. 2

Start with Block number 1. Pick the answer that you think is correct. If you select choice number 1, go to Block number 2. If you select choice number 2, go to Block number 3. Proceed as directed. There is only one correct number for each question.

BLOCK 1

An industrial electronic system that uses a program stored in memory to implement a process is called:

(1) An industrial processor. Go to Block 2.
(2) A programmable controller. Go to Block 3.

BLOCK 2

Your answer to the question in Block 1 is not correct. Go back and read the question again and select another answer.

BLOCK 3

The correct answer to the question in Block 1 is choice (2). There are other systems that fit the definition but, of the two choices, only programmable controller can be correct.

Here is your next question: *Which type of memory is erased by ultraviolet light?*

_____. Go to Block 4.

BLOCK 4

The correct answer to the question in Block 3 is *EPROM*. EPROM stands for Erasable Programmable Read Only Memory. After erasing, it is necessary to place an opaque tape over the window to prevent further erasing by fluorescent lights, sunlight, or other ultraviolet source.

Here is your next question: *With regard to memory, what do the letters DRAM stand for?*

_____. Go to Block 5.

BLOCK 5

The correct answer to the question in Block 4 is *Dynamic Read Only Memory*. This type of memory uses a capacitor to store a logic bit. The capacitor is charged to represent logic 1, and discharged to represent logic 0.

Here is your next question: *With the proper address code you can select any byte of information in:*

(1) A Random Access Memory (RAM). Go to Block 6.
(2) A Read Only Memory (ROM). Go to Block 7.
(3) Either a RAM or a ROM. Go to Block 8.
(4) None of the choices is correct. Go to Block 9.

BLOCK 6

Your answer to the question in Block 5 is not correct. Go back and read the question again and select another answer.

BLOCK 7

Your answer to the question in Block 5 is not correct. Go back and read the question again and select another answer.

BLOCK 8

The correct answer to the question in Block 5 is choice (3). The term *random access memory* is a misnomer. Actually, the RAM and the ROM are both random access. There has been a move to change the term *random access memory* to *read/write memory,* but it has not been able to gather much momentum.

Here is your next question: *A certain memory can be programmed and erased by voltages. It is an example of a/an _____. Go to Block 10.*

BLOCK 9

Your answer to the question in Block 5 is not correct. Go back and read the question again and select another answer.

BLOCK 10

The correct answer to the question in Block 8 is *EEROM*. The letters stand for Electrically Erasable Read Only Memory.

Here is your next question: *A certain motor uses a thermal switch mounted on the frame. It is normally closed, but it opens if the temperature of the frame is too high for normal operation. The thermal switch and the ON/OFF switch must be in the:*

(1) AND configuration. Go to Block 11.
(2) OR configuration. Go to Block 12.
(3) Neither choice is correct. Go to Block 13.

BLOCK 11

The correct answer to the question in Block 10 is choice (1). The thermal switch AND the ON/OFF switch must both be closed (logic 1) to get an output (motor run).

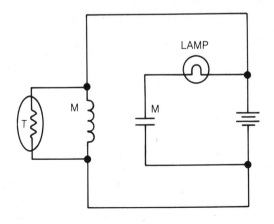

Here is your next question: *For the system shown in this block you would expect the lamp to be ON when the ambient temperature is:*

(1) Cold. Go to Block 14.
(2) Hot. Go to Block 15.

BLOCK 12

Your answer to the question in Block 10 is not correct. Go back and read the question again and select another answer.

BLOCK 13

Your answer to the question in Block 10 is not correct. Go back and read the question again and select another answer.

BLOCK 14

The correct answer to the question in Block 11 is choice (1). The temperature of the thermistor is high when the system is cold, so most of the current flows through the relay coil. The relay is energized and the lamp is ON. (Note: unless otherwise stated, the thermistors in circuits are presumed to have a negative temperature coefficient.)

Here is your next question: *The speed of a certain motor is controlled in a closed-loop system. To sense the existing speed, a:*

(1) Tachometer is used. Go to Block 16.
(2) Speedometer is used. Go to Block 17.

BLOCK 15

Your answer to the question in Block 11 is not correct. Go back and read the question again and select another answer.

BLOCK 16

The correct answer to the question in Block 14 is choice (1). A speedometer is used for measuring *linear* rate of change of distance.

Here is your next question: *Which of the following increases the stability of a closed-loop control?*

(1) Increase the gain. Go to Block 18.
(2) Decrease the gain. Go to Block 19.
(3) Stability is not related to gain. Go to Block 20.

BLOCK 17

Your answer to the question in Block 14 is not correct. Go back and read the question again and select another answer.

BLOCK 18

Your answer to the question in Block 16 is not correct. Go back and read the question again and select another answer.

BLOCK 19

The correct answer to the question in Block 16 is choice (2). Think of it this way. If the gain is equal to 1, you would have perfect stability. Anything above 1 starts to approach instability.

Here is your next question: *Which of the following converts an electrical signal to a mechanical action?*

(1) A transductor. Go to Block 21.
(2) An actuator. Go to Block 22.
(3) Both answers are correct. Go to Block 23.

BLOCK 20

Your answer to the question in Block 16 is not correct. Go back and read the question again and select another answer.

BLOCK 21

Your answer to the question in Block 19 is not correct. Go back and read the question again and select another answer.

BLOCK 22

The correct answer to the question in Block 19 is choice (2). There are other devices that convert electrical signals to mechanical action, but of the ones listed actuator is the only correct choice.

Here is your next question: *An automated drill press can position a drill bit on a workpiece and then drill the hole to a predetermined depth. Which of the following is related to the depth of the hole?*

(1) X-axis. Go to Block 24.
(2) Y-axis. Go to Block 25.
(3) Z-axis. Go to Block 26.
(4) D-axis. Go to Block 27.

BLOCK 23

Your answer to the question in Block 19 is not correct. Go back and read the question again and select another answer.

BLOCK 24

Your answer to the question in Block 22 is not correct. Go back and read the question again and select another answer.

BLOCK 25

Your answer to the question in Block 22 is not correct. Go back and read the question again and select another answer.

BLOCK 26

The correct answer to the question in Block 22 is choice (3). There is no such thing as a D-axis.

Here is your next question: *Which of the following is measured by using zero pressure as a reference?*

(1) Absolute pressure. Go to Block 28.
(2) Differential pressure. Go to Block 29.

BLOCK 27

Your answer to the question in Block 22 is not correct. Go back and read the question again and select another answer.

BLOCK 28

The correct answer to the question in Block 26 is choice (1). Be sure you know the difference between relative and absolute measurements. Relative is with reference to another value and absolute is with reference to zero.

Here is your next question: *Which of the following uses a change in wire length and diameter as a sensing element?*

(1) Manometer. Go to Block 30.
(2) Strain gauge. Go to Block 31.
(3) Neither choice is correct. Go to Block 32.

BLOCK 29

Your answer to the question in Block 26 is not correct. Go back and read the question again and select another answer.

BLOCK 30

Your answer to the question in Block 28 is not correct. Go back and read the question again and select another answer.

BLOCK 31

The correct answer to the question in Block 28 is choice (2). The strain gauge must be deformed in order to make a measurement. With the type that has wire bounded to its surface that deformation causes the wire to stretch and its diameter to decrease.

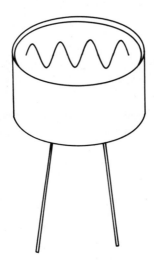

Here is your next question: *Is the following statement correct? The transducer shown in this block is a photocell.*

(1) Correct. Go to Block 33.
(2) Not correct. Go to Block 34.

BLOCK 32

Your answer to the question in Block 28 is not correct. Go back and read the question again and select another answer.

BLOCK 33

Your answer to the question in Block 31 is not correct. Go back and read the question again and select another answer.

BLOCK 34

The correct answer to the question in Block 31 is choice (2). For many years this device was sold as a photocell by a large supplier in the United States. Recently, they have changed their catalog and marked it correctly to be a photoresistor.

Here is your next question: *When infrared is used to activate a PIN diode transducer, the light shines on the:*

(1) N-region. Go to Block 35.
(2) P-region. Go to Block 36.
(3) Neither choice is correct. Go to Block 37.

BLOCK 35

Your answer to the question in Block 34 is not correct. Go back and read the question again and select another answer.

BLOCK 36

Your answer to the question in Block 34 is not correct. Go back and read the question again and select another answer.

BLOCK 37

The correct answer to the question in Block 34 is choice (3). The letters PIN stand for Positive—Intrinsic—Negative. The intrinsic layer between P and N is a nonconductor until light strikes it. Without light, no current can pass through the diode. This type of diode requires infrared light. You will also see pin diodes used extensively at microwave frequencies because of their low junction capacitance.

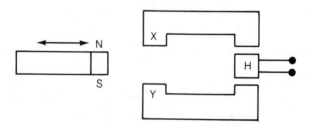

Here is your next question: *For the system in this block, only the output of the Hall (H) sensor is shown. When the bar moves the mag-*

net between X and Y, the output of the Hall sensor in this position indicator is:

 (1) A voltage. Go to Block 38.
 (2) A change in resistance. Go to Block 39.
 (3) A decrease in current. Go to Block 40.

BLOCK 38

The correct answer to the question in Block 37 is choice (1). Although a current flows through a Hall device in its normal operation, its output is a voltage related to the presence of a magnetic field.

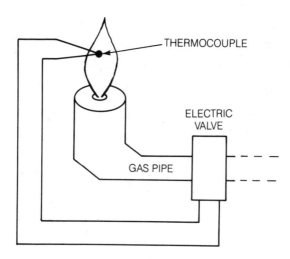

Here is your next question: *For the system in this block, the output of the thermocouple holds the valve open. If the flame dies, there is no thermocouple output and the valve closes. That, in turn, prevents gas from getting into the region. This is an example of an:*

 (1) Adaptive control. Go to Block 41.
 (2) Open-loop control. Go to Block 42.
 (3) Neither choice is correct. Go to Block 43.

BLOCK 39

Your answer to the question in Block 37 is not correct. Go back and read the question again and select another answer.

BLOCK 40

Your answer to the question in Block 37 is not correct. Go back and read the question again and select another answer.

BLOCK 41

Your answer to the question in Block 38 is not correct. Go back and read the question again and select another answer.

BLOCK 42

Your answer to the question in Block 38 is not correct. Go back and read the question again and select another answer.

BLOCK 43

The correct answer to the question in Block 38 is choice (3). This is an ON/OFF control.

Here is your next question: *Refer again to the illustration in Block 38. The system shown is an example of:*

(1) Proportional control. Go to Block 44.
(2) Process control. Go to Block 45.

BLOCK 44

Your answer to the question in Block 43 is not correct. Go back and read the question again and select another answer.

BLOCK 45

The correct answer to the question in Block 43 is choice (2). This is a typical ON/OFF process control.

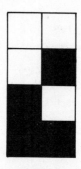

Here is your next question: *For the two-bit coding shown in this block, the black areas represent logic 1 and the white areas represent logic 0. The code shown:*

(1) Counts to four in binary numbers. Go to Block 46.
(2) Makes three binary counts. Go to Block 47.
(3) Neither choice is correct. Go to Block 48.

BLOCK 46

Your answer to the question in Block 45 is not correct. Go back and read the question again and select another answer.

BLOCK 47

Your answer to the question in Block 45 is not correct. Go back and read the question again and select another answer.

BLOCK 48

The correct answer to the question in Block 45 is choice (3). The code (reading from the top) is 00, 01, 10, and 11. This is the binary code from 0 to 3. That makes a total of four counts.

Here is your next question: *A resistive hygrometer changes its resistance when there is a change in:*

(1) Salinity. Go to Block 49.
(2) Humidity. Go to Block 50.

BLOCK 49

Your answer to the question in Block 48 is not correct. Go back and read the question again and select another answer.

BLOCK 50

The correct answer to the question in Block 48 is choice (2). There are a number of different ways to make a hygrometer. The one referred to in the question has a chemical coating that reduces its resistance in the presence of moisture.

You have now completed Programmed Review No. 2.

KEY WORDS

Absolute measurement
Actuator

Adaptive control
Bit slice

Cathode, grid, plate
Closed loop control
Common base
Common collector
Common drain
Common emitter
Common gate
Common source
Crowbar
Current differencing amplifier
Dedicated computer
Differential transformer
Differentiator
DRAM
EEROM
Emitter follower
EPROM
Ferroresonant

Hygrometer
Integrator
Load cell
Maximum power transfer theorem
Memory
PLA
Polling
Process control
Programmable controller
Proportional control
Regulation
Relative measurement
ROM
RAM
Series-pass regulator
Single stepping
Source follower
Surge-limiting

PRACTICE TEST

1. Which of the following would be used to accurately measure a voltage?

 (A) Potentiometer.
 (B) Wheatstone bridge.

2. Is the following statement correct? A differential transformer can be used to sense the direction of a motion.

 (A) Correct.
 (B) Not correct.

3. An ON/OFF control is an example of a:

 (A) Process control.
 (B) Continuous feedback loop control.

4. Which of the following might be used for a temperature sensor?

 (A) Thermistor.
 (B) Thermocouple.
 (C) Both choices are correct.

5. Is the following statement correct? All thermistors have a negative temperature coefficient.

(A) Correct.
(B) Not correct.

6. Which of the following is used in a load cell?

(A) Piezoelectric device.
(B) Stress gauge.

7. High currents in electronic devices are sometimes produced by:

(A) Using feedback.
(B) Avalanching.

8. When the input signal is to the source and the output signal is from the drain, the amplifier is:

(A) A common source type.
(B) A common gate type.
(C) A common drain type.

9. Four input lines to a decoder can produce:

(A) 16 possible outputs.
(B) 8 possible outputs.

10. Flow charts are used for programming and for:

(A) Troubleshooting charts.
(B) Graphing.

ANSWERS TO PRACTICE TEST

1. (A)   The potentiometer is a voltage measuring instrument that is not often discussed in schools.

2. (A)   A soft iron slug is moved between the two differential outputs to affect the output balance.

3. (A)

4. (C)

5. (B)   Unless otherwise noted, the negative temperature coefficient is assumed.

6. (A)   There is no such thing as a stress gauge.

7. (B)

8. (B)

9. (A)   It is two raised to the fourth power.

10. (A)

8
Robotics

EVEN THOUGH YOU may not expect to work in robotics and you may not be working in robotics now, there are some important aspects of robotic technology that you should understand before taking the CET test.

Robotics is a relatively minor part of the overall subject of industrial electronics. However, it is an example of a complete *system* that employs *components* (such as resistors and capacitors) and *circuits* (such as oscillators and amplifiers).

It is difficult to pick an industrial electronic system that is simple enough to be included in one chapter and, at the same time, complex enough to demonstrate some industrial electronic technology. Robotics is a subject that works well.

When you are discussing robotics there are three types of power applications, or power supplies, that you should be familiar with. *Electric* robots are usually electronically controlled. They can be very precisely positioned. *Pneumatic* robots are powered by air or other gas pressure. They have the advantage that a return line is not needed, but the disadvantage is that air is compressible. Therefore, there can be a certain amount of bounce that prohibits highly accurate positioning.

Hydraulic robots are by far the strongest in terms of being able to lift and maneuver heavy objects. There are some maintenance problems associated with hydraulic robots. For example, the fluid filters and the fluid must be replaced periodically. Hydraulic and pneumatic robots are not easy to interface with computers, microprocessors, and other electronic control systems.

The type of robot that has caught the imagination of science fiction writers and writers of today's technical literature is the one called *anthropomorphic*. This robot can closely simulate the motions and activities of a human.

Human activity can be performed in three dimensions: *horizontal, vertical*, and *depth*. These three motions are normally called X, Y, and Z. Not all robots can operate in all three dimensions. For example, some of them can only operate in the X and Y dimension.

The complexity of a robot depends on the amount of money that can be spent and the type of job to be performed. As a rule the simplest and least expensive robot is the best for a job, provided it can do that job.

An important feature of robots is that they can be programmed. In other words, they can be designed to do a wide variety of jobs depending on the programs that are operating them. This makes them very flexible. A robot may be controlling a paint sprayer one day and a riveter the next day.

Of course, you cannot change from one type of operation to another without changing the program. Changing the program can be very expensive in terms of *downtime* on an assembly line or other type of manufacturing process.

Some robots are directly controlled by computers. Others may be controlled by punched tape or magnetic tape. The tapes or the computer serve as memory for the operation that is being performed by the robot. In other words, they hold the program that the robot will follow in some form of memory.

In some cases the program is nothing more complicated than a stop that the robot moves against. The mechanical stop limits its travel, and therefore determines its path of operation.

An activity sometimes described for a robot is to take eggs out of a box and place them in a basket. The reason this application is so important is because it involves very complex technology. It must be able to handle the egg without breaking it. It must also be able to turn the egg so that the large part is at the bottom. It must be able to move the egg safely from one point to the other.

Just the simple process of picking the egg out of the basket is very complicated. It must be able to pick up the egg without breaking the other eggs around it.

The example simply illustrates how complex a robotic job can be. It is not an example of the typical application of robots in industry. Certainly there are many parts in industry that have to be moved that are as delicate as the eggs and that have shapes that are as difficult for the robot to recognize.

If a human is performing the job, that human can easily pick a golf ball out of a box of eggs. If a robot is performing the job, unless special provisions are made, it will put the golf ball in the egg crate in place of the egg that should be there.

Of course, the robot has the advantage that it does not get tired. Robots can work all day without getting tired. They do not need coffee breaks, lunch breaks, or sick leave. Also, it can work in dangerous areas where explosives or poisonous gases are present.

A very important advantage of robots is that they don't get bored. They can perform the same repetitive task day after day without the mental fatigue normal for a human.

An important classification for robots is the *LERT* system. Those letters stand for Linear, Extensional, Rotational, and Twisting. They are the four basic types of robotic actions. A LERT robot can handle all of those motions.

Robots can also be classified according to the *envelope* that they can trace. For example, a rectangular robot can trace horizontal and vertical directions as well as depth.

Robots are sometimes classified by the technology that is used in programming them and in using them. Closed-loop feedback systems are needed for very accurate positioning of electric robots. Closed-loop electronic controls can very accurately control the robot's motions. *Feedback controls* are sometimes called servo control.

Sensors are sometimes used with electronically controlled robots. The types of sensors are the same as the sensors used in other industrial applications, specifically in measurements and controls.

If a robot is anthropomorphic it must be able to perform wrist motions. Wrist motions do not change the envelope of the robotic motion, but they do make the robot more versatile. There are three wrist motions that you must be able to recognize. They are *roll, yaw,* and *pitch*.

The part of the robot that actually picks up and handles the object is called the *end effector*. It is also called by the names *manipulator* or gripper.

PROGRAMMED REVIEW NO. 1

Start with Block number 1. Pick the answer that you think is correct. If you select choice number 1, go to Block 13. If you select choice number 2, go to Block 15. Proceed as directed. There is only one correct answer for each question.

BLOCK 1

Which type of motor is very well suited for applications in robotics because it can be made to turn in small, accurately defined angles?

(1) Stepping motor. Go to Block 13.
(2) Compound-wound dc motor. Go to Block 15.

BLOCK 2

The correct answer to the question in Block 3 is choice (1). Robots and any other type of controlled machine can be very dangerous. Be sure to follow the safety rules set up by your company. Always be *alert*!

Here is your next question: *When a program is delivered from the computer to the robot it is said to be:*

(1) Dumped. Go to Block 7.
(2) Downloaded. Go to Block 11.

BLOCK 3

The correct answer to the question in Block 19 is choice (1). When suction is used to pick up an object it is an example of pickup by *force*. It is an ON/OFF method.

Here is your next question: *Is the following statement correct? You can always feel safe around a robot because all robots are designed to automatically protect people.*

(1) Wrong! Go to Block 2.
(2) Right! Go to Block 12.

BLOCK 4

Your answer to the question in Block 22 is not correct. Go back and read the question again and select another answer.

BLOCK 5

Your answer to the question in Block 23 is not correct. Go back and read the question again and select another answer.

BLOCK 6

The correct answer to the question in Block 11 is choice (2). Of course, all electronic equipment needs a power supply. However, it has become traditional to use the term power supply to mean the source of power for the robot.

Here is your next question: *What three types of power are used for operating robots?*

_____.
_____.
_____. Go to Block 24.

BLOCK 7

Your answer to the question in Block 2 is not correct. Go back and read the question again and select another answer.

BLOCK 8

Your answer to the question in Block 10 is not correct. Go back and read the question again and select another answer.

BLOCK 9

Your answer to the question in Block 16 is not correct. Go back and read the question again and select another answer.

BLOCK 10

The correct answer to the question in Block 20 is choice (1). It is obvious that the end effector must be able to release the workpiece. Turning is a wrist motion, not a motion of the end effector.

Here is your next question: *What is the name of the system that determines the action of the end effectors?*

(1) Robot controller. Go to Block 23.
(2) Hand-held operator. Go to Block 8.

BLOCK 11

The correct answer to the question in Block 2 is choice (2). *Dumped* is a slang expression often used. Textbooks and instruction manuals call it downloading.

Here is your next question: *In robotics terminology, the power supply:*

(1) Provides dc for the electronics. Go to Block 21.
(2) Operates the robot. Go to Block 6.

BLOCK 12

Your answer to the question in Block 3 is not correct. Go back and read the question again and select another answer.

BLOCK 13

The correct answer to the question in Block 1 is choice (1). The position of a stepping motor can be accurately controlled with pulses from the control circuitry. That makes them useful for applications in electrically powered robots used for precise positioning.

Here is your next question: *A robot's limit of reach is called the:*

(1) Outreach. Go to Block 18.
(2) Envelope. Go to Block 20.

BLOCK 14

Your answer to the question in Block 19 is not correct. Go back and read the question again and select another answer.

BLOCK 15

Your answer to the question in Block 1 is not correct. Go back and read the question again and select another answer.

BLOCK 16

The correct answer to the question in Block 23 is choice (1). Spring-loaded end effectors pick up an object by releasing the holder. The springs push the holders against the object.

Here is your next question: *Which of the following can be the more complicated tool for the end of a robot arm?*

(1) Gripper. Go to Block 22.

(2) Drill and countersink. Go to Block 9.

BLOCK 17

Your answer to the question in Block 20 is not correct. Go back and read the question again and select another answer.

BLOCK 18

Your answer to the question in Block 13 is not correct. Go back and read the question again and select another answer.

BLOCK 19

The correct answer to the question in Block 22 is choice (2). Lead-through programming is the simplest method. The technician moves the end effector through the paths it is supposed to take. The system memory puts the motions into the proper codes. After that, it can go by itself.

The disadvantage of this system is that production must be stopped while the programming is performed.

Here is your next question: *Suction-type end effectors can be used for very delicate work, but it is not possible to accurately control their:*

(1) Force. Go to Block 3.

(2) Position. Go to Block 14.

BLOCK 20

The correct answer to the question in Block 13 is choice (2). The word *outreach* is not used in robotic terminology.

The envelope is the limit of reach of the end effector. All maneuvers of the robot can be performed within the envelope.

Here is your next question: *End effectors perform these three functions: grip, lift, and:*

(1) Release. Go to Block 10.

(2) Turn. Go to Block 17.

BLOCK 21

Your answer to the question in Block 11 is not correct. Go back and read the question again and select another answer.

BLOCK 22

The correct answer to the question in Block 16 is choice (1). Grippers may have built-in sensors that help in locating the object being lifted. They may also be needed for turning the object. An example is in turning an egg so that its larger end is down into the crate.

Here is your next question: *You program a certain robot by physically moving its end effector through the path that you want it to go. This is called:*

(1) On-line programming. Go to Block 4.
(2) Lead-through programming. Go to Block 19.

BLOCK 23

The correct answer to the question in Block 10 is choice (1). *Hand-held operator* is not a term used in robotics.

In some very delicate and precise robots there is a method of moving anthropomorphic end effectors by inserting a human hand into the controller. Motions of the human hand are translated into motion of the end effector. This type is used in moving radioactive workpieces and in some medical applications.

Remember that robots are not only useful in manufacturing, but there are many fields where they are the only sensible method of moving an object. Radioactive and medical applications are just two examples.

For the Mars landing, a robotic arm picked up samples of the surface material and carried them inside for analysis. This is another example of nonhuman applications.

Here is your next question: *The simplest end effectors are:*

(1) Spring loaded. Go to Block 16.
(2) Controlled by a stepper motor. Go to Block 5.

BLOCK 24

The correct answer to the question in Block 6 is *electric, hydraulic, and pneumatic*.

You have now completed Programmed Review No. 1.

PROGRAMMED REVIEW NO. 2

Start with Block number 1. Pick the answer that you think is correct. If you select choice number 1, go to Block 13. If you select choice number 2, go to Block 15. Proceed as directed. There is only one correct answer for each question.

BLOCK 1

Is the following statement correct? It is not a robot unless it uses electronic controls.

(1) It is correct. Go to Block 13.
(2) It is not correct. Go to Block 15.

BLOCK 2

Your answer to the question in Block 11 is not correct. Go back and read the question again and select another answer.

BLOCK 3

Your answer to the question in Block 11 is not correct. Go back and read the question again and select another answer.

BLOCK 4

Your answer to the question in Block 11 is not correct. Go back and read the question again and select another answer.

BLOCK 5

Your answer to the question in Block 8 is not correct. Go back and read the question again and select another answer.

BLOCK 6

The correct answer to the question in Block 12 is choice (2). Paint spraying requires accurate positioning of the robot end effectors.

Here is your next question: *The robot in this block will have:*

(1) A rectangular envelope. Go to Block 18.
(2) A spherical envelope. Go to Block 10.

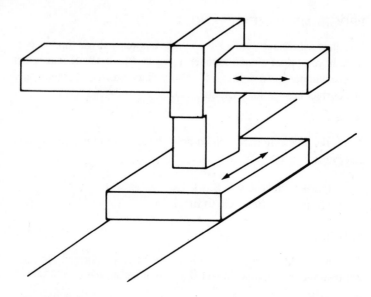

BLOCK 7

Your answer to the question in Block 18 is not correct. Go back and read the question again and select another answer.

BLOCK 8

The correct answer to the question in Block 21 is choice (2). You should know the types of wrist motion and how they are produced. Study the illustration in Block 6.

Here is your next question: *Continuous path motion is the same as the:*

(1) Bang-bang method of moving. Go to Block 19.
(2) Straight-line method of moving. Go to Block 5.

BLOCK 9

Your answer to the question in Block 19 is not correct. Go back and read the question again and select another answer.

BLOCK 10

Your answer to the question in Block 6 is not correct. Go back and read the question again and select another answer.

BLOCK 11

The correct answer to the question in Block 20 is choice (2). It is important to learn the terms used in your field.

Here is your next question: *Which of the following types of robots can be easily interfaced for computer control?*

(1) Hydraulic. Go to Block 3.
(2) Pneumatic. Go to Block 4.
(3) Neither. Go to Block 21.
(4) Both. Go to Block 2.

BLOCK 12

The correct answer to the question in Block 15 is

<u>electric</u> and
<u>hydraulic</u>.

Here is your next question: *Which type of program would normally be used for paint spraying?*

(1) Continuous path. Go to Block 24.
(2) Control path. Go to Block 6.

BLOCK 13

Your answer to the question in Block 1 is not correct. Go back and read the question again and select another answer.

BLOCK 14

Your answer to the question in Block 9 is not correct. Go back and read the question again and select another answer.

BLOCK 15

The correct answer to the question in Block 1 is choice (2). As an electronics technician your work may be specialized in electronic controls. However, there are nonelectronic robots that are also being used in industry.

Here is your next question: *Which types of power are used for pick and place robots?*

_____ and _____. Go to Block 12.

BLOCK 16

Your answer to the question in Block 20 is not correct. Go back and read the question again and select another answer.

BLOCK 17

The correct answer to the question in Block 19 is choice (1). Anthropomorphic robots are the most interesting to fiction writers.

Here is your next question: *Which of the following is an example of on-line programming?*

(1) The computer method. Go to Block 25.
(2) The teach pendant method. Go to Block 14.

BLOCK 18

The correct answer to the question in Block 6 is choice (1). Remember that the envelope is traced by the *maximum* reach of the robot arm.

Here is your next question: *A teach pendant is used for:*

(1) Programming a robot. Go to Block 20.
(2) Training a robotics technician. Go to Block 7.

BLOCK 19

The correct answer to the question in Block 8 is choice (1). Continuous path motion is the easiest to produce. Straight-line motion gives faster results, but it is more difficult to produce.

Here is your next question: *Robots that closely simulate human motions and activities are called:*

(1) Anthropomorphic. Go to Block 17.
(2) Humanoids. Go to Block 9.

BLOCK 20

The correct answer to the question in Block 18 is choice (1). Teach pendants are like remote controls. The operator puts the robot through the required motions using the teach pendant. The motions are put into memory. The robot can then go through the motions from the memory.

Here is your next question: *Another name for an end effector is:*

(1) Hand. Go to Block 16.
(2) Gripper. Go to Block 11.

BLOCK 21

The correct answer to the question in Block 11 is choice (3). This does not mean that it is impossible to use electronic controls in a hydraulic or pneumatic robot. However, it is not as simple as controlling electric robots with electronics.

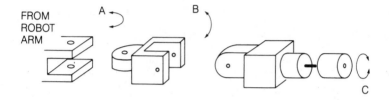

Here is your next question: *Which of the wrist actions illustrated in this block will produce pitch action?*

(1) The one marked A. Go to Block 23.
(2) The one marked B. Go to Block 8.
(3) The one marked C. Go to Block 22.

BLOCK 22

Your answer to the question in Block 21 is not correct. Go back and read the question again and select another answer.

BLOCK 23

Your answer to the question in Block 21 is not correct. Go back and read the question again and select another answer.

BLOCK 24

Your answer to the question in Block 12 is not correct. Go back and read the question again and select another answer.

BLOCK 25

The correct answer to the question in Block 9 is choice (1). Remember that an important advantage of computer programming is that it greatly reduces downtime of the assembly line or processing section of the company. With computer programming, all of the work is done on the computer and it is quickly downloaded to the robot.

Here is your next question: *Name the four types of motion defined by the LERT system of classification.*

_____   _____

_____   _____

Go to Block 26.

BLOCK 26

The four types of motion defined by the LERT system of classification are linear, extensional, rotation, and twisting.

You have now completed Programmed Review No. 2.

KEY WORDS

Anthropomorphic	LERT
Axes	Manipulator
Bang bang	Pick and place
Circuits	Pitch
Components	Pneumatic
Computer programming	Robots
Continuous path	Roll
Downloaded	Spring loaded
Dumped	Stepping motor
Elbow	Systems
End effector	Teach pendant
Envelope	Waste
Gripper	Wrist motion
Hydraulic	Yaw
Lead-through programming	

PRACTICE TEST

1. Three robotic wrist motions are pitch, roll, and:

    (A) Yaw.
    (B) Level out.

2. For a pneumatic robot, increasing the payload:

    (A) Increases the accuracy of arm motion.
    (B) Decreases the accuracy of arm motion.

3. If a robot is classified as being RZE, it is:

   (A) Retractable.
   (B) Rotational.

4. Which of the following types of robots is used for the most delicate and highly-accurate job?

   (A) Electric.
   (B) Pneumatic.
   (C) Hydraulic.

5. Which of the following does not affect the work envelope of a robot?

   (A) Twisting motion.
   (B) Rotational motion.

6. Which type of robot listed here can be used to lift the heaviest payload?

   (A) Electric.
   (B) Hydraulic.

7. Is the following statement correct? The motion of a true robot is programmed.

   (A) The statement is correct.
   (B) The statement is not correct.

8. Which of the following is an important rating of robots?

   (A) Its ability to store programs.
   (B) Its range of motions and types of motions.

9. The motion of a robot is always defined by starting:

   (A) At the base and working outward.
   (B) At the farthest reach and working toward the base.

10. The rotational part of a robot, where it is mounted, is called the:

   (A) Waist.
   (B) Base.

ANSWERS TO PRACTICE TEST

1. (A)   Not all robots can perform all wrist motions. In fact, the three motions can only be used on more expensive systems. Some robots have no wrist motion.

2. (B)   The greater the payload the greater the tendency for bounce due to the compressibility of the air.

3. (B)

4. (A)   Electronic feedback circuits and electric transducers are better adapted for electronic systems.

5. (A)

6. (B)

7. (A)   Programming can be with a teach pendant, physical motion of the arm, or by a computer. Even the simplest robots have their motion fixed by physical limits. Setting those physical limits is a very basic form of programming.

8. (B)

9. (A)

10. (A)

9

Tests and Measurements Used in Industrial Electronics

IN MOST CASES, the first step in troubleshooting is to make a measurement. The measurement can be a simple visual observation, or it might be highly complex using advanced test equipment. In any case, the information from the measurement tells the technician whether additional work should be done on the subject of investigation.

Measurements, of course, are also important in the study of test equipment. This covers a broad range of subjects including industrial electronics. You will find questions in this section that do not appear to be directly related to measurements. Keep in mind that some of the earlier sections are reviewed in these chapters, which is the reason for those questions.

PROGRAMMED REVIEW NO. 1

Start with Block number 1. Pick the answer that you think is correct. If you select choice number 1, go to Block 13. If you select choice number 2, go to Block 15. Proceed as directed. There is only one correct number for each question.

BLOCK 1

What value of R_x is needed to balance the Wheatstone bridge in the circuit in this block?

(1) 476.7 ohms. Go to Block 13.
(2) 420.8 ohms. Go to Block 15.

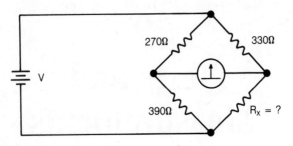

BLOCK 2

Your answer to the question in Block 25 is not correct. Go back and read the question again and select another answer.

BLOCK 3

Your answer to the question in Block 31 is not correct. Go back and read the question again and select another answer.

BLOCK 4

The correct answer to the question in Block 22 is choice (1). There are π radians in 180, and $\pi/2$ radians in 90.

Here is your next question: *For the circuit shown in this block, the voltage:*

(1) Leads the current. Go to Block 18.
(2) Lags the current. Go to Block 50.

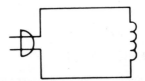

BLOCK 5

Your answer to the question in Block 13 is not correct. Go back and read the question again and select another answer.

BLOCK 6

Your answer to the question in Block 36 is not correct. Go back and read the question again and select another answer.

BLOCK 7

Your answer to the question in Block 25 is not correct. Go back and read the question again and select another answer.

BLOCK 8

Your answer to the question in Block 11 is not correct. Go back and read the question again and select another answer.

BLOCK 9

Your answer to the question in Block 32 is not correct. Go back and read the question again and select another answer.

BLOCK 10

Your answer to the question in Block 13 is not correct. Go back and read the question again and select another answer.

BLOCK 11

The correct answer to the question in Block 40 is choice (2). Always remember that whenever two or more capacitors are connected in series across a voltage source the higher voltage drop is across the capacitor with the lower capacitance.

Here is your next question: *Which of the following has the higher input impedance.*

(1) A 50,000 ohms/volt analog voltmeter. Go to Block 35.
(2) A digital multimeter. Go to Block 8.
(3) An electrostatic voltmeter. Go to Block 36.

BLOCK 12

Your answer to the question in Block 31 is not correct. Go back and read the question again and select another answer.

BLOCK 13

The correct answer to the question in Block 1 is choice (1). The value of R_x is determined by the following ratio:

$$\frac{270}{390} = \frac{330}{R_x}$$

This ratio is solved for R_x:

$$R_x = \frac{300 \times 390}{270} = 476.6 \text{ ohms.}$$

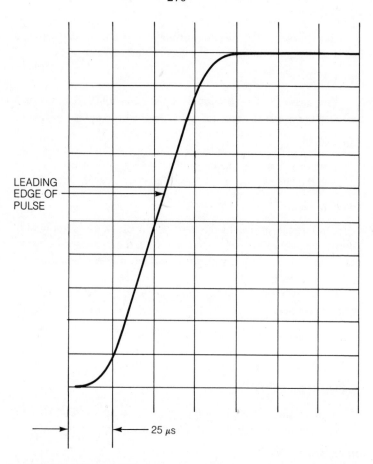

Here is your next question: *What is the rise time of the pulse leading edge shown in this block?*

(1) 100 μs. Go to Block 5.
(2) 80 μs. Go to Block 28.
(3) 50 μs. Go to Block 48.
(4) None of these choices is correct. Go to Block 10.

BLOCK 14

Your answer to the question in Block 37 is not correct. Go back and read the question again and select another answer.

BLOCK 15

Your answer to the question in Block 1 is not correct. Go back and read the question again and select another answer.

BLOCK 16

Your answer to the question in Block 25 is not correct. Go back and read the question again and select another answer.

BLOCK 17

The correct answer to the question in Block 41 is choice (1). The empirical equation is:

$$\text{Bandwidth} = \frac{0.35}{\text{rise time}}$$

Where the bandwidth is in hertz when the rise time is in seconds.

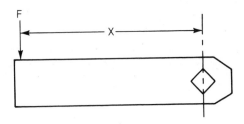

Here is your next question: *The torque exerted by the wrench in the illustration for this block is:*

(1) (F)(X). Go to Block 37.

(2) $\dfrac{(F)(X)}{2} \times 32$. Go to Block 21.

(3) Neither choice is correct. Go to Block 43.

BLOCK 18

The correct answer to the question in Block 4 is choice (1). Be sure you know the phase angle relationships between voltage and current in different types of ac circuits.

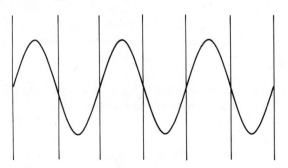

Here is your next question: *For the oscilloscope display in this block, the trace is calibrated for 100 μs per division. The frequency of the waveform is:*

(1) 100,000 Hz. Go to Block 34.
(2) 10,000 Hz. Go to Block 23.
(3) 5000 Hz. Go to Block 42.

BLOCK 19

Your answer to the question in Block 38 is not correct. Go back and read the question again and select another answer.

BLOCK 20

Your answer to the question in Block 42 is not correct. Go back and read the question again and select another answer.

BLOCK 21

Your answer to the question in Block 17 is not correct. Go back and read the question again and select another answer.

BLOCK 22

The correct answer to the question in Block 44 is choice (1). Not all ohmmeters have a low-power feature. In that case, it is sometimes possible to avoid forward biasing a junction by taking care with the ohmmeter connection. Knowing which ohmmeter lead is positive and which is negative, it is possible to make measurements without forward biasing the semiconductor junctions.

Here is your next question: *How many radians are in a circle?*

(1) 2π. Go to Block 4.
(2) π. Go to Block 39.
(3) $\pi/2$. Go to Block 47.

BLOCK 23

Your answer to the question in Block 18 is not correct. Go back and read the question again and select another answer.

BLOCK 24

Your answer to the question in Block 48 is not correct. Go back and read the question again and select another answer.

BLOCK 25

The correct answer to the question in Block 36 is choice (2). When the power supply is obtained from the ac commercial source there is a chance for ripple. Also, any noise on the power line can get into the output of the rf generator.

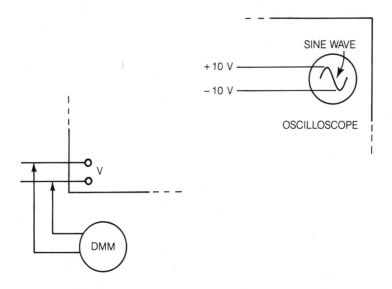

Here is your next question: *The meter in the circuit for this block should display:*

(1) 20 V. Go to Block 7.
(2) 10 V. Go to Block 2.
(3) 14.14 V. Go to Block 16.
(4) None of these choices is correct. Go to Block 44.

BLOCK 26

The correct answer to the question in Block 52 is choice (1). The switch shown is activated by a Bourdon tube.

Here is your next question: *Complete the power triangle shown in this block.* Go to Block 53.

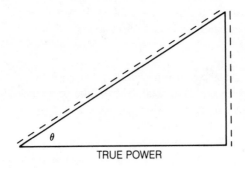

TRUE POWER

BLOCK 27

Your answer to the question in Block 48 is not correct. Go back and read the question again and select another answer.

BLOCK 28

Your answer to the question in Block 13 is not correct. Go back and read the question again and select another answer.

BLOCK 29

Your answer to the question in Block 40 is not correct. Go back and read the question again and select another answer.

BLOCK 30

The correct answer to the question in Block 32 is choice (1). When the voltage and current are out of phase the power company's generators can be damaged. Manufacturers can cause this problem if they present a reactive load to the power companies.

Here is your next question: *What method is sometimes used by manufacturers to correct a voltage/current phase angle problem?*

(1) Large capacitors in series with the transmission line. Go to Block 33.

(2) A synchronous generator across the line. Go to Block 52.

BLOCK 31

The correct answer to the question in Block 42 is choice (2). Distinguish between stress and strain. Stress is the force that deforms a body. Strain is the deformation. A strain gauge is deformed—that is, twisted or bent—during a measurement.

Here is your next question: *The precision method of measuring an unknown voltage by balancing it against a known voltage is called:*

(1) The voltist method. Go to Block 3.

(2) The potentiometer method. Go to Block 38.

(3) The bridge method. Go to Block 12.

BLOCK 32

The correct answer to the question in Block 38 is choice (1). The display is obtained by comparing two sinewave voltages. One is delivered to the x axis and the other to the y axis. One of the voltages can be in phase with the current. In that case, ϕ is the phase angle between voltage and current.

Here is your next question: *Is the following statement correct? A manufacturer can be fined for causing a phase angle to exist on power company lines.*

(1) Correct. Go to Block 30.

(2) Not correct. Go to Block 9.

BLOCK 33

Your answer to the question in Block 30 is not correct. Go back and read the question again and select another answer.

BLOCK 34

Your answer to the question in Block 18 is not correct. Go back and read the question again and select another answer.

BLOCK 35

Your answer to the question in Block 11 is not correct. Go back and read the question again and select another answer.

BLOCK 36

The correct answer to the question in Block 11 is choice (2). The idea behind an electrostatic voltmeter is illustrated in this block. The unknown voltage causes the upper plate to be attracted to the lower plate. The amount of attraction (and the amount of movement) depends on the magnitude of the voltage being measured. This type of voltmeter is used in industrial labs for voltages greater than 500.

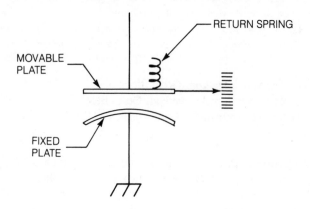

Here is your next question: *Which of the following is a reason for using a battery-operated signal generator?*

(1) Lower cost of operation. Go to Block 6.
(2) A cleaner (noise free) signal. Go to Block 25.

BLOCK 37

The correct answer to the question in Block 17 is choice (1). Torque is the turning effort of a force. It is an important characteristic of motors that are used in industrial applications.

Here is your next question: *A clamp-on ammeter measures current indirectly by measuring the strength of its:*

(1) Electric field. Go to Block 14.
(2) Magnetic field. Go to Block 40.

BLOCK 38

The correct answer to the question in Block 31 is choice (2). Potentiometers are used in industrial applications when a highly accurate voltage measurement is important. However, digital meters can be made with comparable accuracy and they are easier to use.

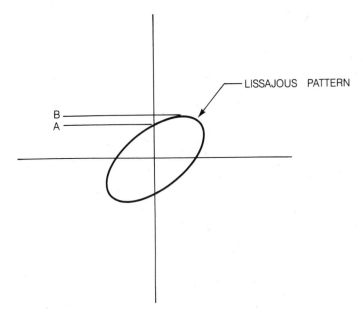

LISSAJOUS PATTERN

Here is your next question: *The illustration in this block shows how a lissajous pattern displays phase angle. The phase angle can be computed from the equation:*

(1) $\phi\text{-Sin}^{-1}\dfrac{A}{B}$. Go to Block 32.

(2) $\phi\text{-Sin}^{-1}\dfrac{B}{A}$. Go to Block 19.

(3) $\phi\text{-Cos}^{-1}\dfrac{A}{B}$. Go to Block 46.

BLOCK 39

Your answer to the question in Block 22 is not correct. Go back and read the question again and select another answer.

BLOCK 40

The correct answer to the question in Block 37 is choice (2). The strength of a magnetic field around a current-carrying conductor is directly related to the amount of current. The clamp-on ammeter measures the strength of the magnetic field and converts that value to the current value.

```
        ○  + 100 V
        │
       ─┴─
       ─┬─   C1
        │    0.01 μF
        │
       ─┴─
       ─┬─   C2
        │    0.1 μF
        │
       ╱777  COMMON
```

Here is your next question. *In the capacitive voltage divider in this block, the voltage across C, is about:*

(1) 91 V. Go to Block 29.
(2) 9 V. Go to Block 11.

BLOCK 41

The correct answer to the question in Block 48 is choice (2). The ×10 expander *increases* the speed of the sweep ten times. You have to divide the calibrated scope sweep by ten to get the rise time.

Here is your next question: *What is the bandwidth of an amplifier that delivers a 10 μs output rise time when a perfect step voltage is applied to its input?*

(1) About 35 kHz. Go to Block 17.
(2) About 100 kHz. Go to Block 45.

BLOCK 42

The correct answer to the question in Block 18 is choice (2). One cycle occurs in 200 μs. The frequency is the reciprocal of the time (T) for one cycle is

$$f = \frac{1}{T} = \frac{1}{200 \ \mu s} = 5000 \text{ Hz}$$

Here is your next question: *A measure of how much a body is deformed is called:*

(1) Stress. Go to Block 20.
(2) Strain. Go to Block 31.

BLOCK 43

Your answer to the question in Block 17 is not correct. Go back and read the question again and select another answer.

BLOCK 44

The correct answer to the question in Block 25 is choice (4). The meter displays the RMS value of the peak voltage (not the peak-to-peak voltage).

$$\text{RMS voltage} = 0.707 \times V_{max}$$

In this case, that is 7.07 V.

Here is your next question: *Which of the following makes the low-power ohms feature of an ohmmeter useful:*

(1) Doesn't forward bias semiconductor junctions. Go to Block 22.
(2) Won't burn out resistors. Go to Block 51.

BLOCK 45

Your answer to the question in Block 41 is not correct. Go back and read the question again and select another answer.

BLOCK 46

Your answer to the question in Block 38 is not correct. Go back and read the question again and select another answer.

BLOCK 47

Your answer to the question in Block 22 is not correct. Go back and read the question again and select another answer.

BLOCK 48

The correct answer to the question in Block 13 is choice (3). Rise time is the time that it takes a step voltage to go from 10% to

90% of the maximum voltage. Decay time is the time that it takes a step voltage to go from 90% to 10% of the maximum voltage.

Here is your next question: *It is necessary to use an oscilloscope sweep expander to measure the rise time of a step voltage. The sweep expander is marked ×10 and the rise time measures 80 μs. The actual rise time is:*

(1) 800 μs. Go to Block 24.
(2) 8 μs. Go to Block 41.
(3) 80 μs. Go to Block 27.

BLOCK 49

Your answer to the question in Block 52 is not correct. Go back and read the question again and select another answer.

BLOCK 50

Your answer to the question in Block 4 is not correct. Go back and read the question again and select another answer.

BLOCK 51

Your answer to the question in Block 44 is not correct. Go back and read the question again and select another answer.

BLOCK 52

The correct answer to the question in Block 30 is choice (2). The synchronous generator automatically corrects phase angle problems.

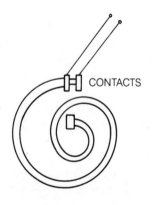

Here is your next question: *The switch in this block is activated by:*

(1) Pressure. Go to Block 26.
(2) Current. Go to Block 49.

BLOCK 53

The correct answer to the question in Block 26 is shown in the illustration for this block.

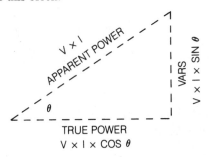

You have now completed Programmed Review No. 1

PROGRAMMED REVIEW NO. 2

Start with Block number 1. Pick the answer that you think is correct. If you select choice number 1, go to Block 13. If you select choice number 2, go to Block 15. Proceed as directed. There is only one correct answer for each question.

BLOCK 1

In the MKS system, the unit of magnetomotive force is the:

(1) Ampere-turn. Go to Block 15.
(2) Weber per square meter. Go to Block 13.

BLOCK 2

Your answer to the question in Block 46 is not correct. Go back and read the question again and select another answer.

BLOCK 3

Your answer to the question in Block 21 is not correct. Go back and read the question again and select another answer.

BLOCK 4

Your answer to the question in Block 23 is not correct. Go back and read the question again and select another answer.

BLOCK 5

Your answer to the question in Block 36 is not correct. Go back and read the question again and select another answer.

BLOCK 6

The correct answer to the question in Block 14 is choice (3). There are 746 W in one hp.

Here is your next question: *A certain impedance is represented as 27.6 + j 27.6. What is the phase angle between the voltage and current?*

(1) 37°. Go to Block 49.
(2) 45°. Go to Block 25.
(3) 60°. Go to Block 32.

BLOCK 7

Your answer to the question in Block 25 is not correct. Go back and read the question again and select another answer.

BLOCK 8

Your answer to the question in Block 35 is not correct. Go back and read the question again and select another answer.

BLOCK 9

Your answer to the question in Block 36 is not correct. Go back and read the question again and select another answer.

BLOCK 10

Your answer to the question in Block 48 is not correct. Go back and read the question again and select another answer.

BLOCK 11

The correct answers to the questions in Block 29 are given here:

$$\mu = \frac{B}{H}$$

(B is flux density and H is magnetic intensity)

$$mmf = flux \times reluctance$$

Here is your next question: *How much power is dissipated by a 3.2 Henry coil having a one-ampere ac current flowing through it? Assume a frequency of 60 Hz.* Go to Block 33.

BLOCK 12

Your answer to the question in Block 31 is not correct. Go back and read the question again and select another answer.

BLOCK 13

The correct answer to the question in Block 1 is choice (1). The unit of induction—that is, *flux density*—is the Weber per square meter.

Magnetism is a very important part of all types of electronic circuits. Understanding magnetism is helpful in understanding how many of these circuits work.

Here is your next question: *Which of the following is more likely to be used as an electromagnetic shield against a field around an ac current?*

(1) Cobalt. Go to Block 24.
(2) Aluminum. Go to Block 36.

BLOCK 14

The correct answer to the question in Block 38 is choice (1). The equation in choice (2) has no meaning.

Here is your next question: *How many watts are there in one horsepower?*

(1) 764. Go to Block 18.
(2) 100. Go to Block 28.
(3) Neither choice is correct. Go to Block 6.

BLOCK 15

Your answer to the question in Block 1 is not correct. Go back and read the question again and select another answer.

BLOCK 16

Your answer to the question in Block 31 is not correct. Go back and read the question again and select another answer.

BLOCK 17

Your answer to the question in Block 41 is not correct. Go back and read the question again and select another answer.

BLOCK 18

Your answer to the question in Block 14 is not correct. Go back and read the question again and select another answer.

BLOCK 19

The correct answer to the question in Block 39 is choice (2). The capacitor shifts the phase by 90° and that provides two-phase power for starting. When the motor is up to speed the capacitor is switched out and the motor operates on single phase. You have now completed the programmed section.

BLOCK 20

Your answer to the question in Block 42 is not correct. Go back and read the question again and select another answer.

BLOCK 21

The correct answer to the question in Block 50 is $0.159 \ \mu F$. It is calculated as shown here.

$$X_c = R = 10\Omega$$

$$X_c = \frac{1}{2\pi fc}$$

therefore,

$$C = \frac{1}{2\pi fx_C}$$

$$= \frac{1}{2\pi \times (10 \times 10^3) \times 10}$$

$$C = 0.159 \ \mu F$$

Here is your next question: *Which of the following could be used for measuring current with an oscilloscope?*

(1) A one-ohm resistor. Go to Block 44.

(2) A one-megaohm resistor. Go to Block 3.

(3) Oscilloscopes cannot be used to measure current. Go to Block 22.

BLOCK 22

Your answer to the question in Block 21 is not correct. Go back and read the question again and select another answer.

BLOCK 23

The correct answer to the question in Block 44 is choice (2). Load cells measure the weight of large equipment. They also measure vibration.

A piezoelectric transducer is used to produce a voltage related to the weight or vibration. Strain gauges are more likely to be used for this application.

Here is your next question: *A certain 3 φ delta-to-wye transformer has a turn ratio of one-to-one for each branch. If the primary voltage across each winding is 220 V, the voltage across the secondary branch is:*

(1) 220 V. Go to Block 4.

(2) 381 V. Go to Block 39.

(3) Neither choice is correct. Go to Block 26.

BLOCK 24

Your answer to the question in Block 13 is not correct. Go back and read the question again and select another answer.

BLOCK 25

The correct answer to the question in Block 6 is choice (2). Many of today's calculators have an easy algorithm for converting from rectangular coordinate to polar coordinates. (Algorithm is the name used for the math procedure.)

The impedance triangle for $27.6 + j\,27.6$ is shown in this block. The phase angle is $45°$.

Also,

$$\phi = \text{Tan}^{-1} \frac{27.6}{27.6}$$

$$\phi = 45°$$

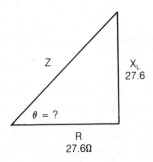

Here is your next question: *A synchro-generator/synchro-receiver combination can be used:*

(1) To drive very heavy mechanical loads. Go to Block 7.
(2) For remote indication. Go to Block 46.

BLOCK 26

Your answer to the question in Block 23 is not correct. Go back and read the question again and select another answer.

BLOCK 27

Your answer to the question in Block 36 is not correct. Go back and read the question again and select another answer.

BLOCK 28

Your answer to the question in Block 14 is not correct. Go back and read the question again and select another answer.

BLOCK 29

The correct answer to the question in Block 45 is choice (2). The measurand is sensed by the *transducer*. Transducers are also called sensors.

Here is your next question: *Write the equation for permeability* (*μ*) *and the equation called ohms law for magnetism.* Go to Block 11.

BLOCK 30

Your answer to the question in Block 33 is not correct. Go back and read the question again and select another answer.

BLOCK 31

The correct answer to the question in Block 42 is choice (2). You can see the Bode plot of an amplifier by using a sweep generator to cover the range of frequencies. Function generators with a VCO (voltage-controlled oscillator) input can be used as a sweep generator.

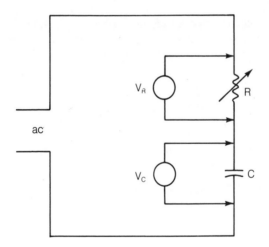

Here is your next question: *The circuit in this block is being used to measure capacitance. The variable resistance is adjusted until $V_R = V_C$. If the voltages each equal 10 volts it follows that the ac voltage applied is equal to:*

(1) 20 volts. Go to Block 16.
(2) It cannot be determined. Go to Block 12.
(3) Neither choice is correct. Go to Block 50.

BLOCK 32

Your answer to the question in Block 6 is not correct. Go back and read the question again and select another answer.

BLOCK 33

The correct answer to the question in Block 11 is no power is dissipated. There is no resistance given so it can be presumed to be negligible. Inductors (and capacitors) do not dissipate power.

Here is your next question: *The direction of rotation of a dc motor can be reversed by:*

(1) Reversing the field or armature current. Go to Block 38.
(2) Reversing the field and armature current. Go to Block 30.

BLOCK 34

Your answer to the question in Block 39 is not correct. Go back and read the question again and select another answer.

BLOCK 35

The correct answer to the question in Block 41 is choice (1). There is no meter called the insultester. (There could be a meter with that trade name, but the question asks for a type of meter.)

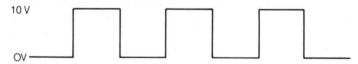

Here is your next question: *The average value of voltage for the perfect square wave shown in this block is:*

(1) 5 V. Go to Block 45.
(2) About 7 V. Go to Block 37.
(3) About 6.36 V. Go to Block 8.

BLOCK 36

The correct answer to the question in Block 13 is choice (2). The electromagnetic waves induce currents in the aluminum. The magnetic fields of those currents repel the oncoming magnetic field.

Here is your next question: *Which of the following can be used as a sensor for detecting heat?*

(1) A thermistor. Go to Block 27.
(2) A thermocouple. Go to Block 5.
(3) Both choices are correct. Go to Block 48.
(4) Tungsten wire. Go to Block 9.

BLOCK 37

Your answer to the question in Block 35 is not correct. Go back and read the question again and select another answer.

BLOCK 38

The correct answer to the question in Block 33 is choice (1). If the field current and the armature currents are both reversed, the motor will continue to flow in the same direction.

Here is your next question: *The percent efficiency of a motor (or any other device) is equal to:*

(1) $\dfrac{\text{total output power}}{\text{total input power}} \times 100.$ Go to Block 14.

(2) $\dfrac{\text{total output power})^2}{\text{total resistance}}$. Go to Block 40.

BLOCK 39

The correct answer to the question in Block 23 is choice (2). The secondary voltage is calculated as follows:

$$V_S = \left(\frac{N_S}{N_P} \right) \times V_P \times \sqrt{3}$$

For the values in Block 23:

$$V_S = (1) \times 220 \times \sqrt{3}$$

$$V_S = 381 \text{ V}$$

As an industrial electronics technician you are expected to know about single-phase and three-phase power systems. It is especially important to know the various types of transformers and rectifier circuits in single-phase and three-phase systems.

Here is your next question: *A capacitor start motor is actually starting on:*

(1) Three-phase power. Go to Block 47.
(2) Two-phase power. Go to Block 19.
(3) Single-phase power. Go to Block 34.

BLOCK 40

Your answer to the question in Block 38 is not correct. Go back and read the question again and select another answer.

BLOCK 41

The correct answer to the question in Block 48 is choice (2). The method of determining frequency from the lissahours pattern is illustrated in this block. A line (V) is drawn across the top so that it touches each point of the pattern. Another line (H) is drawn vertically and it also touches each point. The vertical input to the scope is what drives the beam to touch the line marked V. The horizontal line drives the beam to touch the line marked H.

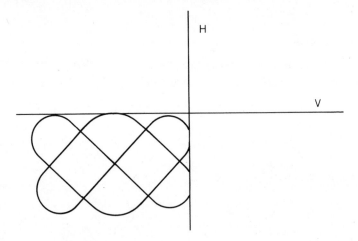

Here is the equation:

$$\frac{\text{Number of Times the Pattern Touches Line V}}{\text{Number of Times the Pattern Touches Line H}} = \frac{\text{Vertical Frequency}}{\text{Horizontal Frequency}}$$

For the problem at hand the vertical frequency is known to be 1200 Hz. Filling in the rest of the equation from the illustration in this block:

$$\frac{V}{H} = \frac{f_V}{f_H}$$

$$\frac{3}{2} = \frac{1200}{f_H}$$

Setting the product of the means equal to the product of the extremes:

$$3f_H = 2 \times 1200$$
$$f_H = \frac{2 \times 1200}{3}$$
$$f_H = 800 \text{ Hz}$$

Here is your next question: *Which of the following types of meters is used to check the resistance of insulating materials?*

(1) Megohmmeter. Go to Block 35.
(2) Insultester. Go to Block 17.

BLOCK 42

The correct answer to the question in Block 46 is choice (2). The Ward-Leonard speed control is an efficient nonelectronic method of controlling speed. It is represented by the illustration in this block.

An ac motor turns a dc generator that has a separate field control. The generator output runs the dc motor. Since the field control

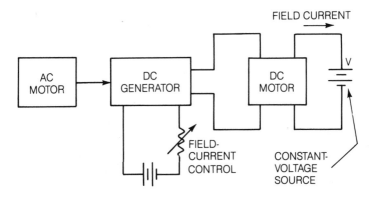

of the motor is a fixed current, the output of the dc generator controls the speed of the shunt-wound dc motor. A small change in the field current of the dc generator controls a large change in the armature current of the dc motor.

This system is sometimes called a Ward-Leonard *amplifier* because the small change in generator current controls a large change in motor speed.

Here is your next question: *The output voltage and phase of an amplifier are plotted against the frequency. This is called a/an:*

(1) F LINE diagram. Go to Block 20.
(2) Bode plot. Go to Block 31.

BLOCK 43

Your answer to the question in Block 45 is not correct. Go back and read the question again and select another answer.

BLOCK 44

The correct answer to the question in Block 21 is choice (1). The one-ohm resistor is connected in series with the unknown current. The oscilloscope is used to measure the peak voltage across that resistor. The peak value of current is numerically the same as the peak value of voltage. If the current has a sinusoidal waveform

$$I = 0.707 \ V_{max}.$$

Here is your next question: *Which of the following is used to make a load cell?*

(1) Thermoelectric transducer. Go to Block 51.
(2) Piezoelectric transducer. Go to Block 23.

BLOCK 45

The correct answer to the question in Block 35 is choice (1). The square wave is on and off for equal times. Its average value is one-half the peak value. You can think of it this way. If you cut off the pulse above the 5 V line, the pieces you cut off would exactly fit in the spaces between the pulses. Thus, you would get a 5 Vdc line.

The half-cycle average of a *sine wave* is 0.636 times the peak value. The RMS value of a sine wave is 0.707 times the peak value.

Here is your next question: *The value being sensed by a transducer is called the:*

(1) Measuree. Go to Block 43.
(2) Measurand. Go to Block 29.

BLOCK 46

The correct answer to the question in Block 25 is choice (2). *Servo* drives are used for very heavy loads. The generator/receiver combination can be used whenever it is desirable to know the position of a rotating device from a position where it can't be seen.

Here is your next question: *A Ward-Leonard system is used to control:*

(1) Position. Go to Block 2.
(2) Speed. Go to Block 42.

BLOCK 47

Your answer to the question in Block 39 is not correct. Go back and read the question again and select another answer.

BLOCK 48

The correct answer to the question in Block 36 is choice (3). Thermistors have a large change of resistance for a relatively small change in temperature.

A thermocouple is a junction of two metals. It produces a voltage when heated.

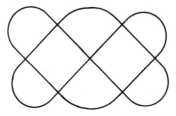

Here is your next question: *Consider the oscilloscope lissajous pattern shown in this block. If the vertical frequency is 1200 Hz, then the horizontal frequency is:*

(1) 1800 Hz. Go to Block 10.
(2) 800 Hz. Go to Block 41.

BLOCK 49

Your answer to the question in Block 6 is not correct. Go back and read the question again and select another answer.

BLOCK 50

The correct answer to the question in Block 31 is choice (3). The voltages across R and C are in quadrature. The equation for the applied voltage is:

$$V = \sqrt{V_R^2 + V_C^2}$$

For the values given:

$$V = \sqrt{(10)^2 + 10^2}$$

$$= \sqrt{200}$$

$$V = 14.14$$

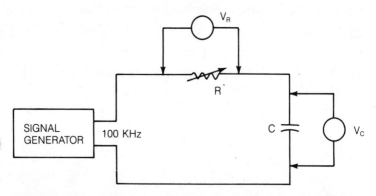

Here is your next question: *The test setup in this circuit is used to determine the value of C. The resistor is adjusted until* $V_C = V_R = 1$ V; *that occurs when R = 10 ohms. What is the capacitance value of C?* Go to Block 21.

BLOCK 51

Your answer to the question in Block 44 is not correct. Go back and read the question again and select another answer.

You have now completed Programmed Review No. 2.

KEY WORDS

Algorithm
Ampere-turn (amperes × turns)
Apparent power
Bandwidth vs rise time
Bourdon tube
Bode plot
Capacitor start
Clamp-on ammeter
Delta-to-wye
Electromagnetic shield
Electrostatic voltmeter
Flux density
Horsepower
Lissajous pattern
Load cell
Low-power ohms
Magnetic intensity
Measurand
Mechanical loads
Megohmmeter
MKS (meter-kilogram-second)
Ohms-per-volt rating
Permeability

Phase angle
Potentiometer voltage
  measurement
Power triangle
Rise time
Servo
Shield
Strain
Strain gauge
Stress
Synchro
Synchronous generator
Thermistor
Thermocouple
Torque
True power
Vars
Ward-Leonard amplifier
Ward-Leonard control
Weber
Weber per square meter
Wheatstone bridge
Wye-to-delta

PRACTICE TEST

1. How many radians are there in 90°?

   (A) π.
   (B) $\frac{\pi}{2}$.

2. What is the amount of current required for full-scale deflection on a 50,000 ohms-per-volt meter movement?

   (A) 50 microamperes.
   (B) 20 microamperes.

3. Assuming a step-voltage input, if the rise time of an output pulse from an amplifier is 0.02 μs, the approximate bandwidth of the

amplifier is:

    (A) 17.5 MHz.
    (B) 10 MHz.

4. Two capacitors—0.5 μF and 1.0 μF are connected in series across a 100 Vdc course. Which will have the higher voltage across it?

    (A) The 0.5 μF capacitor.
    (B) The 1.0 μF capacitor.

5. A force of 16 ounces is exerted on a wrench at a point that is 12 inches from the center of rotation. The torque exerted is:

    (A) 38 ounce inches.
    (B) 1 pound-foot.

6. If a wheel is turning at a rate of 2π radians per second, how many degrees will it turn in one second?

    (A) 180°.
    (B) 360°.

7. In a conventional Class A transistor amplifier the collector voltage should usually be:

    (A) About half the supply voltage.
    (B) Equal the supply voltage.

8. The power that is actually dissipated by an inductor or capacitor is zero watts. The voltage across the reactance multiplied by the current through it is called the reactive volt amperes, or:

    (A) Apparent power.
    (B) Vars.

9. Companies can be fined because of the phase angle they create on power lines. They can avoid this by using a:

    (A) Synchronous generator.
    (B) Foldback regulator.

10. Electrostatic voltmeters are used for voltage:

   (A) Above 500 V.
   (B) Below 500 V.

ANSWERS TO PRACTICE TEST

1. (B)

2. (B)

3. (A)

4. (A)

5. (B)

6. (B)

7. (A)

8. (B)

9. (A)

10. (A)

10
Troubleshooting Procedures

THE CET TEST that you take may be divided into sections: "Trouble-shooting Procedures" is an example. The titles are somewhat arbitrary. For example, in troubleshooting you would need to know what voltage polarities should be on the leads of an amplifier. A question on that subject might be in this chapter, or it might be in a previous chapter.

You might find a question on measurements in this chapter or in the previous chapter. Troubleshooting involves making a measurement, analyzing the measured value, and determining whether the trouble exists at that location. Measurements are a very important part of troubleshooting.

In the troubleshooting section, more than any other section in the CET test, you will find catch-all questions that just did not seem to fit any other place. For example, you may be asked about a ferrite bead and its purpose. Of course, if you do not know its purpose, you cannot tell if it is working or not. That is an important presumption of troubleshooting questions in the CET test.

The CET test is not designed to test you about troubleshooting specific pieces of equipment. Instead, it is a general test of trouble-shooting ability. It is based on the idea that if you are going to troubleshoot something effectively you should know how it works. That way you can better tell what is wrong if it is not working.

You can be sure that you will be asked questions on power supplies in the troubleshooting section (if that section actually exists in the test you take). The reason for that is that the power supply is used in all types of electronic systems. No matter what system you are working on, you will at least encounter a power supply. It might be just a battery, or it might be a stiffly-regulated supply, or it might be a simple brute force supply. You will be asked some typical power supply questions in this Programmed Review.

Remember that it is not possible to thoroughly test you on all facets of a CET test. This is simply a study guide. It is used primarily to flag areas that you need to review more in depth.

Another subject that is universal for all systems is the amplifier. In the early days, vacuum tube amplifiers were most important. You may still be asked a question about a vacuum tube amplifier. Remember that it has the same voltage polarities as an N-channel JFET. It is connected in almost identical circuitry. The only difference is in the magnitude of the voltage. If you know how a JFET works you should be able to troubleshoot a vacuum tube amplifier. (There are still many tube systems being used in industry.)

Being able to troubleshoot also implies that you are able to make repairs. If you replace a transformer with a dot notation and you replace it incorrectly, you can cause a failure in the system.

Be sure you know how to read ladder diagrams.

It is assumed that you can recognize the various symbols used on schematics. Also, it is assumed that you can make the measurements necessary for troubleshooting.

PROGRAMMED REVIEW NO. 1

Start with Block number 1. Pick the answer that you think is correct. If you select choice number 1, go to Block 13. If you select choice number 2, go to Block 15. Proceed as directed. There is only one correct number for each question.

BLOCK 1

The emitter-base voltage of a conducting silicon power transistor is measured and found to be 0.95 V. Which of the following is correct?

(1) The transistor is defective. Go to Block 13.
(2) The transistor is OK. Go to Block 15.

BLOCK 2

The correct answer to the question in Block 46 is choice (1). The collector of a PNP transistor must be *negative* with respect to its emitter. Therefore, its emitter must be *positive* with respect to its collector.

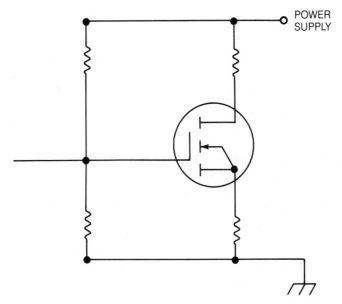

Here is your next question: *The power supply with the circuit of this block must be:*

(1) Positive. Go to Block 31.
(2) Negative. Go to Block 8.

BLOCK 3

The correct answer to the question in Block 55 is choice (1). The rapid change in voltage produces oscillation in the amplifier. This indicates excessive high-frequency response.

Here is your next question: *The lissajous pattern in this block is obtained by comparing two sine waves on an oscilloscope screen. Which of the following will give the phase angle (ϕ) between the voltages?*

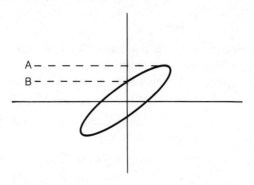

(1) $\phi = \text{Sin}^{-1} \dfrac{A}{B}$ Go to Block 51.

(2) $\phi = \text{Cos}^{-1} \dfrac{A}{B}$ Go to Block 23.

(3) $\phi = \text{Tan}^{-1} \dfrac{A}{B}$ Go to Block 54.

(4) None of the choices is correct. Go to Block 4.

BLOCK 4

The correct answer to the question in Block 3 is choice (4). The correct equation for the phase angle (ϕ) is

$$\phi = \text{Sin}^{-1} \frac{B}{A}$$

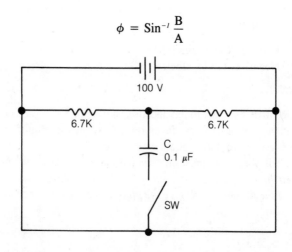

Here is your next question: *How long will it take the capacitor in this block to charge to one time constant?*

(1) $T = RC = 6700 \times 0.1 \times 10^{-6} = 670 \ \mu s$. Go to Block 39.

(2) $T = RC = 3350 \times 0.1 \times 10^{-6} = 33.5 \ \mu s$. Go to Block 57.

(3) Neither choice is correct. Go to Block 26.

BLOCK 5

Your answer to the question in Block 48 is not correct. Go back and read the question again and select another answer.

BLOCK 6

Your answer to the question in Block 18 is not correct. Go back and read the question again and select another answer.

BLOCK 7

Your answer to the question in Block 11 is not correct. Go back and read the question again and select another answer.

BLOCK 8

Your answer to the question in Block 2 is not correct. Go back and read the question again and select another answer.

BLOCK 9

The correct answer to the question in Block 19 is choice (2). If you have to replace a transformer that is shown with dots on the schematic be very careful to wire it in compliance with the dot notation. In other words, do not get the secondary connected in the wrong phase.

Here is your next question: *In which of the following would you expect to find a Faraday shield?*

(1) Power transformer. Go to Block 53.

(2) Nonpolarized electrolytic capacitor. Go to Block 14.

BLOCK 10

Your answer to the question in Block 50 is not correct. Go back and read the question again and select another answer.

BLOCK 11

The correct answer to the question in Block 25 is choice (2). The time constant is calculated as follows:

$$T = L/R$$

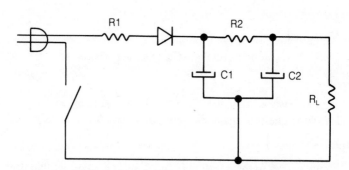

Here is your next question: *In the power supply for this block, R1 is open and shows signs of having been overheated. This might be the result of:*

(1) Defective filter capacitors. Go to Block 33.
(2) A sudden increase in the resistance of R_L. Go to Block 7.

BLOCK 12

The correct answer to the question in Block 37 is choice (4). The sawtooth voltage across the capacitor represents its charge and discharge.

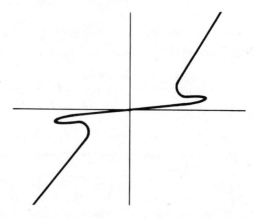

Here is your next question: *Which of the following components has a characteristic curve like the one shown in this block?*

(1) Diac. Go to Block 50.
(2) Varistor. Go to Block 17.
(3) Schottky diode. Go to Block 35.
(4) Schockley diode. Go to Block 41.

BLOCK 13

Your answer to the question in Block 1 is not correct. Go back and read the question again and select another answer.

BLOCK 14

Your answer to the question in Block 9 is not correct. Go back and read the question again and select another answer.

BLOCK 15

The correct answer to the question in Block 1 is choice (2). The typical voltage is 0.7 V. However, higher voltages are common in power transistors. If you suspect something may be wrong in the stage, conduct further tests before squawking the transistor.

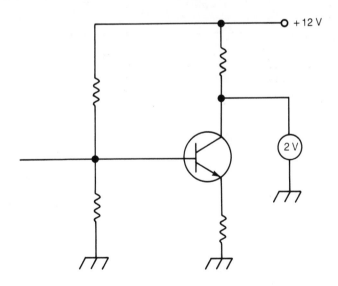

Here is your next question: *With no signal applied, the Class A amplifier shown in this block is:*

(1) Working properly. Go to Block 30.
(2) Conducting too much current. Go to Block 18.
(3) Not conducting enough current. Go to Block 40.

BLOCK 16

Your answer to the question in Block 37 is not correct. Go back and read the question again and select another answer.

BLOCK 17

Your answer to the question in Block 12 is not correct. Go back and read the question again and select another answer.

BLOCK 18

The correct answer to the question in Block 15 is choice (2). The collector voltage should be about half the power supply voltage. (This is true also for tube and FET circuits.)

The current through the transistor is too high, so the voltage drop across R_L is too high. The collector voltage is equal to the supply voltage minus the drop across R_L.

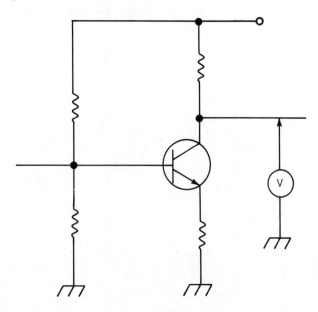

Here is your next question: *The circuit shown in this block is operating Class A. With no signal applied V equals 15 V. When a pure 500 Hz sine wave voltage is applied to the base, the voltage being measured should:*

(1) Not change. Go to Block 28.
(2) Increase. Go to Block 49.
(3) Decrease. Go to Block 6.

BLOCK 19

The correct answer to the question in Block 26 is choice (2). The counter voltage generated by the coil can destroy the transistor. The diode is used to protect the transistor from the kickback voltage.

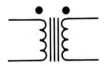

Here is your next question: *The dots on the transformer in this block indicate points that have:*

(1) Equal voltages. Go to Block 34.
(2) Equal phase. Go to Block 9.

BLOCK 20

Your answer to the question in Block 33 is not correct. Go back and read the question again and select another answer.

BLOCK 21

Your answer to the question in Block 36 is not correct. Go back and read the question again and select another answer.

BLOCK 22

Your answer to the question in Block 55 is not correct. Go back and read the question again and select another answer.

BLOCK 23

Your answer to the question in Block 3 is not correct. Go back and read the question again and select another answer.

BLOCK 24

Your answer to the question in Block 48 is not correct. Go back and read the question again and select another answer.

BLOCK 25

The correct answer to the question in Block 28 is choice (2). When the emitter of Q_1 is shorted to its base no collector current flows and there is no voltage drop across R_3. The collector voltage of Q_1 rises to a high value and destroys Q_2.

Here is your next question: *In an R-L time constant circuit, increasing the value of R will:*

(1) Increase the time constant. Go to Block 32.
(2) Decrease the time constant. Go to Block 11.

BLOCK 26

The correct answer to the question in Block 4 is choice (3). The battery is short circuited. There is no voltage across the capacitor. If you are asked to troubleshoot a prototype spend some time looking at the circuit.

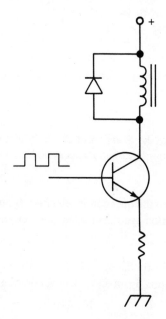

Here is your next question: *The diode in the circuit for this block is open. Which of the following is likely?*

(1) The coil will likely burn out. Go to Block 47.
(2) The transistor will likely be destroyed. Go to Block 19.

BLOCK 27

The correct answer to the question in Block 48 is choice (3). When the switch is closed the motor will stop and the lamp will be ON.

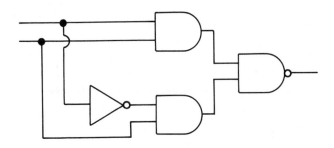

Here is your next question: *For the logic circuit shown in this block, the output is:*

(1) Always at logic 0. Go to Block 56.
(2) Always at logic 1. Go to Block 36.
(3) A pulse, but no glitch. Go to Block 52.

BLOCK 28

The correct answer to the question in Block 18 is choice (1). The full-cycle average of a sine wave is zero. The output voltage should not change when the signal is applied. If it does change there is something wrong in the amplifier stage.

Here is your next question: *During the course of a troubleshooting procedure, a technician shorts the emitter of Q_1 in the illustration in this block to its base and measures the collector voltage. This is:*

(1) A good troubleshooting step. Go to Block 38.
(2) Not a good troubleshooting step. Go to Block 25.

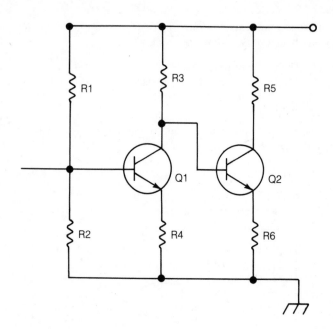

BLOCK 29

Your answer to the question in Block 46 is not correct. Go back and read the question again and select another answer.

BLOCK 30

Your answer to the question in Block 15 is not correct. Go back and read the question again and select another answer.

BLOCK 31

The correct answer to the question in Block 2 is choice (1). An N-channel enhancement MOSFET is shown. It requires a positive drain. Note the forward-biased gate as required for this type of FET.

Here is your next question: *Consider the circuit in this block. The dc connection shows that this is a common collector circuit.*

(1) That is correct. Go to Block 43.
(2) That is not correct. Go to Block 37.

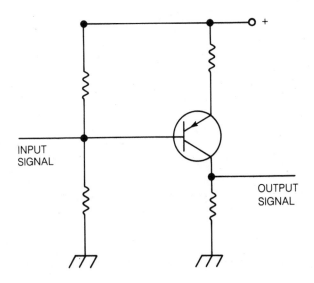

BLOCK 32

Your answer to the question in Block 25 is not correct. Go back and read the question again and select another answer.

BLOCK 33

The correct answer to the question in Block 11 is choice (1). A defective filter capacitor will cause a parallel path for current around R_L. The excessive current can destroy the surge limiting resistor.

Never replace the surge limiting resistor or diode without checking the electrolytic capacitors!

Here is your next question: *Is the following statement correct? The problem with electrolytic capacitors is no longer leakage current. Instead, it is the series resistance of the capacitor.*

(1) Not correct. Go to Block 46.
(2) Correct. Go to Block 20.

BLOCK 34

Your answer to the question in Block 19 is not correct. Go back and read the question again and select another answer.

BLOCK 35

Your answer to the question in Block 12 is not correct. Go back and read the question again and select another answer.

BLOCK 36

The correct answer to the question in Block 27 is choice (2). Here is the truth table for the circuit:

A	B	AB	A	A B	AB × A B
0	0	0	1	0	1
0	1	0	1	1	1
1	0	0	0	0	1
1	1	1	0	0	1

A glitch might occur due to the propagation delay of the inverter.

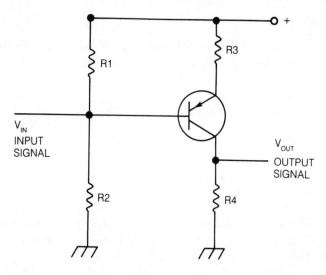

Here is your next question: *An emitter-to base short test is applied to the transistor circuit for this block. The dc voltage at the collector should be:*

(1) Positive while the short is applied. Go to Block 21.
(2) Negative while the short is applied. Go to Block 44.
(3) Neither choice is correct. Go to Block 55.

BLOCK 37

The correct answer to the question in Block 31 is choice (2). The amplifier configuration is based on the input and output signals. It has nothing to do with the dc voltages. Note that the input signal goes to the base and the output signal comes from the collector. So, it is a common emitter circuit.

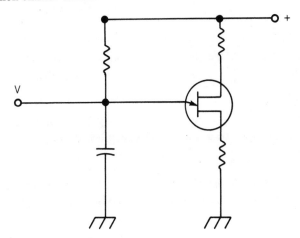

Here is your next question: *For the circuit in this block you would expect the voltage at the terminal marked V to be:*

(1) A positive pulse. Go to Block 16.
(2) A negative pulse. Go to Block 58.
(3) A dc voltage. Go to Block 46.
(4) A sawtooth voltage. Go to Block 12.

BLOCK 38

Your answer to the question in Block 28 is not correct. Go back and read the question again and select another answer.

BLOCK 39

Your answer to the question in Block 4 is not correct. Go back and read the question again and select another answer.

BLOCK 40

Your answer to the question in Block 15 is not correct. Go back and read the question again and select another answer.

BLOCK 41

Your answer to the question in Block 12 is not correct. Go back and read the question again and select another answer.

BLOCK 42

Your answer to the question in Block 46 is not correct. Go back and read the question again and select another answer.

BLOCK 43

Your answer to the question in Block 31 is not correct. Go back and read the question again and select another answer.

BLOCK 44

Your answer to the question in Block 36 is not correct. Go back and read the question again and select another answer.

BLOCK 45

Your answer to the question in Block 37 is not correct. Go back and read the question again and select another answer.

BLOCK 46

The correct answer to the question in Block 33 is choice (1). Test equipment measures *equivalent* series resistance. It is the *combined* leakage and series resistance.

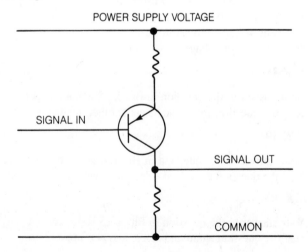

Here is your next question: *The power supply connection for the PNP transistor in this block must be:*

(1) A positive voltage. Go to Block 2.
(2) A negative voltage. Go to Block 42.
(3) Zero volts. Go to Block 29.

BLOCK 47

Your answer to the question in Block 26 is not correct. Go back and read the question again and select another answer.

BLOCK 48

The correct answer to the question in Block 50 is choice (2). Infrared components are preferred in many light-operated systems because they are not affected by daylight.

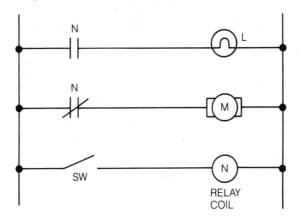

Here is your next question: *Consider the ladder diagram shown in this block. When the switch is closed:*

(1) The motor will start and the lamp will be ON. Go to Block 24.
(2) The motor will stop and the lamp will go OFF. Go to Block 5.
(3) Neither choice is correct. Go to Block 27.

BLOCK 49

Your answer to the question in Block 18 is not correct. Go back and read the question again and select another answer.

BLOCK 50

The correct answer to the question in Block 12 is choice (1). Of the components listed, only the diac will break over in either direction. Diacs are used in SCR gate circuits. They prevent conduction before the voltage reaches a certain value.

Here is your next question: *Which of the following will conduct when exposed to infrared light?*

(1) An optical coupler. Go to Block 10.
(2) A PIN diode. Go to Block 48.

BLOCK 51

Your answer to the question in Block 3 is not correct. Go back and read the question again and select another answer.

BLOCK 52

Your answer to the question in Block 27 is not correct. Go back and read the question again and select another answer.

BLOCK 53

The correct answer to the question in Block 9 is choice (1). A braided wire out of the transformer case connects to the Faraday shield. It should be grounded. Its purpose is to prevent electrostatic coupling from the primary to the secondary. That, in turn, prevents noise spikes from passing through the transformer.

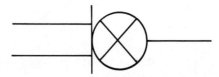

Here is your next question: *What logic gate is represented by the NEMA symbol in this block?*

_____. Go to Block 56.

BLOCK 54

Your answer to the question in Block 3 is not correct. Go back and read the question again and select another answer.

BLOCK 55

The correct answer to the question in Block 36 is choice (3). The emitter-to-base short stops conduction through the transistor. That, in turn, stops current flow through R_4 and the dc voltage at V_{OUT} goes to zero.

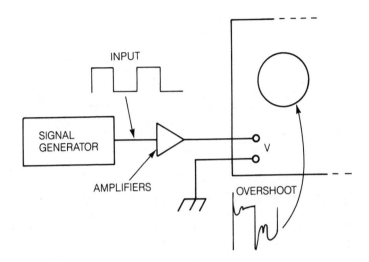

Here is your next question: *The overshoot on the square wave display in this block indicates:*

(1) Excessive high-frequency response. Go to Block 3.
(2) Poor low-frequency response. Go to Block 22.

BLOCK 56

Your answer to the question in Block 27 is not correct. Go back and read the question again and select another answer.

BLOCK 57

Your answer to the question in Block 4 is not correct. Go back and read the question again and select another answer.

BLOCK 58

Your answer to the question in Block 37 is not correct. Go back and read the question again and select another answer.

BLOCK 59

It is a NOR Gate.

You have now completed Programmed Review No. 1.

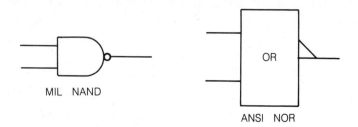

MIL NAND

ANSI NOR

PROGRAMMED REVIEW NO. 2

Start with Block number 1. Pick the answer that you think is correct. If you select choice number 1, go to Block 13. If you select choice number 2, go to Block 15. Proceed as directed. There is only one correct answer for each question.

BLOCK 1

Is the following statement correct? Conduction in UJTs takes place when the emitter voltage reaches a predetermined value such as 1.4 V.

(1) Not correct. Go to Block 13.
(2) Correct. Go to Block 15.

BLOCK 2

The correct answer to the question in Block 17 is choice (1). The lower dc voltage is chopped, or used to operate an oscillator. The output of the oscillator goes to a step-up transformer. The secondary voltage of that transformer is rectified and filtered. The *converter* changes the lower dc voltage to a higher dc voltage. Without the secondary rectifier and filter it is an *inverter*. In other words, it converts dc to ac.

Here is your next question: *Between a digital counter and a seven-segment display for the counter you need:*

(1) An encoder. Go to Block 8.
(2) A decoder. Go to Block 43.

BLOCK 3

Your answer to the question in Block 36 is not correct. Go back and read the question again and select another answer.

BLOCK 4

Your answer to the question in Block 18 is not correct. Go back and read the question again and select another answer.

BLOCK 5

Your answer to the question in Block 28 is not correct. Go back and read the question again and select another answer.

BLOCK 6

Your answer to the question in Block 13 is not correct. Go back and read the question again and select another answer.

BLOCK 7

Your answer to the question in Block 40 is not correct. Go back and read the question again and select another answer.

BLOCK 8

Your answer to the question in Block 2 is not correct. Go back and read the question again and select another answer.

BLOCK 9

Your answer to the question in Block 53 is not correct. Go back and read the question again and select another answer.

BLOCK 10

The correct answer to the question in Block 27 is choice (3). An important advantage of three-phase rectifiers is that their output voltage is easier to filter. You should know all facets of three-phase operation in industrial electronic systems.

Here is your next question: *Which of the following can be used as an accurate timer?*

(1) Asynchronous counter. Go to Block 57.
(2) Multiplexer. Go to Block 47.
(3) Demultiplexer. Go to Block 11.

BLOCK 11

Your answer to the question in Block 10 is not correct. Go back and read the question again and select another answer.

BLOCK 12

The correct answer to the question in Block 45 is choice (1). If any of the inputs, or all of the inputs are at logic 1 the output is at logic 1. Diode logic is used when a single gate or operation is needed.

Here is your next question: *A certain type of control automatically tries to improve the processes for completing a task. This is called:*

(1) An adaptive control. Go to Block 18.
(2) A memory feedback process control. Go to Block 41.

BLOCK 13

The correct answer to the question in Block 1 is choice (1). Conduction in the UJT depends on the ratio of the emitter voltage to the supply voltage. That ratio is called the intrinsic standoff ratio.

Here is your next question: *What is the equation for time constant in an R-L circuit?*

(1) $T = \dfrac{R}{L}$ Go to Block 6.

(2) $T = \dfrac{L}{R}$ Go to Block 26.

(3) Neither choice is correct. Go to Block 31.

BLOCK 14

Your answer to the question in Block 25 is not correct. Go back and read the question again and select another answer.

BLOCK 15

Your answer to the question in Block 1 is not correct. Go back and read the question again and select another answer.

BLOCK 16

Your answer to the question in Block 27 is not correct. Go back and read the question again and select another answer.

BLOCK 17

The correct answer to the question in Block 55 is choice (2). Moving the switch to point Y increases the turns ratio. That returns the secondary voltage to a higher voltage.

Here is your next question: *Which of the following types of power supplies require an oscillator for its operation?*

(1) Converter. Go to Block 2.

(2) Doubler. Go to Block 42.

BLOCK 18

The correct answer to the question in Block 12 is choice (1). Adaptive controls are more expensive, but they are very useful in some operations.

Here is your next question: *Another name for sensor is:*

(1) Touch plate. Go to Block 58.

(2) Perceptor. Go to Block 4.

(3) Neither choice is correct. Go to Block 53.

BLOCK 19

Your answer to the question in Block 38 is not correct. Go back and read the question again and select another answer.

BLOCK 20

Your answer to the question in Block 57 is not correct. Go back and read the question again and select another answer.

BLOCK 21

Your answer to the question in Block 36 is not correct. Go back and read the question again and select another answer.

BLOCK 22

Your answer to the question in Block 44 is not correct. Go back and read the question again and select another answer.

BLOCK 23

The correct answer to the question in Block 46 is choice (2). When light strikes the photoresistor its resistance drops to a low value. The low-resistance path around the relay coil causes it to deenergize, the contacts open, and the lamp is OFF.

Here is your next question: *A defective crowbar circuit can affect the output of a:*

(1) Power supply. Go to Block 55.

(2) Drive motor. Go to Block 34.

BLOCK 24

Your answer to the question in Block 53 is not correct. Go back and read the question again and select another answer.

BLOCK 25

The correct answer to the question in Block 26 is choice (2). Here is the calculation:

$$120 \, \frac{\text{Rev}}{\text{Min}} \times \frac{1 \text{ min}}{60 \text{ sec}} \times \frac{2\pi\text{rad}}{\text{rev}} = 4 \, \pi \, \frac{\text{rad}}{\text{sec}}$$

The value of 4π is 12.6.

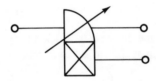

Here is your next question: *The symbol in this block represents:*

(1) A variable inverter. Go to Block 14.
(2) Delay. Go to Block 28.

BLOCK 26

The correct answer to the question in Block 13 is choice (2). Time constant is measured in seconds or parts of a second. It is the time required for coil current to rise to 63% of maximum or drop to 37% of maximum.

Here is your next question: *A motor is turning at a rate of 120 rpm. How many radians per second is it turning?*

(1) 126 radians per second. Go to Block 52.
(2) 12.6 radians per second. Go to Block 25.

BLOCK 27

The correct answer to the question in Block 28 is choice (3). The voltage between the legs of the Y-connected transformer secondary is 1.732 times the voltage across a leg, or 173 V. The diodes conduct to the voltage across the legs.

The voltage across a leg is set by the transformer turns ratio. If the secondary-to-primary turns ratio is two-to-one, then the voltage across R_L will peak at twice the line voltage peak.

Here is your next question: *What is the ripple frequency of the voltage across R_L in the half-wave power supply of Block 28?*

(1) The same as the power line frequency. Go to Block 16.

(2) One-third the power line frequency. Go to Block 48.

(3) Three times the power line frequency. Go to Block 10.

BLOCK 28

The correct answer to the question in Block 25 is choice (2). It is very important for industrial electronics technicians to know and understand the use of all types of schematic symbols.

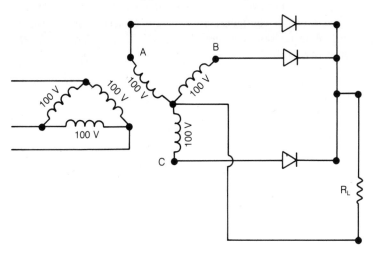

Here is your next question: *The voltage across one leg of the 3ϕ secondary in this block is 100 V. What is the voltage between A and C?*

(1) 200 V. Go to Block 5.

(2) 50 V. Go to Block 32.

(3) Neither choice is correct. Go to Block 27.

BLOCK 29

Your answer to the question in Block 55 is not correct. Go back and read the question again and select another answer.

BLOCK 30

Your answer to the question in Block 44 is not correct. Go back and read the question again and select another answer.

BLOCK 31

Your answer to the question in Block 13 is not correct. Go back and read the question again and select another answer.

BLOCK 32

Your answer to the question in Block 28 is not correct. Go back and read the question again and select another answer.

BLOCK 33

The correct answer to the question in Block 57 is choice (1). The bridged-T circuit configuration is sometimes seen in power supply filters. With resistors (as shown in Block 57) it is identical to the Wheatstone Bridge.

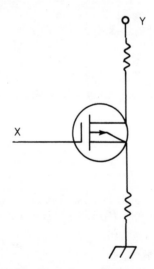

Here is your next question: *Part of a Class A amplifier circuit is shown in this block. You would expect to measure a positive voltage at:*

(1) Point X. Go to Block 38.
(2) Point Y. Go to Block 51.

BLOCK 34

Your answer to the question in Block 23 is not correct. Go back and read the question again and select another answer.

BLOCK 35

Your answer to the question in Block 45 is not correct. Go back and read the question again and select another answer.

BLOCK 36

The correct answer to the question in Block 53 is choice (2). The induction heating coil must carry a high ac current to induce eddy currents into the metal block. Nonconducting materials are heated by using them as a capacitor dielectric.

Here is your next question: *Which of the following can be used as an ultrasonic generator?*

(1) Piezoelectric transducer. Go to Block 56.
(2) Magnetostrictive transducer. Go to Block 21.
(3) Either can be used. Go to Block 44.
(4) Neither can be used. Go to Block 3.

BLOCK 37

Your answer to the question in Block 43 is not correct. Go back and read the question again and select another answer.

BLOCK 38

The correct answer to the question in Block 33 is choice (1). A P-channel MOSFET is shown. It is a depletion type and you would expect a positive gate voltage and a negative drain voltage.

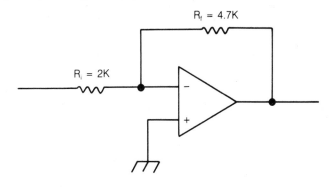

Here is your next question: *If operated within its proper frequency range, the gain of the op amp in this block should be:*

(1) $\dfrac{(2 \times 4.7)K}{2K} = 3.35$

Go to Block 19.

(2) $\dfrac{(24.7K)}{4.7K} = 1.43$

Go to Block 54.

(3) Neither choice is correct. Go to Block 40.

BLOCK 39

Your answer to the question in Block 46 is not correct. Go back and read the question again and select another answer.

BLOCK 40

The correct answer to the question in Block 38 is choice (3). The gain of the op amp is simply:

$$A_V = \frac{R_f}{R_i} = \frac{4.7}{2} = 2.35$$

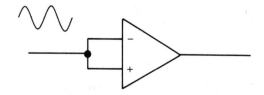

Here is your next question: *The op amp in this block is:*

(1) Connected as a buffer. Go to Block 7.
(2) Connected for a common mode input. Go to Block 46.

BLOCK 41

Your answer to the question in Block 12 is not correct. Go back and read the question again and select another answer.

BLOCK 42

Your answer to the question in Block 17 is not correct. Go back and read the question again and select another answer.

BLOCK 43

The correct answer to the question in Block 2 is choice (2). The seven-segment decoder takes the binary count from the counter and delivers voltages to light the proper segments in the display.

Here is your next question: *An Eccles-Jordan circuit can be used as a:*

(1) Power amplifier. Go to Block 37.
(2) Binary counter. Go to Block 45.

BLOCK 44

The correct answer to the question in Block 36 is choice (3). Ultrasonics is used for cleaning parts with irregular shapes. It is also used for inspecting castings for bubbles.

Here is your next question: *In a 60-Hz three-phase system the ripple frequency of a bridge rectifier is:*

(1) 60 Hz. Go to Block 30.
(2) 120 Hz. Go to Block 22.
(3) 360 Hz. Go to Block 59.
(4) 180 Hz. Go to Block 49.

BLOCK 45

The correct answer to the question in Block 43 is choice (2). The Eccles-Jordan circuit is a flip flop that can be easily triggered.

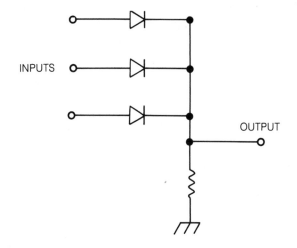

Here is your next question: *The inputs to the diode logic circuit in the circuit for this block are either logic 0 or logic 1. This is an example of:*

(1) An OR circuit. Go to Block 12.
(2) An AND circuit. Go to Block 50.
(3) A 3-state control. Go to Block 35.

BLOCK 46

The correct answer to the question in Block 40 is choice (2). The common mode connection is used for evaluating operational amplifiers. The output should be zero volts (ac) when the input signal is a sine wave. A measure of how well the op amp accomplishes this is called the *common mode rejection ratio*.

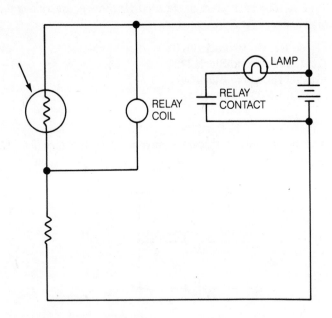

Here is your next question: *When light strikes the photoresistor in this circuit, the lamp is:*

(1) ON. Go to Block 39.
(2) OFF. Go to Block 23.

BLOCK 47

Your answer to the question in Block 10 is not correct. Go back and read the question again and select another answer.

BLOCK 48

Your answer to the question in Block 27 is not correct. Go back and read the question again and select another answer.

BLOCK 49

Your answer to the question in Block 44 is not correct. Go back and read the question again and select another answer.

BLOCK 50

Your answer to the question in Block 45 is not correct. Go back and read the question again and select another answer.

BLOCK 51

Your answer to the question in Block 33 is not correct. Go back and read the question again and select another answer.

BLOCK 52

Your answer to the question in Block 26 is not correct. Go back and read the question again and select another answer.

BLOCK 53

The correct answer to the question in Block 18 is choice (3). *Transducer* is the name that is sometimes used to mean sensor.

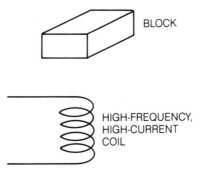

BLOCK

HIGH-FREQUENCY, HIGH-CURRENT COIL

Here is your next question: *In the illustration for this block the coil is used to heat the block. Which of the following is correct?*

(1) The block must be made of a nonconducting material. Go to Block 24.
(2) The block is heated by eddy currents. Go to Block 36.
(3) A high-current dc must flow through the coil. Go to Block 9.

BLOCK 54

Your answer to the question in Block 38 is not correct. Go back and read the question again and select another answer.

BLOCK 55

The correct answer to the question in Block 23 is choice (1). When in operation, a crowbar circuit connects a short across a power supply output. It is a very fast-acting circuit for protecting against an output overvoltage.

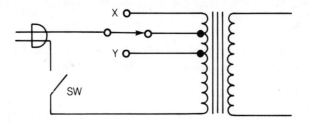

Here is your next question: *The transformer shown schematically in this block can be used to adjust for small changes in line voltage. If the line voltage drops, compensate by moving the switch to terminal:*

(1) X. Go to Block 29.
(2) Y. Go to Block 17.

BLOCK 56

Your answer to the question in Block 36 is not correct. Go back and read the question again and select another answer.

BLOCK 57

The correct answer to the question in Block 10 is choice (1). The clock for the asynchronous counter is crystal controlled. The counter operates at a precise number of counts per second. For example, the crystal oscillator can be counted down to one count per second. The asynchronous counter is jammed at the desired count (number of seconds). Synchronous counters can also be used.

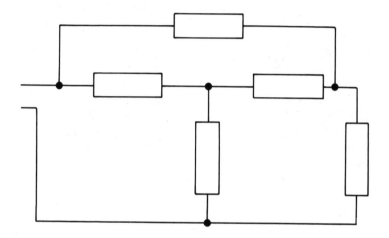

Here is your next question: *The* bridged-T *circuit shown in this block is the same as:*

(1) A Wheatstone Bridge. Go to Block 33.
(2) The circuit used in A/D converters. Go to Block 20.

BLOCK 58

Your answer to the question in Block 18 is not correct. Go back and read the question again and select another answer.

BLOCK 59

The correct answer to the question in Block 44 is choice (3). The high ripple frequency is very easy to filter. However, some circuits can use the dc output without filtering.

You have now completed Programmed Review No. 2.

KEY WORDS

Asynchronous counter
Bridged-T
Class A amplifier (also Class B,
Class AB, and Class C)
Common mode
Common mode rejection ratio
Crowbar
Decoder
Depletion MOSFET
Dielectric heating
Dot notation
Eccles-Jordan (triggered) flip
  flop
Eddy currents
Encoder
Enhancement MOSFET
ESR
Faraday Shield

Glitch
Induction heating
Infrared
Ladder diagrams
L-R time constant
Magnetostrictive
Multiplexer/demultiplexer
Nonpolarized electrolytic
  capacitor
Optical coupler
Photoresistor
Piezoelectric
PIN diode
Surge-limiting resistor
Synchronous counter
Three-state (also tristate) buffer
  or inverter
Transducer

PRACTICE TEST

1. In an NPN transistor amplifier the base is:

    (A) Positive with respect to the collector.
    (B) Negative with respect to the collector.

2. In an Enhancement MOSFET amplifier the gate is:

    (A) Forward biased with respect to the source.
    (B) Reverse biased with respect to the source.

3. Increasing the value of L in an L-R time constant circuit:

    (A) Increases the time constant.
    (B) Decreases the time constant.

4. Which of the following can be determined from a lissajous pattern?

    (A) Peak-to-peak voltage.

(B) Peak-to-peak current.

(C) Both choices are correct.

(D) Neither choice is correct.

5. If the peak-to-peak value of a sawtooth waveform is measured on a scope and found to be 10 V, the RMS voltage will be:

(A) About 7 volts.

(B) About 3.5 volts.

(C) Neither choice is correct.

6. Which of the following choices is correct regarding bipolar transistor amplifier troubleshooting?

(A) Always use the emitter-base short test for direct-coupled amplifiers.

(B) Never use the emitter-base short test for direct-coupled amplifiers.

7. In a Class A amplifier the efficiency is:

(A) Maximum compared to other classes of amplifiers.

(B) Poor compared to other classes of amplifiers.

8. You want to view a modulated waveform on a oscilloscope but its bandwidth is too narrow. So, you use a:

(A) Demodulator probe.

(B) Decoupling probe.

9. A perfect step voltage is delivered to the input of an amplifier. The rise time of the output signal is $0.35\ \mu s$. Should the amplifier be able to pass a 500-kHz signal?

(A) Yes

(B) No

10. To display a glitch, an oscilloscope:

(A) Must have a good dc response.

(B) Must have a good high-frequency response.

ANSWERS TO PRACTICE TEST

1. (B)   The collector must be more positive than the base, so the base is negative with respect to the collector.

2. (A)

3. (A) $T = L/R$.

4. (D)   Lissajous patterns are used for determining frequency or phase.

5. (C)   RMS values are 0.707 times the peak for sine wave voltages and currents.

6. (B)   There are exceptions. However, if you get in the habit of using the emitter-base short test for direct-coupled amplifiers you will eventually destroy a transistor.

7. (B)   Class A amplifiers deliver an output signal with minimum distortion. However, the circuit efficiency is low.

8. (A)   This question is included in this test to remind you that you may be asked about probes in the CET test.

9. (A)   Bandwidth $= 0.35/\text{rise time}$
   $= 0.35/0.35$ MHz
   $= 1$ MHz.

10. (B)   The greater the bandwidth the better your chances of catching a glitch. Remember that a good logic probe does an excellent job of catching glitches.

Appendix

Practice CET Test:
Industrial Electronics Option

THE CET TEST that you take may be divided into the following sections:

- Components for Industrial Electronics,
- Analog Circuits and Systems,
- Digital and Microprocessor Circuits and Systems,
- Dc Power Supplies,
- Ac Power Supplies, and
- Troubleshooting and Circuit Analysis.

These subjects have been reviewed in this book. Also, they will be covered in this Practice Test. However, this test is not divided into those sections. The number of questions on each subject is related to the difficulty and number of times questions on the subjects have been missed rather than on sections in the test.

As with all practice tests, this one covers the range of subjects. These are not the questions you will actually get when you take the test.

1. The circuit in Fig. A-1 can be used as:

   (A) A low-pass filter.
   (B) An integrator.
   (C) A differentiator.
   (D) None of these choices is correct.

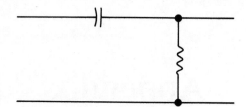

Fig. A-1

2. Which of the following is not correct?

   (A) $I = V/R$.
   (B) The parallel resistance of two resistors in parallel $= 1/R_1 + 1/R_2$.
   (C) $f = 1/T$.
   (D) Transformer primary turns ratio is equal to secondary Z_1/Z_2.

3. In a VCO circuit you would expect to find:

   (A) A varistor.
   (B) An avalanche diode.
   (C) A Shockley diode.
   (D) A varactor.

4. The power supply regulator in Fig. A-2 is a/an:

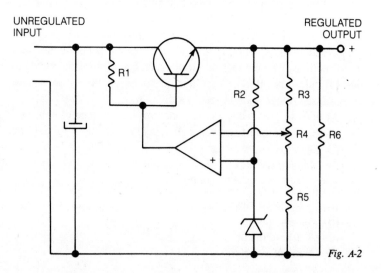

Fig. A-2

(A) Analog type.
(B) Digital type.
(C) Positive feedback type.
(D) Differential type.

5. For the power supply circuit in Fig. A-2, the sense circuit is:

(A) R_1.
(B) R_2 and D_1.
(C) R_3, R_4, and R_5.
(D) R_6.

6. The rate of change of output signal voltage for a step-voltage input is called:

(A) Differential gain.
(B) Integral output.
(C) Acceleration recovery.
(D) Slewing rate.

7. In the circuit of Fig. A-2, the $+$ and $-$ signs on the op amp refer to:

(A) The polarities of the inputs.
(B) The connection of the op amp for inverting or noninverting operation.
(C) Both choices are correct.

8. In a certain system a logic 1 delivered to the input of the flip flop results in a logic 1 at Q. When a logic 0 is delivered to the input of the same flip flop there is a logic 0 at Q.

What type of flip flop is in this system?

(A) R-S.
(B) Eccles Jordan.
(C) Reed Lowey.
(D) None of these choices is correct.

9. The transistor arrangement in Fig. A-3 is often made with two matched transistors in the same case. The difficulty with this arrangement is:

(A) Poor power gain.

(B) False triggering.
(C) Very high input power requirement.
(D) High internal heat.

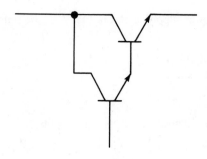

Fig. A-3

10. The transistor arrangement in Fig. A-3 is used as a power supply series-pass regulator. It is called:

    (A) Daytona.
    (B) Darlington.
    (C) Complementary.
    (D) Operational.

11. Refer again to the transistor arrangement in Fig. A-3; this arrangement can also be called:

    (A) Divide-by-beta.
    (B) Parallel-connected.
    (C) Beta squared.
    (D) Beta + beta.

12. Refer to the circuits shown in Fig. A-4. Assume the power amplifiers are working properly. Which diode connection protects the transistor from inductive kickback?

    (A) The one shown in A.
    (B) The one shown in B.
    (C) Neither choice is correct because the diodes have nothing to do with inductive kickback.

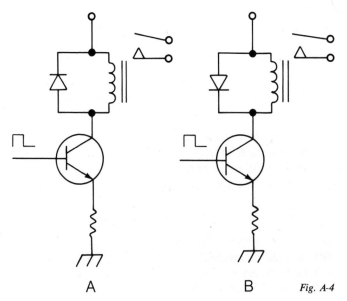

A   B   *Fig. A-4*

13. An advantage of a relay over an SCR for controlling power is that:

    (A) It is faster.
    (B) It has a higher fan-out capability.

14. The output of the PLL in Fig. A-5 is:

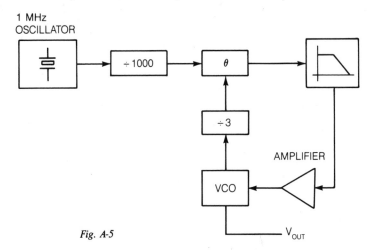

Fig. A-5

(A) 1000 Hz.
(B) 3 MHz.
(C) 3000 Hz.
(D) 333-$^1/_3$ Hz.

15. Which of the following will reverse the direction of rotation of an induction motor?

(A) Reverse the armature leads.
(B) Reverse the field leads.
(C) Reverse the armature and field leads.
(D) None of the choices is correct.

16. You would expect to find a rotating magnetic field inside:

(A) A capacitor-start ac motor.
(B) An induction motor.
(C) Both choices are correct.
(D) Neither choice is correct.

17. Power amplifiers:

(A) Are not as much affected by power supply ripple as voltage amplifiers.
(B) Are more affected by power supply ripple than voltage amplifiers.

18. What number is represented by binary decimal code 10010011?

(A) 147.
(B) 43.
(C) Neither choice is correct.

19. You would expect to find a crowbar circuit in a:

(A) Phase-locked loop.
(B) DMA circuit.
(C) Power supply.
(D) Dynamic random access memory.

20. Which of the following is represented by the truth table in Fig. A-6?

    (A) $\overline{A} + \overline{B} = L$.
    (B) $\overline{A\,B}$ $= L$.
    (C) $A\,B$ $= L$.
    (D) $A + B = L$.

A	B	L	
0	0	1	
0	1	0	
1	0	0	
1	1	0	*Fig. A-6*

21. Which of the following gates is represented by the truth table in Fig. A-6?

    (A) AND.
    (B) OR.
    (C) NAND.
    (D) NOR.

22. In this discussion the turns ratio of a transformer is the number of secondary turns divided by the number of primary turns. This is often written $N_s{:}N_p$.
    Which of the following is correct for a power transformer?

    (A) $N_s{:}N_p = I_s{:}I_p$.
    (B) $N_s{:}N_p = Z_s{:}Z_p$.
    (C) $N_s{:}N_p = V_p{:}V_s$.
    (D) None of these choices is correct.

    (Note: Make sure you know the relationships between turns ratio and current ratio, voltage ratio, and impedance ratio.)

23. Which of the following gates is represented by the circuit in Fig. A-7?

    (A) Inverter.
    (B) NOR.
    (C) EXCLUSIVE OR.
    (D) None of these choices is correct.

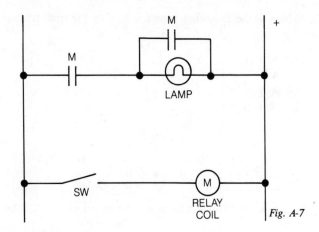

Fig. A-7

24. Refer to Fig. A-7.

    (A) The lamp will be ON when the switch is closed.
    (B) The lamp is ON when the switch is opened.
    (C) Neither choice is correct.

25. A tachometer measures:

    (A) Torque.
    (B) RPM.
    (C) Linear speed.
    (D) Input power.

26. Refer to the illustration in Fig. A-8. The output signal at V_{out} should be a:

    (A) Sawtooth waveform.
    (B) Positive pulse.
    (C) Negative pulse.
    (D) Square wave.

27. The intrinsic standoff ratio of the UJT in Fig. A-8 is 0.63. The frequency of oscillation should be about:

    (A) 1000 Hz.
    (B) 2000 Hz.
    (C) 3000 Hz.
    (D) 5000 Hz.

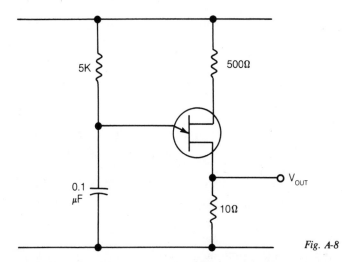

Fig. A-8

28. The symbol shown in the box in Fig. A-9 represents the same device as the one shown in:

(A) A.
(B) B.
(C) C.
(D) D.

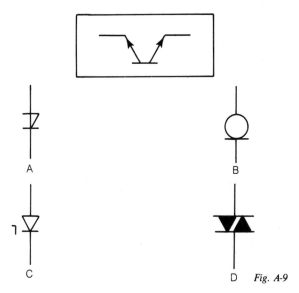

D   *Fig. A-9*

29. Which of the following diodes is sometimes used as a very fast switch?

    (A) Esaki (tunnel) diode.
    (B) Shockley (four-layer) diode.
    (C) Schottky (hot carrier) diode.
    (D) Point contact diode.

    (Important note: Make sure you know about all of the choices in this question.)

30. Refer to the circuit in Fig. A-10. The output (V_{out}) should be a:

    (A) Pure dc at a predetermined level.
    (B) Positive-going pulse waveform.
    (C) Negative-going pulse waveform.
    (D) Sawtooth waveform.

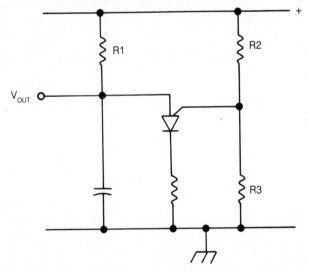

Fig. A-10

31. Figure A-10 shows a PUT oscillator circuit. The purpose of R_2 and R_3 is:

    (A) To lower the anode voltage.
    (B) To set the dc output voltage.
    (C) To set the intrinsic standoff ratio.
    (D) None of the choices is correct.

32. Refer to the circuit of Fig. A-11. When the arm of R is moved all the way to X:

    (A) The SCR will be destroyed.
    (B) The lamp will glow at full brightness.
    (C) The lamp will glow at half brightness.
    (D) The lamp will be OFF.

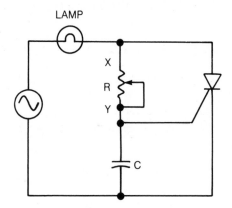

Fig. A-11

33. Which of the following is true about the symbol in Fig. A-12?

    (A) $\overline{A}\,B + A\,\overline{B} = L$.
    (B) $\overline{A}\,\overline{B} + A\,B = L$.
    (C) $\overline{A + B} = L$.
    (D) $\overline{A} + \overline{B} = L$.

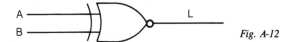

Fig. A-12

34. Is the following statement correct? A Hall device can be used to measure the strength of a magnetic field.

    (A) Correct.
    (B) Not correct.

35. Form A contacts on a relay (or other switch) are:

    (A) Normally open.
    (B) Normally closed.

36. You cannot write information into:

    (A) An EPROM.
    (B) A ROM.
    (C) An EEROM.
    (D) A RAM.

37. Which of the following is the conjugate of 23 - j17?

    (A) 23.
    (B) j17.
    (C) 23 - j17.
    (D) 23 + j17.

38. What approximate voltage reading would you expect to get at Point A in the circuit of Fig. A-13?

    (A) 0.7 V.
    (B) 1.7 V.
    (C) 2.7 V.
    (D) 3.7 V.

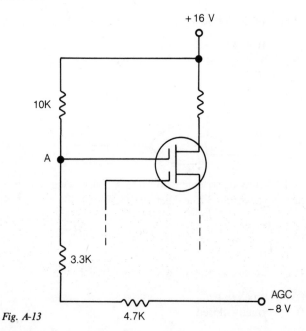

Fig. A-13

39. A 1500-Hz square wave is applied to the input of an amplifier circuit. The output signal is displayed on an oscilloscope and it looks like the waveform in Fig. A-14. The amplifier has:

(A) Poor low-frequency response.
(B) Poor high-frequency response.

Fig. A-14

40. To troubleshoot a closed-loop system:

(A) Short circuit the output and look for excessive power dissipation.
(B) Provide a step change in the input and look for oscillation.
(C) Provide a step change in the output impedance and look for oscillation.
(D) Open the loop and provide the proper substitute voltage or frequency.

41. In the simple arrangement shown in Fig. A-15 the dc motor speed can be varied by:

(A) Changing the pulse frequency.
(B) Changing the pulse width.

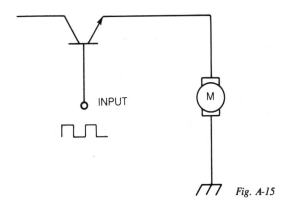

Fig. A-15

42. Brightness on an oscilloscope can be controlled by the proper input to the:

   (A) X-axis.
   (B) Y-axis.
   (C) Z-axis.
   (D) None of these choices is correct.

43. A rotary converter is used for:

   (A) Increasing ac voltage.
   (B) Increasing ac power.
   (C) Increasing dc voltage.
   (D) Correcting phase angle.

44. Which of the following is true?

   (A) Power factor must be greater than 1.0.
   (B) Power factor $= \sin \phi$—where ϕ is the phase angle between voltage and current.
   (C) Power factor $= \cos \phi$—where ϕ is the phase angle between voltage and current.
   (D) Power factor $= V \times I \times \tan \phi$—where ϕ is the phase angle between voltage and current.

45. Both inputs of the circuit in Fig. A-16 are at logic 0. The output:

   (A) Is logic 1.
   (B) Is logic 0.
   (C) Cannot be determined from the information given.

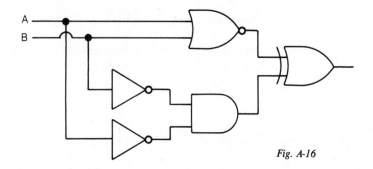

Fig. A-16

46. Which of the components represented in Fig. A-17 can be used as a power supply preregulator?

    (A) The one marked A.
    (B) The one marked B.
    (C) Neither choice is correct.
    (D) Both choices are correct.

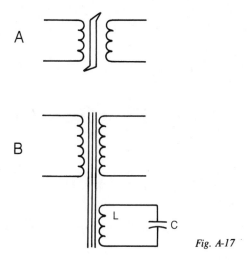

Fig. A-17

47. Which of the following is used for power amplification?

    (A) VMOS.
    (B) CMOS.
    (C) JFET.
    (D) Depletion MOSFET.

48. If the input signal is delivered to the gate and the output signal is at the source, the amplifier is:

    (A) A follower.
    (B) An inverter.
    (C) A Class B amplifier with phase inversion.
    (D) None of these choices is correct.

49. The op amp shown in Fig. A-18 is connected as a simple:

    (A) Differentiator.
    (B) Integrator.
    (C) Noninverting amplifier.
    (D) Inverting amplifier.

    (Important note: Make sure you know all of the op amp connections mentioned in this question.)

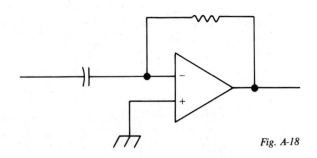

Fig. A-18

50. Which of the following components could be used to eliminate inductive kickback from a relay coil in a VMOS drain circuit?

    (A) VDR.
    (B) Diode.
    (C) Both choices are correct.
    (D) Neither choice is correct.

51. Form B contacts on a relay (or other switch) are:

    (A) Normally open.
    (B) Normally closed.

52. To interface CMOS logic with a 40-V display:

    (A) Use a directional coupler.
    (B) Use an optical coupler.
    (C) No special coupler is needed.
    (D) None of the choices is correct.

53. A shunt-wound motor:

    (A) Will operate on ac or dc.

(B) Will operate on ac only.

(C) Will operate on dc only.

(D) Has a higher starting torque than a series-wound motor.

54. An advantage of a relay over an SCR for controlling power is that:

(A) It is faster.

(B) It has a high input/output circuit isolation.

55. You would expect an electronic dc converter circuit to have:

(A) An oscillator.

(B) A duplexer.

(C) A synchronizer.

(D) A directional coupler.

56. In Fig. A-19 the driven wheel is A. Which of the following is true?

(A) A, B, and C turn at the same speed because of the idler wheels.

(B) A, B, and C turn in the same direction.

(C) B turns faster than C.

(D) C turns faster than A.

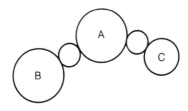

Fig. A-19

57. You would expect to find a snubber in:

(A) A converter.

(B) An inverter.

(C) A J-K flop flop.

(D) An SCR circuit.

58. Which of the following is not a thyristor?

(A) SCR.
(B) VARIAC.
(C) DIAC.
(D) UJT.

59. The components illustrated in Fig. A-20 are:

(A) Depletion MOSFETS.
(B) JFETS.
(C) Enhancement MOSFETS.
(D) CFETS.

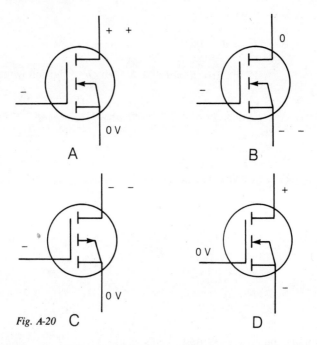

Fig. A-20

60. Refer again to Fig. A-20. Which of the components is improperly biased?

(A) The one marked A.
(B) The one marked B.
(C) The one marked C.
(D) The one marked D.

61. Refer again to Fig. A-20. Identify the N-channel device.

    (A) The ones marked A, B, and D.
    (B) The one marked C.
    (C) All are N-channel devices.
    (D) None are N-channel devices.

62. You are picking a component for a low-frequency clock signal, which of the following could be used for that clock signal?

    (A) Toggled J-K flip flop.
    (B) D flip flop.
    (C) PUT.
    (D) Triac.

63. A certain power supply has an output of 12 V when there is no load connected. With a full load connected the output is still 12 V. The power supply percent regulation is:

    (A) 0%.
    (B) 100%.

64. A program for a drill press is stored in machine language, which of the following could be used for storing it?

    (A) Punched tape.
    (B) Magnetic tape.
    (C) Magnetic discs (called floppy discs).
    (D) Hard disc.
    (E) Any of these could be used.

65. The calibration of the scope is given with the waveform in Fig. A-21. Determine the RMS voltage and the frequency of the waveform.

    (A) 7.1 V and 2 MHz.
    (B) 7.1 V and 5 MHz.
    (C) 17.4 V and 1.25 MHz.
    (D) 10.6 V and 0.833 MHz.

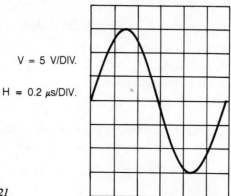

V = 5 V/DIV.

H = 0.2 μs/DIV.

Fig. A-21

66. The circuit shown in Fig. A-22 is an example of:

(A) A common collector amplifier.
(B) A common base amplifier.
(C) A common emitter amplifier.

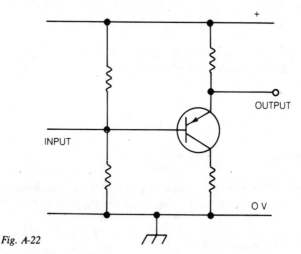

Fig. A-22

67. The operational amplifier in Fig. A-23 is connected for:

(A) Maximum voltage gain.
(B) Maximum current gain.
(C) Common-mode operation.
(D) Buffer operation.

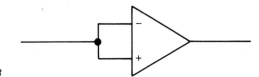

Fig. A-23

68. Which of the following is used to start large dc motors?

   (A) A simple ON/OFF switch can be used.
   (B) An SCR circuit (a thyratron circuit in older systems).
   (C) A manual starter.
   (D) None of the above choices is correct.

69. Each time a pulse is delivered to a certain motor its shaft turns 15°. It is:

   (A) A synchronous motor.
   (B) A motor with a shaded pole.
   (C) A stepping motor.
   (D) An incremental induction motor.

70. A Ward-Leonard control is used for adjusting:

   (A) Oscillator frequency.
   (B) Motor speed.
   (C) Generator output power.
   (D) Current in a varying load.

71. Which of the following is not a logic family?

   (A) RCL.
   (B) TTL.
   (C) I^2L.
   (D) CMOS.

72. The output of the op amp in Fig. A-24 should be:

   (A) 0.2 V, peak to peak.
   (B) 0.08 V, peak to peak.
   (C) 0.5 V, peak to peak.
   (D) None of the choices are correct.

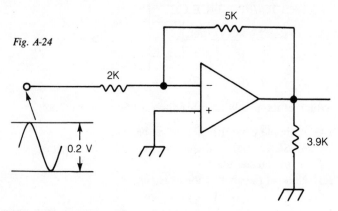

Fig. A-24

73. The operation of a triac is the same as the operation of:

    (A) A thyratron.
    (B) A diac.
    (C) Back-to-back SCRs.
    (D) Back-to-back neon lamps.

74. In a Class A bipolar PNP transistor amplifier, the dc base voltage is:

    (A) Positive with respect to the collector.
    (B) Negative with respect to the collector.
    (C) The same voltage as the collector.

75. Which of the following can be turned ON and OFF with input signals?

    (A) SCR.
    (B) SCS.
    (C) Both choices are correct.
    (D) Neither choice is correct.

ANSWERS TO PRACTICE CET TEST

Industrial Electronics Option

1. (C)	26. (B)	51. (B)
2. (D)	27. (B)	52. (B)
3. (D)	28. (D)	53. (C)
4. (A)	29. (A)	54. (B)
5. (C)	30. (D)	55. (A)
6. (D)	31. (C)	56. (D)
7. (B)	32. (C)	57. (D)
8. (D)	33. (B)	58. (B)
9. (D)	34. (A)	59. (C)
10. (B)	35. (A)	60. (A)
11. (C)	36. (B)	61. (A)
12. (A)	37. (D)	62. (C)
13. (B)	38. (C)	63. (A)
14. (C)	39. (B)	64. (E)
15. (C)	40. (D)	65. (D)
16. (C)	41. (B)	66. (A)
17. (A)	42. (C)	67. (C)
18. (C)	43. (C)	68. (C)
19. (C)	44. (C)	69. (C)
20. (B)	45. (B)	70. (B)
21. (D)	46. (D)	71. (A)
22. (D)	47. (A)	72. (C)
23. (D)	48. (A)	73. (C)
24. (C)	49. (A)	74. (A)
25. (B)	50. (C)	75. (B)

Index

Other Bestsellers of Related Interest

TROUBLESHOOTING AND REPAIRING VCRs—Gordon McComb

It's estimated that 50% of all American households today have at least one VCR. *Newsweek* magazine reports that most service operations charge a minimum of $40 just to look at a machine, and in some areas there's a minimum repair charge of $95 *plus the cost of any parts*. Now this time- and money-saving sourcebook gives you complete schematics and step-by-step details on general up-keep and repair of home VCRs—from the simple cleaning and lubricating of parts, to troubleshooting power and circuitry problems. 336 pages, 300 illustrations. Book No. 2960, $17.95 paperback, $27.95 hardcover

TROUBLESHOOTING AND REPAIRING ELECTRONIC CIRCUITS —2nd Edition—Robert L. Goodman

Here are easy-to-follow, step-by-step instructions for troubleshooting and repairing all major brands of the latest electronic equipment, with hundreds of block diagrams, specs, and schematics to help you do the job right the first time. You will find expert advice and techniques for working with both old and new circuitry, including tube-type, transistor, IC, microprocessor, and analog and digital logic circuits. 320 pages, 236 illustrations. Book No. 3258, $18.95 paperback, $27.95 hardcover

INDUSTRIAL ELECTRONICS FOR TECHNICIANS—Sam Wilson

Industrial Electronics for Technicians provides an effective overview of the topics covered in the industrial electronics CET test, as well as being a valuable reference on industrial electronics in general. It covers the theory and applications of industrial hardware from the technician's perspective, giving you the explanations you need to fully understand all of the areas needed to qualify for CET accreditation. This book is also an ideal workbench companion. 350 pages, 120 illustrations. Book No. 3321, $16.95 paperback, $24.95 hardcover

TROUBLESHOOTING AND REPAIRING THE NEW PERSONAL COMPUTERS—Art Margolis

A treasury of time- and money-saving tips and techniques that show personal computer owners and service technicians how to troubleshoot and repair today's new 8- and 16-bit computers (including IBM PC/XT/AT and compatibles, the Macintosh, the Amiga, the Commodores, and other popular brands). Margolis examines the symptoms, describes the problem, and indicates which chips or circuits are most likely to be the source of the trouble. 416 pages, 351 illustrations. Book No. 2809, $19.95 paperback, $29.95 hardcover

THE CET STUDY GUIDE—2nd Edition—Sam Wilson

Written by the Director of CET Testing for ISCET (International Society of Certified Electronics Technicians), Sam Wilson, this completely up-to-date and practical guide gives you a comprehensive review of all topics covered in the Associate and Journeyman exams. Example questions help you pinpoint your own strengths and weaknesses. Most important, the author provides the answers to all the questions and offers valuable hints on how you can avoid careless errors when you take the actual CET exams. 336 pages, 179 illustrations. Book No. 2941, $15.95 paperback, $23.95 hardcover

INTERNATIONAL ENCYCLOPEDIA OF INTEGRATED CIRCUITS
—Stan Gibilisco

How would you like to have the answers to just about any IC or IC application question in one easy-to-use "master" source? Now you can, with the new, all-inclusive *International Encyclopedia of Integrated Circuits*. This convenient quick-reference source provides pin-out diagrams, internal block diagrams and schematics, characteristic curves, desciptions and applications—for foreign and domestic ICs! 1,000 pages, 4,500 illustrations. Book No. 3100, $75.00 hardcover only

ELECTRONICS EQUATIONS HANDBOOK—Stephen J. Erst

Here is immediate access to equations for nearly every imaginable application! In this book, Stephen Erst provides an extensive compilation of formulas from his 40 years' experience in electronics. He covers 21 major categories and more than 600 subtopics in offering the over 800 equations. This broad-based volume includes equations in everything from basic voltage to microwave system designs. 280 pages, 219 illustrations. Book No. 3241, $16.95 paperback, $24.95 hardcover

COMPUTER TECHNICIAN'S HANDBOOK—3rd Edition
—Art Margolis

"This is a clear book, with concise and sensible language and lots of large diagrams . . . use [it] to cure or prevent problems in [your] own system . . . the [section on troubleshooting and repair] is worth the price of the book." —*Science Software Quarterly*

MORE than just a how-to manual of do-it-yourself fix-it techniques, this book offers complete instructions on interfacing and modification that will help you get the most out of your PC. 580 pages, 97 illustrations. Book No. 3279, $24.95 paperback, $36.95 hardcover

TROUBLESHOOTING AND REPAIRING SOLID-STATE TVs
—Homer L. Davidson

Packed with case study examples, photos of solid-state circuits, and circuit diagrams. You'll learn how to troubleshoot and repair all the most recent solid-state TV circuitry used by the major manufacturers of all brands and models of TVs. This workbench reference is filled with tips and practical information that will get you right to the problem! 448 pages, 516 illustrations. Book No. 2707, $17.95 paperback, $26.95 hardcover

TROUBLESHOOTING AND REPAIRING AUDIO EQUIPMENT
—Homer L. Davidson

When your telephone answering machine quits . . . when your cassette player grinds to a stop . . . when your TV remote control loses control . . . or when your compact disc player goes berserk . . . you don't need a degree in electronics or even any experience. Everything you need to troubleshoot and repair most common problems in almost any consumer audio equipment is here in a servicing guide that's guaranteed to save you time and money! 336 pages, 354 illustrations. Book No. 2867, $18.95 paperback, $25.95 hardcover

THE DIGITAL IC HANDBOOK—Michael S. Morley

This book will make it easier for you to determine which digital ICs are currently available, how they work, and in what instances they will function most effectively. The author examines ICs from many major manufacturers and compares them not only by technology and key specification but by package and price as well. If you've ever been overwhelmed by the number of choices, this book will help you sort through the hundreds of circuits and evaluate your options. 624 pages, 273 illustrations. Book No. 3002, $40.50 hardcover only

TROUBLESHOOTING AND REPAIRING COMPACT DISC PLAYERS—Homer L. Davidson

Here's all the expert guidance you need to maintain and repair your CD player! Repairs can be a very costly proposition. With this book, you can learn to troubleshoot and repair this complicated electronic unit yourself, saving money and time. Davidson guides you through CD players, showing each section, circuit, and component and explains how they all work together. 368 pages, 429 illustrations. Book No. 3107, $17.95 paperback, $26.95 hardcover

TROUBLESHOOTING AND REPAIRING YOUR COMMODORE™ 128—Art Margolis

Hundreds of easy repairs save you time, money, and computer down time! This sourcebook is probably the most important "add-on" you'll ever buy for your C-128! Packed with maintenance tips, troubleshooting procedures, and do-it-yourself repair techniques, it can save you time, money, and untold frustration. The simple chip-changing instructions, alone, will enable you to cure at least 50% of the problems that cause breakdowns. 400 pages, 290 illustrations. Book No. 3099, $18.95 paperback, $27.95 hardcover

CAMCORDER MAINTENANCE AND REPAIR—Homer L. Davidson

Homer Davidson offers you the handbook no camcorder owner should be without! Providing money-saving repair tips and simple care procedures, Davidson shows you how to help ensure years of carefree use of your camcorder. Step-by-step instructions, schematics, block diagrams, and photographs guide you through areas previously reserved for service technicians. From general maintenance to troubleshooting to safety, it's all covered here! 304 pages, 386 illustrations. Book No. 3157, $16.95 paperback, $25.95 hardcover

THE CET EXAM BOOK—2nd Edition—Ron Crow and Dick Glass

An excellent source for update or review, this book includes information on practical mathematics, capacitance and inductance, oscillators and demodulators, meters, dependency logic notation, understanding microprocessors, electronics troubleshooting and more! Thoroughly practical, it is an essential handbook for preparing for the Associate CET test! 266 pages, 211 illustrations. Book No. 2950, $13.95 paperback, $21.95 hardcover

Prices Subject to Change Without Notice.

Look for These and Other TAB Books at Your Local Bookstore

To Order Call Toll Free 1-800-822-8158
(in PA and AK call 717-794-2191)

or write to TAB BOOKS, Blue Ridge Summit, PA 17294-0840.

Title	Product No.	Quantity	Price

☐ Check or money order made payable to TAB BOOKS

Charge my ☐ VISA ☐ MasterCard ☐ American Express

Acct. No. _____ Exp. _____

Signature: _____

Name: _____

Address: _____

City: _____

State: _____ Zip: _____

Subtotal	$	_____
Postage and Handling ($3.00 in U.S., $5.00 outside U.S.)	$	_____
Please add appropriate local and state sales tax	$	_____
TOTAL	$	_____

TAB BOOKS catalog free with purchase; otherwise send $1.00 in check or money order and receive $1.00 credit on your next purchase.

Orders outside U.S. must pay with international money order in U.S. dollars.

TAB Guarantee: If for any reason you are not satisfied with the book(s) you order, simply return it (them) within 15 days and receive a full refund. **BC**